Freedom of Association

Freedom of Association

Digest of decisions and principles of the Freedom of Association Committee of the Governing Body of the ILO

Fifth (revised) edition

INTERNATIONAL LABOUR OFFICE GENEVA

ILO
Freedom of Association: Digest of decisions and principles of the Freedom of Association Committee of the Governing Body of the ILO
Geneva, International Labour Office, Fifth (revised) edition, 2006

/Summary/, /Freedom of association/, /Committee/, /ILO Governing Body/. 04.02.2
ISBN 92-2-119031-5 (10-digits)
ISBN 978-92-2-119031-8 (13-digits)

French version: *La liberté syndicale. Recueil de décisions et de principes du Comité de la liberté syndicale du Conseil d'administration du BIT*
(ISBN 92-2-219031-9 et 978-92-2-219031-7), Genève, 2006

Spanish version: *Libertad sindical: Recopilaciôn de decisiones y principios del Comité de Libertad Sindical del Consejo de Administraciôn de la OIT*
(ISBN 92-2-319031-2 y 978-92-2-319031-6), Ginebra, 2006

ILO Cataloguing in Publication Data

ILO publications can be obtained through major booksellers or ILO local offices in many countries, or direct from ILO Publications, International Labour Office, CH-1211 Geneva 22, Switzerland. A catalogue or list of new publications will be sent free of charge from the above address.

Photocomposed in Switzerland WEI
Printed by the International Labour Office, Geneva, Switzerland

Table of contents

Paragraph(s)

Introduction

It has been ten years now since the publication of the previous edition of the Digest of decisions and principles of the Freedom of Association Committee. Since then, the world of work and industrial relations experienced, in all the regions of the world, profound changes linked to the globalization process.

The Committee on Freedom of Association which, as a result of the content of the increasingly more numerous complaints which it receives, is at the heart of current developments concerning the difficulties with which employers' and workers' organisations are faced, could not of course ignore the evolution of the world and the new problems raised in the area of industrial relations. In the course of the last ten years, the Committee had therefore to resolve questions which had been unexplored until then and thus adopt a significant number of new principles in order to give an appropriate, impartial and objective response to the allegations made in the complaints presented by employers' and workers organisations.

While always adapting itself to the continuously changing world which surrounds it, the Committee has nevertheless been guided by the constant values of freedom of association which, by allowing for the establishment of workers' and employers' organisations and vesting them with the means to promote and defend the interests of their members, constitute a source of social justice and one of the main safeguards of sustainable peace. At the same time, freedom of association is the *conditio sine qua non* of the tripartism that the Constitution of the ILO enshrines in its own structures and advocates for member States: without freedom of association, the concept of tripartism would be meaningless.

This explains why, from the outset, the Constitution of the ILO has affirmed the principle of freedom of association and why, over the years, the International Labour Conference has adopted Conventions,[1] Recommendations

[1] The fundamental Conventions on freedom of association and collective bargaining have received a very high number of ratifications: the Freedom of Association and Protection of the Right to Organise Convention, 1948 (No. 87), has received 145 ratifications (as of 1 January 2006), and the Right to Organise and Collective Bargaining Convention, 1949 (No. 98), has received 154 ratifications (as of the same date).

and resolutions, which constitute the most important source of international law in this field and the principles of which, it should be recalled in this context, have been broadly assimilated into the legislation of many countries.

In addition to this standard-setting function of the ILO, which in itself shows how vital freedom of association is for the Organization, it should be emphasized that, pursuant to negotiations and agreements between the Governing Body of the ILO and the United Nations Economic and Social Council, a special procedure was established in 1950-51 for the protection of freedom of association, supplementing the general procedures for the supervision of the application of ILO standards, under the responsibility of two bodies: the Fact-Finding and Conciliation Commission on Freedom of Association and the Freedom of Association Committee of the Governing Body of the ILO. Under this special procedure, governments or organizations of workers and of employers can submit complaints concerning violations of trade union rights by States (irrespective of whether they are Members of the ILO, or Members of the United Nations without being Members of the ILO). The procedure can be applied even when the Conventions on freedom of association and collective bargaining have not been ratified.

The Fact-Finding and Conciliation Commission on Freedom of Association was established in 1950 and is composed of independent persons. Its mandate is to examine any complaint concerning alleged infringements of trade union rights which may be referred to it by the Governing Body of the ILO. Although it is essentially a fact-finding body, it is authorized to discuss with the government concerned the possibilities of securing the adjustment of difficulties by agreement. This Commission, which has dealt with six complaints to date, only requires the consent of the government concerned for its intervention when the country has not ratified the Conventions on freedom of association. The procedure which is set in motion is determined on a case-by-case basis by the Commission itself, and generally includes the hearing of witnesses and a visit to the country concerned. Consisting as it does of a procedure which respects traditional procedural, oral and written guarantees, it is relatively long and costly and has thus only been used in a limited number of cases. Although this Digest does not specifically cover the Fact-Finding and Conciliation Commission, it is only right to emphasize its important contribution in the field of human and trade union rights.

The Committee on Freedom of Association is a tripartite body set up in 1951 by the Governing Body. It is composed of nine members and nine deputies from the Government, Workers' and Employers' groups of the Governing Body, and has an independent Chairman. The Committee on Freedom of Association meets three times a year and, taking into account the observations made by governments, is responsible for carrying out an examination of the complaints submitted under the special procedure, and for recommending to the Governing Body, as appropriate: that a case requires no further examination; that it should draw the attention of the government concerned to the problems that have been found and invite it to take the appropriate measures to resolve them; or, finally, that it should endeavour to obtain the agreement of the government concerned for the case to be referred to the Fact-Finding and Conciliation Commission.

It should be emphasized that the experience acquired through the examination of more than 2,500 cases in its over 50 years of existence has enabled the Committee on Freedom of Association to build up a body of principles on freedom of association and collective bargaining, based on the provisions of the Constitution of the ILO and of the relevant Conventions, Recommendations and resolutions. This body of principles has been created by a specialized and impartial international body of high renown, which adopts a tripartite perspective and whose work is based on real situations, namely concrete, varied and frequently very serious and complex allegations of violations of trade union rights throughout the world; it has therefore acquired recognized authority at both the international and national levels, where it is increasingly being used for the development of national legislation, as well as in the various bodies responsible for the application of law relating to freedom of association, for the resolution of major collective disputes and in publications on jurisprudence.

Herein lies the value of this Digest, which summarizes and brings up to date the decisions and principles of the Committee up to its 339th Report (November 2005) and once again gives effect, in this fifth edition,[2] to the resolution concerning trade union rights and their relation to civil liberties, adopted unanimously by the International Labour Conference at its 54th Session (Geneva, 1970), in which the Governing Body was invited to instruct the Director-General to publish and distribute widely in a concise form the supplementary decisions taken by the Committee on Freedom of Association. The Office is therefore publishing this Digest in the framework of its action to follow up this importance Conference resolution.

[2] The fourth edition was prepared in 1996.

Preliminary remarks

The present compilation is intended as a tool to guide reflection relating to the policies and actions to be adopted so as to ensure the fundamental principles of freedom of association. It cannot be seen as an exhaustive enumeration of these principles as the Committee can only pronounce itself on those cases brought before it. In addition, while setting an important baseline for assessment of achievements in this area, each case is unique and should fully take into account the surrounding circumstances. Through its use of these principles as a basis for its reasoning, the Committee has been able to maintain a continuity in the criteria employed in reaching its conclusions and, as appropriate to the individual case, in finding that the allegations are well-founded or require no further action. Consequently, the application of a principle in a particular case in relation to a country does not necessarily imply that the government of that country has not respected it.

The decisions and principles of the Committee have been developed on the basis of complaints made by organizations of workers or of employers. In this respect, it should be noted that the majority of the complaints examined by the Committee to date have been submitted by organizations of workers, although the number of complaints made by employers' organizations has increased significantly in recent years. This explains why the wording of the Committee's principles and decisions often refers to organizations of workers. Nevertheless, many of these principles are of a general nature and could also be applied, were the case to arise, to organizations of employers.

To guide the reader, for each of the principles and decisions of the Committee contained in this Digest, the corresponding references are given to the previous Digest of 1996 or to the reports, cases and appropriate paragraphs of the Committee's Reports, up to its 339th Report (November 2005).

Procedure in respect of the Committee on Freedom of Association and the social partners

1

Function of the ILO and mandate of the Committee on Freedom of Association

1. The function of the International Labour Organization in regard to freedom of association and the protection of the individual is to contribute to the effectiveness of the general principles of freedom of association, as one of the primary safeguards of peace and social justice. In fulfilling its responsibility in the matter, the Organization must not hesitate to discuss at the international level cases which are of such a character as to affect substantially the attainment of the aims and purposes of the ILO as set forth in the Constitution of the Organization, the Declaration of Philadelphia and the various Conventions concerning freedom of association.

(See the 1996 *Digest*, para. 1; and 332nd Report, Case No. 2227, para. 600.)

2. By virtue of its Constitution, the ILO was established in particular to improve working conditions and to promote freedom of association in the various countries. Consequently, the matters dealt with by the Organization in this connection no longer fall within the exclusive sphere of States and the action taken by the Organization for the purpose cannot be considered to be interference in internal affairs, since it falls within the terms of reference that the ILO has received from its Members with a view to attaining the aims assigned to it.

(See the 1996 *Digest*, para. 2; 329th Report, Case No. 2114, para. 69; and 331st Report, Case No. 2177/2183, para. 548.)

3. The purpose of the procedure of the Committee is to promote respect for trade union rights in law and in fact.

(See the 1996 *Digest*, para. 4; and, for example, 299th Report, Case No. 1772, para. 127; 300th Report, Case No. 1799, para. 205; 305th Report, Case No. 1870, para. 140; 311th Report, Case No. 1873, para. 106; 316th Report, Case No. 1988, para. 386; 321st Report, Case No. 1888, para. 230; 325th Report, Case No. 2052, para. 407; 332nd Report, Case No. 2225, para. 373; 335th Report, Case No. 2111, para. 1169; and 336th Report, Case No. 2321, para. 491.)

4. The object of the special procedure on freedom of association is not to blame or punish anyone, but rather to engage in a constructive tripartite dialogue to promote respect for trade union rights in law and practice.

(See 323rd Report, Case No. 1888, para. 199.)

5. Complaints lodged with the Committee can be submitted whether or not the country concerned has ratified the freedom of association Conventions.

(See the 1996 *Digest*, para. 5; and 332nd Report, Case No. 227, para. 600.)

6. The mandate of the Committee consists in determining whether any given legislation or practice complies with the principles of freedom of association and collective bargaining laid down in the relevant Conventions.

(See the 1996 *Digest*, para. 6; 310th Report, Case No. 1931, para. 494; 311th Report, Case No. 1942, para. 262; 335th Report, Case No. 2187, para. 116; and 337th Report, Case No. 2258, para. 836.)

7. Within the terms of its mandate, the Committee is empowered to examine to what extent the exercise of trade union rights may be affected in cases of allegations of the infringement of civil liberties.

(See the 1996 *Digest*, para. 7.)

8. The Committee's mandate is not linked to the 1998 ILO Declaration on Fundamental Principles and Rights at Work – which has its own built-in follow-up mechanisms – but rather stems directly from the fundamental aims and purposes set out in the ILO Constitution.

(See 332nd Report, Case No. 2227, para. 600.)

9. It is within the mandate of the Committee to examine whether, and to what extent, satisfactory evidence is presented to support allegations; this appreciation goes to the merits of the case and cannot support a finding of irreceivability.

(See 325th Report, Case No. 2106, para. 477.)

10. The Committee always takes account of national circumstances, such as the history of labour relations and the social and economic context, but the freedom of association principles apply uniformly and consistently among countries.

(See 329th Report, Case No. 2177/2183, para. 630.)

11. Where national laws, including those interpreted by the high courts, violate the principles of freedom of association, the Committee has always considered it within its mandate to examine the laws, provide guidelines and offer the ILO's technical assistance to bring the laws into compliance with the principles of freedom of association, as set out in the Constitution of the ILO and the applicable Conventions.

(See the 1996 *Digest*, para. 8; 310th Report, Case No. 1931, para. 494; 318th Report, Case No. 1954, para. 50; 329th Report, Case No. 2114, para. 69, and Case No. 2177/2183, para. 631.)

12. While it is not for the Committee to decide upon questions concerning the occupation or administration of territories, as a Member of the ILO, the Government of the occupying country is bound to respect the principle of freedom of association as contained in the ILO Constitution in respect of the occupied territories where its national legislation does not apply and in respect of which the ratification of the international Conventions on freedom of association does not of itself create an obligation vis-à-vis the ILO. The Committee recalls, in this respect, that its competence in the matter is independent of the ratification of the Conventions on freedom of association.

(See the 1996 *Digest*, para. 9.)

13. The Committee is not competent to consider purely political allegations; it can, however, consider measures of a political character taken by governments in so far as these may affect the exercise of trade union rights.

(See the 1996 *Digest*, para. 200.)

14. The question of representation at the International Labour Conference falls within the competence of the Conference Credentials Committee.

(See the 1996 *Digest*, para. 659.)

Fundamental obligations of member States in respect of human and trade union rights

15. When a State decides to become a Member of the Organization, it accepts the fundamental principles embodied in the Constitution and the Declaration of Philadelphia, including the principles of freedom of association.

(See the 1996 *Digest*, para. 10; 329th Report, Case No. 2177/2183, para. 630; 330th Report, Case No. 2166/2173/2180/2196, para. 288; 333rd Report, Case No. 2268, para. 732; 335th Report, Case No. 2187, para. 116; 336th Report, Case No. 1937/2027, para. 141; 338th Report, Case No. 1890, para. 179, and Case No. 2252, para. 306.)

16. The membership of a State in the International Labour Organization carries with it the obligation to respect in national legislation freedom of association principles and the Conventions which the State has freely ratified.

(See 300th Report, Case No. 1793, para. 263.)

17. The ultimate responsibility for ensuring respect for the principles of freedom of association lies with the Government.

(See 304th Report, Case No. 1852, para. 492.)

18. It is the responsibility of the Government to ensure the application of international labour Conventions concerning freedom of association which have been freely ratified and which must be respected by all state authorities, including the judicial authorities.

(See 313rd Report, Case No. 1952, para. 300; and 318th Report, Case No. 1991, para. 269.)

19. Trade union rights, like other basic human rights, should be respected no matter what the level of development of the country concerned.

(See the 1996 *Digest*, paras. 17 and 41; and 321st report, Case No. 2031, para. 166.)

20. The Committee has referred to the Tripartite Declaration of Principles concerning Multinational Enterprises and Social Policy, adopted by the Governing Body of the ILO in November 1977, which states that (paragraph 46 of the Declaration, as amended in November 2000): "where governments of host countries offer special incentives to attract foreign investment, these incentives should not include any limitation of the workers' freedom of association or the right to organize and bargain collectively".

(See the 1996 *Digest*, para 12.)

21. A State cannot use the argument that other commitments or agreements can justify the non-application of ratified ILO Conventions.

(See the 1996 *Digest*, para. 13; and 330th Report, Case No. 2194, para. 791.)

22. The level of protection for exercising trade union rights which results from the provisions and principles of Conventions Nos. 87 and 98 constitutes a minimum standard which may be complemented and it is desirable that other supplementary guarantees should be added resulting from the constitutional and legal system of any given country, its traditions as regards labour relations, trade union action or bargaining between the parties.

(See the 1996 *Digest*, para. 14.)

23. Faced with allegations against one government of violations of trade union rights, the Committee recalled that a successive government in the same State cannot, for the mere reason that a change has occurred, escape the responsibility deriving from events that occurred under a former government. In any event, the new government is responsible for any continuing consequences which these events may have. Where a change of regime has taken place in a country, the new government should take all necessary steps to remedy any continuing effects which the events on which a complaint is based may have had since its accession to power, even though those events took place under its predecessor.

(See the 1996 *Digest*, para. 18; 306th Report, Case No. 1904, para. 594; 307th Report, Case No. 1905, para. 147, and Case No. 1910, para. 165; 316th Report, Case No. 1970, para. 547; and 335th Report, Case No. 2305, para. 501.)

Obligations of governments relating to the procedure of the Committee on Freedom of Association

24. Governments should recognize the importance for their own reputation of formulating detailed replies to the allegations brought by complainant organizations, so as to allow the Committee to undertake an objective examination.

(See the 1996 *Digest*, para. 20; and, for example, the 304th Report, Case No. 1850, para. 205; 307th Report, Case No. 1864, para. 427; 311th Report, Case No. 1873, para. 106; 318th Report, Case No. 1978, para. 216; 323rd Report, Case No. 2017/2050, para. 301; 324th Report, Case No. 2035, para. 570; 326th Report, Case No. 2103, para. 294; 330th Report, Case No. 2166/2173/2180/2196, para. 289; 334th Report, Case No. 2200, para. 756; and 335th Report, Case No. 2187, para. 116.)

25. In all the cases presented to it since it was first set up, the Committee has always considered that the replies of governments against whom complaints are made should not be limited to general observations.

(See the 1996 *Digest*, para. 21; and 310th Report, Case No. 1929, para. 424.)

The functions of organizations of workers and of employers

(See also paras. 36 and 1069)

26. The development of free and independent organizations and negotiation with all those involved in social dialogue is indispensable to enable a government to confront its social and economic problems and resolve them in the best interests of the workers and the nation.

(See the 1996 *Digest*, para. 24; and 308th Report, Case No. 1934, para. 124; 330th Report, Case No. 2189, para. 466; 332nd Report, Case No. 2090, para. 353; and 337th Report, Case No. 2189, para. 485.)

27. The fundamental objective of the trade union movement should be to ensure the development of the social and economic well-being of all workers.

(See the 1996 *Digest*, para. 27; and 310th Report, Case No. 1929, para. 425.)

28. The occupational and economic interests which workers and their organizations defend do not only concern better working conditions or collective claims of an occupational nature, but also the seeking of solutions to economic and social policy questions and problems facing the undertaking which are of direct concern to the workers.

(See the 1996 *Digest*, para. 29; and 310th Report, Case No. 1929, para. 425.)

29. A trade union's activities cannot be restricted solely to occupational questions. The choice of a general policy, notably in economic affairs, is bound to have consequences on the situation of workers (remuneration, holidays, working conditions).

(See the 1996 *Digest*, para. 30.)

Trade union rights and civil liberties 2

General principles

(See also paras. 7 and 19)

30. The Committee has considered it appropriate to emphasize the importance to be attached to the basic principles set out in the Universal Declaration of Human Rights, considering that their infringement can adversely affect the free exercise of trade union rights.

(See the 1996 *Digest*, para. 32; and 308th Report, Case No. 1934, para. 135.)

31. On many occasions, the Committee has emphasized the importance of the principle affirmed in 1970 by the International Labour Conference in its resolution concerning trade union rights and their relation to civil liberties, which recognizes that "the rights conferred upon workers' and employers' organizations must be based on respect for those civil liberties which have been enunciated in particular in the Universal Declaration of Human Rights and in the International Covenant on Civil and Political Rights, and that the absence of these civil liberties removes all meaning from the concept of trade union rights".

(See the 1996 *Digest*, para. 33; and 300th Report, Case No. 1790, para. 296.)

32. The Committee has considered that a system of democracy is fundamental for the free exercise of trade union rights.

(See the 1996 *Digest*, para. 34; 302nd Report, Case No. 1773, para. 469; and 306th Report, Case No. 1884, para. 684.)

33. A genuinely free and independent trade union movement can only develop where fundamental human rights are respected.

(See the 1996 *Digest*, para. 35; 300th Report, Cases Nos. 1682/1711/1716, para. 173; 302nd Report, Case No. 1773, para. 469; 316th Report, Case No. 1773, para. 614; and 338th Report, Case No. 2378, para. 1153.)

34. The Government has the duty to defend a social climate where respect for the law reigns as the only way of guaranteeing respect for and protection of individuals.

(See 326th Report, Case No. 2027, para. 176.)

35. All appropriate measures should be taken to guarantee that, irrespective of trade union affiliation, trade union rights can be exercised in normal conditions with respect for basic human rights and in a climate free of violence, pressure, fear and threats of any kind.

(See the 1996 *Digest*, para. 36; 306th Report, Case No. 1884, para. 684; 308th Report, Case No. 1934, para. 135; 316th Report, Case No. 1773, para. 614; 332nd Report, Case No. 1888, para. 61; and 333rd Report, Case No. 2268, para. 744.)

36. For the contribution of trade unions and employers' organizations to be properly useful and credible, they must be able to carry out their activities in a climate of freedom and security. This implies that, in so far as they may consider that they do not have the basic freedom to fulfil their mission directly, trade unions and employers' organizations would be justified in demanding that these freedoms and the right to exercise them be recognized and that these demands be considered as coming within the scope of legitimate trade union activities.

(See the 1996 *Digest*, paras. 28, 37 and 459; 334th Report, Case No. 2254, para. 1082; and 337th Report, Case No. 2258, para. 852.)

37. A free trade union movement can develop only under a regime which guarantees fundamental rights, including the right of trade unionists to hold meetings in trade union premises, freedom of opinion expressed through speech and the press and the right of detained trade unionists to enjoy the guarantees of normal judicial procedure at the earliest possible moment.

(See the 1996 *Digest*, para. 38.)

38. The International Labour Conference has pointed out that the right of assembly, freedom of opinion and expression and, in particular, freedom to hold opinions without interference and to seek, receive and impart information and ideas through any media and regardless of frontiers constitute civil liberties which are essential for the normal exercise of trade union rights (resolution concerning trade union rights and their relation to civil liberties, adopted at the 54th Session, 1970).

(See the 1996 *Digest*, para. 39.)

39. It should be the policy of every government to ensure observance of human rights.

(See the 1996 *Digest*, paras. 15 and 40.)

40. Although holders of trade union office do not, by virtue of their position, have the right to transgress legal provisions in force, these provisions should not infringe the basic guarantees of freedom of association, nor should they sanction activities which, in accordance with the principles of freedom of association, should be considered as legitimate trade union activities.

(See the 1996 *Digest*, paras. 42 and 726; 305th Report, Case No. 1870, para. 145; 326th Report, Case No. 2105, para. 448; 329th Report, Case No. 2188, para. 211; 333rd Report, Case No. 2268, para. 744; and 335th Report, Case No. 2276, para. 408.)

41. Allegations of criminal conduct should not be used to harass trade unionists by reason of their union membership or activities.

(See the 1996 *Digest*, para. 43; 305th Report, Case No. 1773, para. 365; 306th Report, Case No. 1884, para. 700; and 327th Report, Case No. 2018, para. 117.)

Right to life, security and the physical and moral integrity of the person

(See also paras. 80 and 1125)

42. The right to life is a fundamental prerequisite for the exercise of the rights contained in Convention No. 87.

(See the 1996 *Digest*, para. 45.)

43. Freedom of association can only be exercised in conditions in which fundamental rights, and in particular those relating to human life and personal safety, are fully respected and guaranteed.

(See the 1996 *Digest*, para. 46; and, for example, 300th Report, Case No. 1649, para. 453; 305th Report, Case No. 1876, para. 322; 307th Report, Case No. 1876, para. 312; 308th Report, Case No. 1892, para. 401; 316th Report, Case No. 1970, para. 548; 324th Report, Case No. 1787, para. 273; 329th Report, Case No. 2201, para. 508; 332nd Report, Case No. 2201, para. 546; 333rd Report, Case No. 1787, para. 450; and 334th Report, Case No. 2254, para. 1088.)

44. The rights of workers' and employers' organizations can only be exercised in a climate that is free from violence, pressure or threats of any kind against the leaders and members of these organizations, and it is for governments to ensure that this principle is respected.

(See the 1996 *Digest*, para. 47; and, for example, 299th Report, Case No. 1512, para. 407; 304th Report, Case No. 1862, para. 81; 308th report, Case No. 1888, para. 342; 321st Report, Case No. 2052, para. 247; 327th Report, Case No. 2017/2050, para. 601; 333rd Report, Case No. 2158, para. 83; 334th Report, Case No. 2254, para. 1088; 336th Report, Case No. 2321, para. 496; 337th Report, Case No. 1787, para. 535; and 338th Report, Case No. 2298, para. 886.)

45. A genuinely free and independent trade union movement cannot develop in a climate of violence and uncertainty.

(See the 1996 *Digest*, para. 48; 302nd Report, Case No. 1849, para. 202; 304th Report, Case No. 1850, para. 207; 326th Report, Case No. 2027, para. 176; and 337th Report, Case No. 2318, para. 340.)

46. A climate of violence, such as that surrounding the murder or disappearance of trade union leaders, or one in which the premises and property of workers and employers are attacked, constitutes a serious obstacle to the exercise of trade union rights; such acts require severe measures to be taken by the authorities.

(See the 1996 *Digest*, para. 49; and 330th Report, Case No. 1888, para. 657.)

47. Facts imputable to individuals bring into play the State's responsibility owing to the State's obligation to prevent violations of human rights. Consequently, governments should endeavour to meet their obligations regarding the respect of individual rights and freedoms, as well as their obligation to guarantee the right to life of trade unionists.

(See the 1996 *Digest*, paras. 19 and 50; and 308th Report, Case No. 1934, para. 135.)

48. The killing, disappearance or serious injury of trade union leaders and trade unionists requires the institution of independent judicial inquiries in order to shed full light, at the earliest date, on the facts and the circumstances in which such actions occurred and in this way, to the extent possible, determine where responsibilities lie, punish the guilty parties and prevent the repetition of similar events.

(See the 1996 *Digest*, para. 51; and, for example, 306th Report, Case No. 1884, para. 699; 310th Report, Case No. 1773, para. 462; 325th Report, Case No. 1888, para. 393; 327th Report, Case No. 2156, para. 202; 328th Report, Case No. 1787, para. 114; 331st Report, Case No. 2158, para. 38; 333rd Report, Case No. 2268, para. 748; 337th Report, Case No. 2318, para. 336, and Case No. 2268, para. 1091; and 338th Report, Case No. 2158, para. 185.)

49. In cases in which the dispersal of public meetings by the police has involved loss of life or serious injury, the Committee has attached special importance to the circumstances being fully investigated immediately through an independent inquiry and to a regular legal procedure being followed to determine the justification for the action taken by the police and to determine responsibilities.

(See the 1996 *Digest*, paras. 52 and 148; 302nd Report, Case No. 1840, para. 353; 304th Report, Case No. 1850, para. 207; 306th Report, Case No. 1884, para. 696; 331st Report, Case No. 2217, para. 200; and 337th Report, Case No. 2323, para. 1030.)

50. In the event of assaults on the physical or moral integrity of individuals, the Committee has considered that an independent judicial inquiry should be instituted immediately with a view to fully clarifying the facts, determining responsibility, punishing those responsible and preventing the repetition of such acts.

(See the 1996 *Digest*, para. 53; and, for example, 299th Report, Case No. 1512, para. 407; 304th Report, Case No. 1719, para. 409; 305th Report, Case No. 1876, para. 324; 306th Report, Case No. 1862, para. 116; 320th Report, Case No. 2048, para. 717; 325th Report, Case No. 2068, para. 314; 326th Report, Case No. 2116, para. 358; and 337th Report, Case No. 2318, para. 340.)

51. In the event that judicial investigations into the murder and disappearance of trade unionists are rarely successful, the Committee has considered it indispensable that measures be taken to identify, bring to trial and convict the guilty parties and has pointed out that such a situation means that, in practice, the guilty parties enjoy impunity which reinforces the climate of violence and insecurity and thus has an extremely damaging effect on the exercise of trade union rights.

(See the 1996 *Digest*, para. 54; and 322nd Report, Case No. 1787, para. 30.)

52. The absence of judgements against the guilty parties creates, in practice, a situation of impunity, which reinforces the climate of violence and insecurity, and which is extremely damaging to the exercise of trade union rights.

(See the 1996 *Digest*, para. 55; and, for example, 304th Report, Case No. 1787, para. 172; 306th Report, Case No. 1843, para. 616; 316th Report, Case No. 1970, para. 548; 320th Report, Case No. 2027, para. 873; 321st Report, Case No. 1813, para. 62; 325th Report, Case No. 2010, para. 28; 330th Report, Case No. 1888, para. 657; 331st Report, Case No. 1937/2027, para. 106; and 337th Report, Case No. 2318, para. 336.)

53. The Committee emphasized the need, in a case in which judicial inquiries connected with the death of trade unionists seemed to be taking a long time to conclude, of proceedings being brought to a speedy conclusion

(See 306th Report, Case No. 1843, para. 615.)

54. The Committee has considered that detained trade unionists, like all other persons, should enjoy the guarantees enunciated in the Universal Declaration of Human Rights and the International Covenant on Civil and Political Rights according to which all persons deprived of their liberty must be treated with humanity and with respect for the inherent dignity of the human person.

(See the 1996 *Digest*, para. 60; and 310th Report, Case No. 1930, para. 361.)

55. As regards allegations of the physical ill-treatment and torture of trade unionists, the Committee has recalled that governments should give precise instructions and apply effective sanctions where cases of ill-treatment are found, so as to ensure that no detainee is subjected to such treatment.

(See the 1996 *Digest*, para. 59; 300th Report, Case No. 1682/1711/1716, para. 175, and Case No. 1818, para. 365; 306th Report, Case No. 1843, para. 616; 318th Report, Case No. 2005, para. 182; 321st Report, Case No. 2031, para. 171; 336th Report, Case No. 2321, para. 495; and 337th Report, Case No. 2249, para. 1495.)

56. In cases of alleged torture or ill-treatment while in detention, governments should carry out inquiries into complaints of this kind so that appropriate measures, including compensation for damages suffered and the sanctioning of those responsible, are taken to ensure that no detainee is subjected to such treatment.

(See the 1996 *Digest*, para. 57; 306th Report, Case No. 1843, para. 616; 309th Report, Case No. 1843, para. 384; 310th Report, Case No. 1930, para. 353; 321st Report, Case No. 2031, para. 171, and Case No. 1965, para. 383; 328th Report, Case No. 1787, para. 114; 331st Report, Case No. 2169, para. 640; and 333rd Report, Case No. 2268, para. 755.)

57. As regards allegations relating to the ill-treatment or any other punitive measures said to have been taken against workers who took part in strikes, the Committee has pointed out the importance that it attaches to the right of trade unionists, like all other persons, to enjoy the guarantees afforded by due process of law in accordance with the principles enunciated in the Universal Declaration of Human Rights and in the International Covenant on Civil and Political Rights.

(See the 1996 *Digest*, para. 58.)

58. A climate of violence, coercion and threats of any type aimed at trade union leaders and their families does not encourage the free exercise and full enjoyment of the rights and freedoms set out in Conventions Nos. 87 and 98. All States have the undeniable duty to promote and defend a social climate where respect of the law reigns as the only way of guaranteeing respect for and protection of life.

(See the 1996 *Digest*, paras. 61 and 62; 306th Report, Case No. 1903, para. 489; 331st Report, Case No. 1937/2027, para. 106; 327th Report, Case No. 1787, para. 342; and 333rd report, Case No. 2268, para. 755.)

59. Attacks against trade unionists and trade union premises and property constitute serious interference with trade union rights. Criminal activities of this nature create a climate of fear which is extremely prejudicial to the exercise of trade union activities.

(See 306th Report, Case No. 1862, para. 112.)

60. The environment of fear induced by threats to the life of trade unionists has inevitable repercussions on the exercise of trade union activities, and the exercise of these activities is possible only in a context of respect for basic human rights and in an atmosphere free of violence, pressure and threats of any kind.

(See the 1996 *Digest*, para. 63; and 337th Report, Case No. 2318, para. 333.)

Arrest and detention of trade unionists

(See also paras. 151, 174, 671, 672, 673 and 674.)

61. The detention of trade union leaders or members for trade union activities or membership is contrary to the principles of freedom of association.

(See the 1996 *Digest*, paras. 69 and 72; 302nd Report, Case No. 1824, para. 155, Case No. 1849, para. 213, and Case No. 1773, para. 476; 304th Report, Case No. 1850, para. 211, and Case No. 1865, para. 245; 305th Report, Case No. 1773, para. 369; 307th Report, Case No. 1864, para. 432; 308th Report, Case No. 1920, para. 524; and 334th Report, Case No. 2249, para. 866.)

62. The arrest, even if only briefly, of trade union leaders and trade unionists, and of the leaders of employers' organizations, for exercising legitimate activities in relation with their right of association constitutes a violation of the principles of freedom of association.

(See the 1996 *Digest*, para. 70; and, for example, 299th Report, Case No. 1772, para. 129; 300th Report, Case No. 1818, para. 363; 309th Report, Case No. 1851/1922, para. 236; 323rd Report, Case No. 1988, para. 53; 326th Report, Case No. 2116, para. 357; 328th report, Case No. 2143, para. 594; 330th Report, Case No. 2189, para. 455; 331st Report, Case No. 2220, para. 575; 336th Report, Case No. 2340, para. 651; and 337th Report, Case No. 2365, para. 1664.)

63. Measures depriving trade unionists of their freedom on grounds related to their trade union activity, even where they are merely summoned or questioned for a short period, constitute an obstacle to the exercise of trade union rights.

(See the 1996 *Digest*, para. 77; and, for example, 305th Report, Case No. 1805, para. 224; 307th Report, Case No. 1863, para. 342; 308th Report, Case No. 1934, para. 131; 311th Report, Case No. 1969, para. 147; 320th Report, Case No. 2023, para. 428; 325th Report, Case No. 2109, para. 461; 326th Report, Case No. 2116, para. 357; 328th Report, Case No. 2129, para. 603; 331st Report, Case No. 2169, para. 638.)

64. The detention of trade unionists for reasons connected with their activities in defence of the interests of workers constitutes a serious interference with civil liberties in general and with trade union rights in particular.

(See the 1996 *Digest*, para. 71; and, for example, 302nd Report, Case No. 1826, para. 413; 316th Report, Case No. 1773, para. 609; 318th Report, Case No. 1994, para. 457; 325th Report, Case No. 2052, para. 410; 330th Report, Case No. 1961, para. 74; 332nd Report, Case No. 2090, para. 354; 334th Report, Case No. 2313, para. 1118; 336th Report, Case No. 2340, para. 651; and 337th Report, Case No. 2189, para. 483, and Case No. 2365, para. 1664.)

65. Measures designed to deprive trade union leaders and members of their freedom entail a serious risk of interference in trade union activities and, when such measures are taken on trade union grounds, they constitute an infringement of the principles of freedom of association.

(See the 1996 *Digest*, para. 74; 323rd Report, Case No. 2079, para. 541; 333rd Report, Case No. 2153, para. 212; and 336th Report, Case No. 2321, para. 494.)

66. The detention of trade unionists on the grounds of trade union activities constitutes a serious obstacle to the exercise of trade union rights and an infringement of freedom of association.

(See the 1996 *Digest*, para. 75; 300th Report, Case No. 1649, para. 454; and 305th Report, Case No. 1870, para. 145.)

67. The arrest of trade unionists and leaders of employers' organizations may create an atmosphere of intimidation and fear prejudicial to the normal development of trade union activities.

(See the 1996 *Digest*, para. 76; 308th Report, Case No. 1888, para. 344; 331st Report, Case No. 2220, para. 575; 332nd Report, Case No. 2090, para. 355, and Case No. 2238, para. 969; 334th Report, Case No. 2313, para. 1118; and 337th Report, Case No. 2189, para. 484.)

68. The apprehension and systematic or arbitrary interrogation by the police of trade union leaders and unionists involves a danger of abuse and could constitute a serious attack on trade union rights.

(See the 1996 *Digest*, para. 78.)

69. The arrest and detention of trade unionists without any charges being laid or court warrants being issued constitutes a serious violation of trade union rights.

(See the 1996 *Digest*, paras. 79 and 82; 299th Report, Case No. 1803, para. 338; 300th Report, Case No. 1818, para. 364; 302nd Report, Case No. 1846, para. 266, and Case No. 1833, para. 552; 331st Report, Case No. 2217, para. 200, and Case No. 2169, para. 638.)

70. The arrest of trade unionists against whom no charge is brought involves restrictions on freedom of association, and governments should adopt measures for issuing appropriate instructions to prevent the danger involved for trade union activities by such arrests.

(See the 1996 *Digest*, paras. 80 and 81; 304th Report, Case No. 1649, para. 391; 308th Report, Case No. 1917, para. 205; 323rd Report, Case No. 2028, para. 212; 326th Report, Case No. 2017/2050, para. 279; 328th Report, Case No. 2158, para. 322; and 331st Report, Case No. 2220, para. 575.)

71. The arrest of employers' officials for reasons linked to actions relating to legitimate demands is a serious restriction of their rights and a violation of freedom of association.

(See 334th Report, Case No. 2254, para. 1084.)

72. While persons engaged in trade union activities or holding trade union office cannot claim immunity in respect of the ordinary criminal law, trade union activities should not in themselves be used by the public authorities as a pretext for the arbitrary arrest or detention of trade unionists.

(See the 1996 *Digest*, para. 83, and, for example, 304th Report, Case No. 1865, para. 246; 318th Report, Case No. 2005, para. 179; 320th Report, Case No. 2048, para. 716; 321st Report, Case No. 1888, para. 233; 323rd Report, Case No. 2074, para. 149; 324th Report, Case No. 2031, para. 47; 327th Report, Case No. 2148, para. 802; 333rd Report, Case No. 2153, para. 213; 337th Report, Case No. 2189, para. 475; and 338th Report, Case No. 2382, para. 531.)

73. Prosecutions, or other forms of sanction, should not in any way be instituted against trade union leaders who bring a case before the Freedom of Association Committee and the charges against them should be withdrawn immediately.

(See 308th Report, Case No. 1920, para. 524.)

74. Union leaders should not be subject to retaliatory measures, and in particular arrest and detention without trial, for having exercised their rights which derive from the ratification of ILO instruments on freedom of association, in this case for having lodged a complaint with the Committee on Freedom of Association.

(See 338th Report, Case No. 2382, para. 532.)

75. The arrest and detention of trade unionists, even for reasons of internal security, may constitute a serious interference with trade union rights unless attended by appropriate judicial safeguards.

(See the 1996 *Digest*, para. 84; 308th Report, Case No. 1888, para. 344; and 333rd Report, Case No. 2268, para. 755.)

Preventive detention

(See also paras. 86 and 120)

76. Measures of preventive detention may involve a serious interference with trade union activities which can only be justified by the existence of a serious situation or emergency and which would be open to criticism unless accompanied by adequate judicial safeguards applied within a reasonable period.

(See the 1996 *Digest*, para. 85; and 305th Report, Case No. 2304, para. 1013.)

77. The preventive detention of trade unionists on the ground that breaches of the law may take place in the course of a strike involves a serious danger of infringement of trade union rights.

(See the 1996 *Digest*, para. 86.)

78. Preventive detention should be limited to very short periods of time intended solely to facilitate the course of a judicial inquiry.

(See the 1996 *Digest*, para. 87; 323rd Report, Case No. 2028, para. 212; and 333rd Report, Case No. 2153, para. 212.)

79. In all cases in which trade union leaders are preventively detained, this can involve a serious interference with the exercise of trade union rights and the Committee has always emphasized the right of all detained persons to receive a fair trial at the earliest possible moment.

(See the 1996 *Digest*, para. 88.)

80. Preventive detention should be accompanied by safeguards and limitations:
(1) to ensure, in particular, that it is not extended beyond the time absolutely necessary and that it is not accompanied by measures of intimidation;
(2) to prevent it being used for purposes other than those for which it is designed and, in particular, to exclude torture and ill-treatment and give protection against situations where the detention is unsatisfactory from the viewpoint of sanitation, unnecessary hardship or the right to defence.

(See the 1996 *Digest*, para. 89.)

81. The prolonged detention of persons without bringing them to trial because of the difficulty of securing evidence under the normal procedure is a practice which involves an inherent danger of abuse; for this reason it is subject to criticism.

(See the 1996 *Digest*, para. 90; 310th Report, Case No. 1929, para. 426; and 338th Report, Case No. 2387, para. 864.)

82. Although the exercise of trade union activity or the holding of trade union office does not provide immunity as regards the application of ordinary criminal law, the continued detention of trade unionists without bringing them to trial may constitute a serious impediment to the exercise of trade union rights.

(See the 1996 *Digest*, para. 91; and 338th Report, Case No. 2382, para. 532.)

Detentions during a state of emergency

83. The Committee, while refraining from expressing an opinion on the political aspects of a state of emergency, has always emphasized that measures involving detention must be accompanied by adequate judicial safeguards applied within a reasonable period and that all detained persons must receive a fair trial at the earliest possible moment.

(See the 1996 *Digest*, para. 99.)

84. Where circumstances approximate to a situation of a civil war, the Committee has emphasized the importance attached to all detained persons receiving a fair trial at the earliest possible moment.

(See the 1996 *Digest*, para. 100.)

85. Due process would not appear to be ensured if, under the national law, the effect of a state of emergency is that a court cannot examine, and does not examine, the merits of the case.

(See the 1996 *Digest*, para. 101.)

86. When examining cases of detention under emergency regulations, the Committee has pointed out that measures of preventive detention should be limited to very short periods intended solely to facilitate the course of a judicial inquiry.

(See the 1996 *Digest*, para. 195.)

System of education through labour

87. The "system of education through labour" with regard to persons who have already been released, constitutes a form of forced labour and administrative detention of people who have not been convicted by the courts and who, in some cases, are not even liable to sanctions imposed by the judicial authorities. This form of detention and forced labour constitutes without any doubt a violation of basic ILO standards which guarantee compliance with human rights and, when applied to people who have engaged in trade union activities, a blatant violation of the principles of freedom of association.

(See the 1996 *Digest*, para. 67; 310th Report, Case No. 1930, para. 358; 321st Report, Case No. 2031, para. 168; and 337th Report, Case No. 2189, para. 480.)

88. The subjection of workers to the education through labour system without any court judgement is a form of administrative detention which constitutes a clear infringement of basic human rights, the respect of which is essential for the exercise of trade union rights, as pointed out by the International Labour Conference in 1970.

(See the 1996 *Digest*, para. 68; and 337th Report, Case No. 2189, para. 480.)

Special bodies and summary procedures

89. In all cases where trade unionists have been the subject of measures or decisions emanating from bodies of a special nature, the Committee has emphasized the importance which it attaches to the guarantees of a normal judicial procedure.

(See the 1996 *Digest*, para. 120.)

90. The Committee has considered that, when trade unionists have been sentenced under summary procedures, they have not enjoyed all the safeguards of a normal procedure. Accordingly, the Committee has suggested that it should be possible to review cases of trade unionists sentenced under such procedures so as to ensure that no one is deprived of their liberty without the benefit of a normal procedure before an impartial and independent judicial authority.

(See the 1996 *Digest*, para. 121; and 337th Report, Case No. 2189, para. 476.)

Internment in psychiatric hospitals

91. All the necessary safeguards should be provided to prevent individuals being committed to psychiatric hospitals as a sanction or a means of pressure against persons who wish to establish a new organization independent of the existing trade union structure.

(See 207th Report, Case No. 905, para. 129; and 310th Report, Case No. 1930, para. 352.)

Bringing of charges and sentencing of trade unionists to imprisonment

92. The Committee has pointed out the danger for the free exercise of trade union rights of sentences imposed on representatives of workers for activities related to the defence of the interests of those they represent.

(See the 1996 *Digest*, para. 44; and 333rd Report, Case No. 2268, para. 744.)

93. The arrest and sentencing of trade unionists to long periods of imprisonment on grounds of the "disturbance of public order", in view of the general nature of the charges, might make it possible to repress activities of a trade union nature.

(See the 1996 *Digest*, para. 64; 305th Report, Case No. 1773, para. 365; 318th Report, Case No. 2005, para. 180; 320th Report, Case No. 2048, para. 721; and 330th Report, Case No. 2189, para. 456.)

94. In cases involving the arrest, detention or sentencing of a trade union official, the Committee, taking the view that individuals have the right to be presumed innocent until found guilty, has considered that it was incumbent upon the government to show that the measures it had taken were in no way occasioned by the trade union activities of the individual concerned.

(See the 1996 *Digest*, para. 65; 305th Report, Case No. 1870, para. 145; 331st Report, Case No. 2169, para. 638; 337th Report, Case No. 2268, para. 1092; and 338th Report, Case No. 2387, para. 863.)

95. Any sentences passed on trade unionists on the basis of the ordinary criminal law should not cause the authorities to adopt a negative attitude towards the organization of which these persons and others are members.

(See the 1996 *Digest*, para. 66; and 335th Report, Case No. 2304, para. 1016.)

Guarantee of due process of law

(See also paras. 57, 75, 76, 78, 79, 81, 82, 83, 89 and 90)

96. Because of the fact that detention may involve serious interference with trade union rights and because of the importance which it attaches to the principle of fair trial, the Committee has pressed governments to bring detainees to trial in all cases, irrespective of the reasons put forward by governments for prolonging the detention.

(See the 1996 *Digest*, para. 92.)

97. It is one of the fundamental rights of the individual that a detained person should be brought without delay before the appropriate judge, this right being recognized in such instruments as the United Nations International Covenant on Civil and Political Rights and the American Declaration of the Rights and Duties of Man. In the case of persons engaged in trade union activities, this is one of the civil liberties which should be ensured by the authorities in order to guarantee the exercise of trade union rights.

(See the 1996 *Digest*, para. 93; and 308th Report, Case No. 1888, para. 344.)

98. It is one of the fundamental rights of the individual that a detainee be brought without delay before the appropriate judge and, in the case of trade unionists, freedom from arbitrary arrest and detention and the right to a fair and rapid trial are among the civil liberties which should be ensured by the authorities in order to guarantee the normal exercise of trade union rights.

(See the 1996 *Digest*, para. 94; 323rd Report, Case No. 2028, para. 212; and 332nd Report, Case No. 2086, para. 123.)

99. Anyone who is arrested should be informed, at the time of the arrest, of the reasons for the arrest and should be promptly notified of any charges brought against her or him.

(See the 1996 *Digest*, para. 95; and 308th Report, Case No. 1888, para. 344.)

100. It should be the policy of every government to ensure observance of human rights and especially of the right of all detained or accused persons to receive a fair trial at the earliest possible moment.

(See the 1996 *Digest*, para. 96; and 310th Report, Case No. 1888, para. 384.)

101. The Committee has emphasized the importance that should be attached to the principle that all arrested persons should be subject to normal judicial procedure in accordance with the principles enshrined in the Universal Declaration of Human Rights, and in accordance with the principle that it is a fundamental right of the individual that a detained person should be brought without delay before the appropriate judge, this right being recognized in such instruments as the International Covenant on Civil and Political Rights, the American Declaration of the Rights and Duties of Man and the American Convention of Human Rights.

(See the 1996 *Digest*, para. 97; and 316th Report, Case No. 1988, para. 389.)

102. Detained trade unionists, like anyone else, should benefit from normal judicial proceedings and have the right to due process, in particular, the right to be informed of the charges brought against them, the right to have adequate time and facilities for the preparation of their defence and to communicate freely with counsel of their own choosing, and the right to a prompt trial by an impartial and independent judicial authority.

(See the 1996 *Digest*, para. 102; 318th Report, Case No. 2005, para. 181; 321st Report, Case No. 1888, para. 233; 323rd Report, Case No. 1888, para. 193; 330th Report, Case No. 2189, para. 457; 331st Report, Case No. 2169, para. 638; and 333rd Report, Case No. 2189, para. 382.)

103. Respect for due process of law should not preclude the possibility of a fair and rapid trial and, on the contrary, an excessive delay may intimidate the employers' leaders concerned, thus having repercussions on the exercise of their activities.

(See the 1996 *Digest*, para. 103.)

104. As concerns allegations that legal proceedings are overly lengthy, the Committee has recalled the importance it attaches to such proceedings being concluded expeditiously, as justice delayed is justice denied.

(See the 1996 *Digest*, para. 104; and 327th Report, Case No. 1962, para. 404.)

105. Justice delayed is justice denied.

(See the 1996 *Digest*, paras. 56 and 105; and, for example, 320th Report, Case No. 1890, para. 56; 325th Report, Case No. 1888, para. 392; 326th Report, Case No. 2017/2050, para. 284; 329th Report, Case No. 1787, para. 376, and Case No. 2201, para. 508; 332nd Report, Case No. 2046, para. 445; 333rd Report, Case No. 2186, para. 350; and 337th Report, Case No. 2249, para. 1472.)

106. The absence of guarantees of due process of law may lead to abuses and result in trade union officials being penalized by decisions that are groundless. It may also create a climate of insecurity and fear which may affect the exercise of trade union rights.

(See the 1996 *Digest*, para. 106; 333rd Report, Case No. 2268, para. 755; and 337th Report, Case No. 2323, para. 1041.)

107. The safeguards of normal judicial procedure should not only be embodied in the law, but also applied in practice.

(See the 1996 *Digest*, para. 107; and 309th Report, Case No. 1851/1922, para. 247.)

108. Due process of law should include the non-retroactive application of the criminal law.

(See the 1996 *Digest*, para. 108; and 332nd Report, Case No. 2086, para. 123.)

109. The Committee has always attached great importance to the principle of prompt and fair trial by an independent and impartial judiciary in all cases, including cases in which trade unionists are charged with political or criminal offences.

(See the 1996 *Digest*, para. 109; 308th Report, Case No. 1773, para. 443; and 337th Report, Case No. 2189, para. 476.)

110. If a government has sufficient grounds for believing that the persons arrested have been involved in subversive activity, these persons should be rapidly tried by the courts with all the safeguards of a normal judicial procedure.

(See the 1996 *Digest*, para. 110.)

111. In cases where the complainants alleged that trade union leaders or workers had been arrested for trade union activities, and the governments' replies amounted to general denials of the allegation or were simply to the effect that the arrests were made for subversive activities, for reasons of internal security or for common law crimes, the Committee has always followed the rule that the governments concerned should be requested to submit further and as precise information as possible concerning the arrests, particularly in connection with the legal or judicial proceedings instituted as a result thereof and the result of such proceedings, in order to be able to make a proper examination of the allegations.

(See the 1996 *Digest*, paras. 98 and 111; 310th Report, Case No. 1929, para. 428; and 337th Report, Case No. 2323, para. 1044.)

112. In many cases, the Committee has asked the governments concerned to communicate the texts of any judgements that have been delivered together with the grounds adduced therefor.

(See the 1996 *Digest*, para. 112.)

113. The Committee has emphasized that when it requests a government to furnish judgements in judicial proceedings, such a request does not reflect in any way on the integrity or independence of the judiciary. The very essence of judicial procedure is that its results are known, and confidence in its impartiality rests on their being known.

(See the 1996 *Digest*, paras. 23 and 113; 327th Report, Case No. 1888, para. 583; 337th Report, Case No. 2189, para. 471, and Case No. 2258, para. 838.)

114. The Committee has pointed out that, where persons have been sentenced on grounds that have no relation to trade union rights, the matter falls outside its competence. It has, however, emphasized that whether a matter is one that relates to the criminal law or to the exercise of trade union rights is not one which can be determined unilaterally by the government concerned. This is a question to be determined by the Committee after examining all the available information and, in particular, the text of the judgement.

(See the 1996 *Digest*, para. 114; 310th Report, Case No. 1888, para. 383, and Case No. 1929, para. 428.)

115. If in certain cases the Committee has reached the conclusion that allegations relating to measures taken against trade unionists did not warrant further examination, this was only after it had received information from the governments showing sufficiently precisely that the measures were in no way occasioned by trade union activities, but solely by activities outside the trade union sphere that were either prejudicial to public order or political in nature.

(See the 1996 *Digest*, para. 115; and 305th Report, Case No. 1858, para. 306.)

116. When it appeared from the information available that the persons concerned had been judged by the competent judicial authorities, with the safeguards of normal procedure, and sentenced on account of actions which were not connected with normal trade union activities or which went beyond the scope of such activities, the Committee has considered that the case called for no further examination.

(See the 1996 *Digest*, para. 116.)

117. Any trade unionist who is arrested should be presumed innocent until proven guilty after a public trial during which he or she has enjoyed all the guarantees necessary for his or her defence.

(See the 1996 *Digest*, para. 117; and 305th Report, Case No. 1773, para. 368.)

118. The Committee has recalled that the International Covenant on Civil and Political Rights, in Article 14, states that everyone charged with a criminal offence shall have the right to adequate time and the necessary facilities for the preparation of his defence and to communicate with counsel of his own choosing.

(See the 1996 *Digest*, para. 118; and 306th Report, Case No. 1884, para. 698.)

119. The Committee is not required to express an opinion on the question of the granting of permission for a foreign lawyer to plead.

(See the 1996 *Digest*, para. 119.)

120. Legislation which permits the Minister at his discretion to impose restrictions on the movement of trade union leaders for a 90-day period, which can be renewed, without trial or without even being charged, is incompatible with the right to perform trade union activities or functions and the right to a fair trial at the earliest possible moment.

(See the 1996 *Digest*, para. 129.)

Freedom of movement

(See also paras. 153, 749 to 754 and 756.)

121. Trade unionists, just like all persons, should enjoy freedom of movement. In particular they should enjoy the right, subject to national legislation, which should not be such so as to violate freedom of association principles, to participate in trade union activities abroad.

(See 302nd Report, Case No. 1849, para. 220.)

122. The Committee has drawn attention to the importance that it attaches to the principle set out in the Universal Declaration of Human Rights that everyone has the right to leave any country, including his own, and to return to his country.

(see 337th Report, Case No. 2268, para. 1100.)

123. Forced exile of trade union leaders and unionists constitutes a serious infringement of human rights and trade union rights since it weakens the trade union movement as a whole when it is deprived of its leaders.

(See the 1996 *Digest*, para. 122; and 300th Report, Case No. 1682/1711/1716, para. 176.)

124. The imposition of sanctions, such as restricted movement, house arrest or banishment for trade union reasons, constitutes a violation of the principles of freedom of association. The Committee has considered it unacceptable that sanctions of this nature should be imposed by administrative action.

(See the 1996 *Digest*, para. 123.)

125. As regards the exile, banishment or the placing under house arrest of trade unionists, the Committee, while recognizing that this procedure may be occasioned by a crisis in a country, has drawn attention to the appropriateness of this procedure being accompanied by all the safeguards necessary to ensure that it shall not be utilized for the purpose of impairing the free exercise of trade union rights.

(See the 1996 *Digest*, para. 124.)

126. The exile of trade unionists, which is in violation of human rights, is particularly grave since it deprives the persons concerned of the possibility of working in their country and of maintaining contacts with their families.

(See the 1996 *Digest*, para. 125.)

127. The granting of freedom to a trade unionist on condition that he leave the country is not compatible with the free exercise of trade union rights.

(See the 1996 *Digest*, para. 126.)

128. The expulsion of trade union leaders from their country for activities connected with the exercise of their functions is not only contrary to human rights but is, furthermore, an interference in the activities of the organization to which they belong.

(See the 1996 *Digest*, para. 127.)

129. The restriction of a person's movements to a limited area, accompanied by the prohibition of entry into the area in which his trade union operates and in which he normally carries on his trade union functions, is inconsistent with the normal enjoyment of the right of association and with the exercise of the right to carry on trade union activities and functions.

(See the 1996 *Digest*, para. 128.)

Rights of assembly and demonstration

(See also para. 511)

A. Meetings of organizations in their premises and in relation to labour disputes

(See also para. 456)

130. The right of occupational organizations to hold meetings in their premises to discuss occupational questions, without prior authorization and interference by the authorities, is an essential element of freedom of association and the public authorities should refrain from any interference which would restrict this right or impede its exercise, unless public order is disturbed thereby or its maintenance seriously and imminently endangered.

(See the 1996 *Digest*, para. 130; 305th Report, Case No. 1893, para. 461; 307th Report, Case No. 1850, para. 116; 321st Report, Case No. 2066, para. 338; 324th Report, Case No. 2014, para. 923; 327th Report, Case No. 2153, para. 158; 329th Report, Case No. 2198, para. 685; 330th Report, Case No. 2144, para. 715; and 334th Report, Case No. 2222, para. 219.)

131. The right to strike and to organize union meetings are essential aspects of trade union rights, and measures taken by the authorities to ensure the observance of the law should not, therefore, prevent unions from organizing meetings during labour disputes.

(See the 1996 *Digest*, para. 131.)

132. Where a representative of the public authorities can attend trade union meetings, this may influence the deliberations and the decisions taken (especially if this representative is entitled to participate in the proceedings) and hence may constitute an act of interference incompatible with the principle of freedom to hold trade union meetings.

(See 299th Report, Case No. 1772, para. 132.)

B. Public meetings and demonstrations

(See also paras. 49 and 196)

133. Workers should enjoy the right to peaceful demonstration to defend their occupational interests.

(See the 1996 *Digest*, para. 132; and, for example, 306th Report, Case No. 1884, para. 695; 307th Report, Case No. 1909, para. 493; 320th Report, Case No. 2023, para. 425; 321st Report, Case No. 2031, para. 174; 326th Report, Case No. 2113, para. 374; 330th Report, Case No. 2189, para. 453; 335th Report, Case No. 2320, para. 664; 336th Report, Case No. 2340, para. 650; 337th Report, Case No. 2318, para. 338, and Case No. 2323, para. 1043.)

134. The right to organize public meetings constitutes an important aspect of trade union rights. In this connection, the Committee has always drawn a distinction between demonstrations in pursuit of purely trade union objectives, which it has considered as falling within the exercise of trade union rights, and those designed to achieve other ends.

(See the 1996 *Digest*, paras. 133 and 464; 300th Report, Case No. 1818, para. 364; 308th Report, Case No. 1934, para. 131; 309th Report, Case No. 1852, para. 340; 311th Report, Case No. 1969, para. 148; 332nd Report, Case No. 2238, para. 968; and 334th Report, Case No. 2222, para. 219.)

135. Protests are protected by the principles of freedom of association only when such activities are organized by trade union organizations or can be considered as legitimate trade union activities as covered by Article 3 of Convention No. 87.

(See 333rd Report, Case No. 2204, para. 228.)

136. The right to organize public meetings and processions, particularly on the occasion of May Day, constitutes an important aspect of trade union rights.

(See the 1996 *Digest*, para. 134; 300th Report, Case No. 1791, para. 339; 302nd Report, Case No. 1840, para. 350; 311th Report, Case No. 1851/1922, para. 478; 335th Report, Case No. 2270, para. 1393; and 337th Report, Case No. 2323, para. 1039.)

137. The holding of public meetings and the voicing of demands of a social and economic nature on the occasion of May Day are traditional forms of trade union action. Trade unions should have the right to organize freely whatever meetings they wish to celebrate on May Day, provided that they respect the measures taken by the authorities to ensure public order.

(See the 1996 *Digest*, para. 135; 308th Report, Case No. 1894, para. 539; 323rd Report, Case No. 2074, para. 148; and 324th Report, Case No. 2055, para. 683.)

138. A demonstration to commemorate the 50th anniversary of Convention No. 87 falls within the exercise of trade union rights.

(See 311th Report, Case No. 1969, para. 148.)

139. Trade union rights include the right to organize public demonstrations. Although the prohibition of demonstrations on the public highway in the busiest parts of a city, when it is feared that disturbances might occur, does not constitute an infringement of trade union rights, the authorities should strive to reach agreement with the organizers of the demonstration to enable it to be held in some other place where there would be no fear of disturbances.

(See the 1996 *Digest*, para. 136; 304th Report, Case No. 1850, para. 213; 309th Report, Case No. 1940, para. 284; 318th Report, Case No. 1994, para. 460; 327th Report, Case No. 2148, para. 802; and 336th Report, Case No. 2340, para. 650.)

140. The authorities should resort to the use of force only in situations where law and order is seriously threatened. The intervention of the forces of order should be in due proportion to the danger to law and order that the authorities are attempting to control and governments should take measures to ensure that the competent authorities receive adequate instructions so as to eliminate the danger entailed by the use of excessive violence when controlling demonstrations which might result in a disturbance of the peace.

(See the 1996 *Digest*, para. 137; and, for example, 300th Report, Case No. 1811/1816, para. 311; 304th Report, Case No. 1837, para. 55; 308th Report, Case No. 1914, para. 670; 311th Report, Case No. 1865, para. 336; 320th Report, Case No. 2027, para. 872; 328th Report, Case No. 2143, para. 593; 330th Report, Case No. 2189, para. 453; 332nd Report, Case No. 2218, para. 422; 336th Report, Case No. 2340, para. 651; and 337th Report, Case No. 2323, para. 1031.)

141. The requirement of administrative permission to hold public meetings and demonstrations is not objectionable per se from the standpoint of the principles of freedom of association. The maintenance of public order is not incompatible with the right to hold demonstrations so long as the authorities responsible for public order reach agreement with the organizers of a demonstration concerning the place where it will be held and the manner in which it will take place.

(See the 1996 *Digest*, para. 138; 334th Report, Case No. 2222, para. 219; 335th Report, Case No. 2285, para. 1184; and 336th Report, Case No. 2358, para. 719.)

142. Permission to hold public meetings and demonstrations, which is an important trade union right, should not be arbitrarily refused.

(See the 1996 *Digest*, para. 139; 316th Report, Case No. 1773, para. 612; and 334th Report, Case No. 2222, para 219.)

143. Although the right of holding trade union meetings is an essential aspect of trade union rights, the organizations concerned must observe the general provisions relating to public meetings, which are applicable to all. This principle is contained in Article 8 of Convention No. 87, which provides that workers and their organizations, like other persons or organized collectivities, shall respect the law of the land.

(See the 1996 *Digest*, para. 140; 332nd Report, Case No. 2187, para. 719; and 334th Report, Case No. 2222, para. 219.)

144. Trade unions must conform to the general provisions applicable to all public meetings and must respect the reasonable limits which may be fixed by the authorities to avoid disturbances in public places.

(See the 1996 *Digest*, para. 141; 300th Report, Case No. 1791, para. 339; 304th Report, Case No. 1865, para. 247; 308th Report, Case No. 1914, para. 670; 327th Report, Case No. 2148, para. 802; 335th Report, Case No. 2285, para. 1184; 336th Report, Case No. 2358, para. 719; and 337th Report, case No. 2318, para. 339.)

145. The right to hold trade union meetings cannot be interpreted as relieving organizations from the obligation to comply with reasonable formalities when they wish to make use of public premises.

(See the 1996 *Digest*, para. 142.)

146. It is for the government, which is responsible for the maintenance of public order, to decide whether meetings, including trade union meetings, may, in particular circumstances, endanger public order and security, and to take any necessary preventive measures.

(See the 1996 *Digest*, para. 143; and 300th Report, Case No. 1791, para. 339.)

147. Trade unions should respect legal provisions which are intended to ensure the maintenance of public order; the public authorities should, for their part, refrain from any interference which would restrict the right of trade unions to organize the holding and proceedings of their meetings in full freedom.

(See the 1996 *Digest*, para. 144; 326th Report, Case No. 2113, para. 372; 335th Report, Case No. 2320, para. 669, and Case No. 2330, para. 878.)

148. The obligation on a procession to follow a predetermined itinerary does not constitute a violation of trade union rights.

(See the 1996 *Digest*, para. 145.)

149. A time restriction placed by legislation on the right to demonstrate is not justified and may render that right inoperative in practice.

(See 320th Report, Case No. 2023, para. 425.)

150. In general, the use of the forces of order during trade union demonstrations should be limited to cases of genuine necessity.

(See the 1996 *Digest*, para. 146; 327th Report, Case No. 2148, para. 802; and 334th Report, Case No. 2222, para. 216.)

151. The police authorities should be given precise instructions so that, in cases where public order is not seriously threatened, people are not arrested simply for having organized or participated in a demonstration.

(See the 1996 *Digest*, para. 147; 300th Report, Case No. 1818, para. 364; and 336th Report, Case No. 2340, para. 651.)

C. *International trade union meetings*

(See also paras. 748, 754 and 758)

152. Trade union meetings of an international character may give rise to special problems, not only because of the nationality of the participants, but also because of the international policy and commitments of the country in which these meetings are to take place. As a result of such commitments, the government of a particular country may consider it necessary to adopt restrictive measures on the grounds of certain special circumstances prevailing at a particular time. Such measures might be justified in exceptional cases, having more regard to specific situations, and provided they conform to the laws of the country. However, it should never be possible to apply measures of a general nature against particular trade union organizations unless in each case sufficient grounds exist to justify the government decision, such as genuine dangers which may arise for the international relations of a State or for security and public order. Otherwise, the right of assembly, the exercise of which by international organizations should also be recognized, would be seriously restricted.

(See the 1996 *Digest*, para. 150.)

153. Participation by trade unionists in international trade union meetings is a fundamental trade union right and governments should therefore abstain from any measure, such as withholding travel documents, that would prevent representatives of workers' organizations from exercising their mandate in full freedom and independence.

(See the 1996 *Digest*, paras. 151 and 645; 300th Report, Case No. 1805, para. 421; and 336th Report, Case No. 2328, para. 885.)

Freedom of opinion and expression

A. *General principles*

(See also para. 745)

154. The full exercise of trade union rights calls for a free flow of information, opinions and ideas, and to this end workers, employers and their organizations should enjoy freedom of opinion and expression at their meetings, in their publications and in the course of other trade union activities. Nevertheless, in expressing their opinions, trade union organizations should respect the limits of propriety and refrain from the use of insulting language.

(See the 1996 *Digest*, para. 152; 304th Report, Case No. 1850, para. 210; 306th Report, Case No. 1885, para. 140; 309th Report, Case No. 1945, para. 67; 324th Report, Case No. 2014, para. 925; and 336th Report, Case No. 2340, para. 652.)

155. The right to express opinions through the press or otherwise is an essential aspect of trade union rights.

(See the 1996 *Digest*, para. 153; 299th Report, Case No. 1640/1646, para. 150; 302nd Report, Case No. 1817, para. 324; 324th Report, Case No. 2065, para. 131; 327th Report, Case No. 2147, para. 865; 328th Report, Case No. 1961, para. 42; 332nd Report, Case No. 2090, para. 354; and 333rd Report, Case No. 2272, para. 539.)

156. The right to express opinions without previous authorization through the press is one of the essential elements of the rights of occupational organizations.

(See the 1996 *Digest*, para. 154.)

157. The freedom of expression which should be enjoyed by trade unions and their leaders should also be guaranteed when they wish to criticize the government's economic and social policy.

(See the 1996 *Digest*, para. 155.)

158. The right of an employers' or workers' organization to express its opinion uncensored through the independent press should in no way differ from the right to express opinions in exclusively occupational or trade union journals.

(See the 1996 *Digest*, para. 156; and 328th Report, Case No. 1961, para. 42.)

159. In a case in which the major communications media had been closed down for months, the Committee emphasized that the right of workers' and employers' organizations to express their views in the press or through other media is one of the essential elements of freedom of association; consequently the authorities should refrain from unduly impeding its lawful exercise.

(See the 1996 *Digest*, para. 157.)

160. With regard to legislation which allowed the temporary or definitive suspension of journals and publications which "compromise the economic stability of the nation", the Committee considered that such restrictions, which amount to a constant threat of suspension of publications, cannot but impede considerably the right of trade union and professional organizations to express their views in the press, in their own publications or through other media, which is one of the essential elements of trade union rights and consequently governments should refrain from unduly impeding the lawful exercise thereof.

(See the 1996 *Digest*, para. 158.)

161. The choice of union insignia falls within the scope of freedom of expression, the respect of which is essential for the normal exercise of trade union rights, and therefore should, as a general principle, be left solely to the internal affairs of the trade union in question.

(See 306th Report, Case No. 1885, para. 140.)

162. The display of union flags at meetings in the workplace, the putting up of union bulletin boards, the distribution of union news and leaflets, the signing of petitions and participation in union rallies constitute legitimate trade union activities.

(See 308th Report, Case No. 1897, para. 475.)

163. The prohibition of the placing of posters stating the point of view of a central trade union organization is an unacceptable restriction on trade union activities.

(See the 1996 *Digest*, para. 467.)

B. Authorization and censorship of publications

(See also paras. 197 and 198)

164. If before being able to publish a newspaper trade unions are required to furnish a substantial bond, this would constitute, especially in the case of smaller unions, such an unreasonable condition as to be incompatible with the exercise of the right of trade unions to express their opinions through the press.

(See the 1996 *Digest*, para. 159; and 328th Report, Case No. 2160, para. 658.)

165. The fear of the authorities of seeing a trade union newspaper serve political ends unrelated to trade union activities or which, at least, lie far outside their normal scope, is not a sufficient reason to refuse to allow such a newspaper to appear.

(See the 1996 *Digest*, para. 160; and 302nd Report, Case No. 1817, para. 324.)

166. The publication and distribution of news and information of general or special interest to trade unions and their members constitutes a legitimate trade union activity and the application of measures designed to control publication and means of information may involve serious interference by administrative authorities with this activity. In such cases, the exercise of administrative authority should be subject to judicial review at the earliest possible moment.

(See the 1996 *Digest*, para. 161; 320th Report, Case No. 2031, para. 172; and 327th Report, Case No. 1787, para. 341.)

167. The discretionary power of the public authorities to revoke the licence granted to a trade union newspaper, without it being possible to appeal against such decisions to a court of law, is not compatible with the provisions of Convention No. 87, which provides that workers' organizations have the right to organize their activities without interference by the public authorities.

(See the 1996 *Digest*, para. 162.)

168. While the imposition of general censorship is primarily a matter that relates to civil liberties rather than to trade union rights, the censorship of the press during an industrial dispute may have a direct effect on the conduct of the dispute and may prejudice the parties by not allowing the true facts surrounding the dispute to become known.

(See the 1996 *Digest*, para. 163.)

C. Publications of a political character

(See also para. 155)

169. When issuing their publications, trade union organizations should have regard, in the interests of the development of the trade union movement, to the principles enunciated by the International Labour Conference at its 35th Session (1952) for the protection of the freedom and independence of the trade union movement and the safeguarding of its fundamental task, which is to ensure the social and economic well-being of all workers.

(See the 1996 *Digest*, para. 165.)

170. In a case in which a trade union newspaper, in its allusions and accusations against the government, seemed to have exceeded the admissible limits of controversy, the Committee pointed out that trade union publications should refrain from extravagance of language. The primary role of publications of this type should be to deal with matters essentially relating to the defence and furtherance of the interests of the unions' members in particular and with labour questions in general. The Committee, nevertheless, recognized that it is difficult to draw a clear distinction between what is political and what is strictly trade union in character. It pointed out that these two notions overlap, and it is inevitable and sometimes normal for trade union publications to take a stand on questions having political aspects, as well as on strictly economic or social questions.

(See the 1996 *Digest*, para. 166.)

171. In a case where the distribution of all the publications of a trade union organization was prohibited, the Committee suggested that the order in question be re-examined in the light of the principle that trade union organizations should have the right to distribute the publications in which their programme is formulated, and so as to distinguish between those trade union publications which deal with problems normally regarded as falling directly or indirectly within the competence of trade unions and those which are obviously political or anti-national in character.

(See the 1996 *Digest*, para. 167.)

D. Seizure of publications

172. The confiscation of May Day propaganda material or other trade union publications may constitute a serious interference by the authorities in trade union activities.

(See the 1996 *Digest*, para. 168.)

173. The attitude adopted by the authorities in systematically seizing a trade union newspaper does not seem to be compatible with the principle that the right to express opinions through the press or otherwise is one of the essential aspects of trade union rights.

(See the 1996 *Digest*, para. 169.)

Freedom of speech at the International Labour Conference

174. The Committee has pointed out that delegates of workers' and employers' organizations to the International Labour Conference deal, in their speeches, with questions which are of direct or indirect concern to the ILO. The functioning of the Conference would risk being considerably hampered and the freedom of speech of the workers' and employers' delegates paralysed if they were to be threatened with prosecution based, directly or indirectly, on the contents of their speeches at the Conference. Article 40 of the Constitution of the Organization provides that delegates to the Conference shall enjoy such "immunities as are necessary for the independent exercise of their functions in connection with the Organisation". The right of delegates to the Conference to express freely their point of view on questions within the competence of the Organization implies that delegates of employers' and workers' organizations have the right to inform their members in their respective countries of their speeches. The arrest and sentencing of a delegate following a speech to the Conference jeopardize freedom of speech for delegates as well as the immunities they should enjoy in this regard.

(See the 1996 *Digest*, para. 170.)

Protection against disclosure of information on trade union membership and activities

(See also paras. 782 and 803)

175. Tampering with correspondence is an offence which is incompatible with the free exercise of trade union rights and civil liberties; the International Labour Conference in its 1970 resolution on trade union rights and their relation to civil liberties stated that particular attention should be given to the right to the inviolability of correspondence and telephonic conversations.

(See the 1996 *Digest*, para. 171.)

176. In one case where it was alleged that the military police had sent out a questionnaire to undertakings in which it was asked whether there were any natural leaders among the employees, strike instigators, trade union delegates or workers' organizations in the undertaking, the Committee considered that such an inquiry could involve a risk of being put to improper use by the military authorities or the police in the event of a labour dispute. For example, workers might be taken into custody simply because they were on a list of persons thus established, even though they had not committed any offence. The Committee also considered that, because of the atmosphere of mistrust that it created, such a procedure was hardly favourable for the development of harmonious industrial relations.

(See the 1996 *Digest*, para. 172.)

177. The establishment of a register containing data on trade union members does not respect rights of the person (including privacy rights) and such a register may be used to compile blacklists of workers.

(See 326th Report, Case No. 2067, para. 512.)

Protection of trade union premises and property

(See also para. 345)

178. The inviolability of trade union premises is a civil liberty which is essential to the exercise of trade union rights.

(See 300th Report, Case No. 1795, para. 189, and Case No. 1791, para. 342.)

179. The occupation of trade union premises by the security forces, without a court warrant authorizing such occupation, is a serious interference by the authorities in trade union activities.

(See the 1996 *Digest*, para. 174; 300th Report, Case No. 1791, para. 342; 321st Report, Case No. 2052, para. 249; 325th Report, Case No. 2052, para. 411; and 338th Report, Case No. 2364, para. 980.)

180. The right of the inviolability of the premises of organizations of workers and employers also necessarily implies that the public authorities may not insist on entering such premises without prior authorization or without having obtained a legal warrant to do so.

(See the 1996 *Digest*, para. 175; and, for example, 299th Report, Case No. 1772, para. 131; 300th Report, Case No. 1790, para. 296; 305th Report, Case No. 1858, para. 308; 308th Report, Case No. 1920, para. 552; 311th Report, Case No. 1954, para. 409; 316th Report, Case No. 1888, para. 497; 320th Report, Case No. 1961, para. 615; 321st Report, Case No. 2020, para. 48; 329th Report, Case No. 2184, para. 828; and 331st Report, Case No. 2081, para. 109.)

181. The entry by police or military forces into trade union premises without a judicial warrant constitutes a serious and unjustifiable interference in trade union activities.

(See the 1996 *Digest*, para. 176; 300th Report, Case No. 1799, para. 211; 302nd Report, Case No. 1849, para. 214; 305th Report, Case No. 1874, para. 271; 311th Report, Case No. 1954, para. 409; 318th Report, Case No. 2005, para. 185; 329th Report, Case No. 2184, para. 828; and 336th Report, Case No. 2321, para. 493.)

182. Any search of trade union premises, or of unionists' homes, without a court order constitutes an extremely serious infringement of freedom of association.

(See the 1996 *Digest*, para. 177; 300th Report, Case No. 1649, para. 455; 304th Report, Case No. 1851, para. 284; 309th Report, Case No. 1851/1922, para. 245; 320th Report, Case No. 1961, para. 615; 323rd Report, Case No. 2081, para. 568; 326th Report, Case No. 2090, para. 239; 331st Report, Case No. 2081, para. 109; and 337th Report, Case No. 2388, para. 1344.)

183. With regard to searches of trade union premises, it is stated in the resolution on trade union rights and their relation to civil liberties, adopted by the International Labour Conference at its 54th Session (1970), that the right to adequate protection of trade union property is one of those civil liberties which are essential for the normal exercise of trade union rights.

(See the 1996 *Digest*, para. 178; 300th Report, Case No. 1799, para. 211, and Case No. 1649, para. 455; and 302nd Report, Case No. 1849, para. 214 .)

184. When examining allegations of attacks carried out against trade union premises and threats against trade unionists, the Committee has recalled that activities of this kind create among trade unionists a climate of fear which is extremely prejudicial to the exercise of trade union activities and that the authorities, when informed of such matters, should carry out an immediate investigation to determine who is responsible and punish the guilty parties.

(See the 1996 *Digest*, para. 179; 306th Report, Case No. 1908, para. 458; 308th Report, Case No. 1908, para. 359; 318th Report, Case No. 1994, para. 461; and 320th Report, Case No. 2027, para. 874.)

185. Searches of trade union premises should be made only following the issue of a warrant by the ordinary judicial authority where that authority is satisfied that there are reasonable grounds for supposing that evidence exists on the premises material to a prosecution for a penal offence and on condition that the search be restricted to the purpose in respect of which the warrant was issued.

(See the 1996 *Digest*, para. 180; 300th Report, Case No. 1783, para. 286; 304th Report, Case No. 1850, para. 212; 323rd Report, Case No. 2081, para. 568; 331st Report, Case No. 2081, para. 109; and 333rd Report, Case No. 2246, para. 935.)

186. If trade union premises are used as a refuge by persons who have committed serious crimes, or as a meeting place for a political organization, the trade unions concerned cannot claim any immunity against the entry of the authorities into these premises.

(See the 1996 *Digest*, para. 181.)

187. Even if police intervention in trade union premises may be justified in particularly serious circumstances, such intervention should in no case entail the ransacking of the premises and archives of an organization.

(See the 1996 *Digest*, para. 182; and 304th Report, Case No. 1850, para. 212.)

188. The occupation or sealing of trade union premises should be subject to independent judicial review before being undertaken by the authorities in view of the significant risk that such measures may paralyse trade union activities.

(See the 1996 *Digest*, para. 183; 304th Report, Case No. 1851, para. 284; 316th Report, Case No. 1888, para. 497, and Case No. 1972, para. 707; 326th Report, Case No. 2090, para. 239; 332nd Report, Case No. 2199, para. 162; 333rd Report, Case No. 2153, para. 205; 334th Report, Case No. 2267, para. 659; and 338th Report, Case No. 2364, para. 980.)

189. The Committee has drawn attention to the importance of the principle that the property of trade unions should enjoy adequate protection.

(See the 1996 *Digest*, para. 184; 304th Report, Case No. 1850, para. 212; 307th Report, Case No. 1851, para. 268; 308th Report, Case No. 1920, para. 522; 316th Report, Case No. 1972, para. 707; 327th Report, Case No. 2118, para. 643; 330th Report, Case No. 2144, para. 708; 331st Report, Case No. 2199, para. 704; 333rd Report, Case No. 2153, para. 205; and 335th Report, Case No. 2304, para. 1016.)

190. The confiscation of trade union property by the authorities, without a court order, constitutes an infringement of the right of trade unions to own property and undue interference in trade union activities.

(See 310th Report, Case No. 1957, para. 132.)

191. A climate of violence, in which attacks are made against trade union premises and property, constitutes serious interference with the exercise of trade union rights; such situations call for severe measures to be taken by the authorities, and in particular the arraignment of those presumed to be responsible before an independent judicial authority.

(See the 1996 *Digest*, para. 185; 307th Report, Case No. 1851, para. 268; 308th Report, Case No. 1920, para. 522; and 318th Report, Case No. 2020, para. 320.)

192. The access of trade union members to their union premises should not be restricted by the state authorities.

(See 326th Report, Case No. 2090, para. 239.)

State of emergency and the exercise of trade union rights

193. The Committee on Freedom of Association has recalled that the Committee of Experts on the Application of Conventions and Recommendations has emphasized that the freedom of association Conventions do not contain any provision permitting derogation from the obligations arising under the Convention, or any suspension of their application, based on a plea that an emergency exists.

(See the 1996 *Digest*, para. 186; 318th Report, Case No. 2006, para. 347; 323rd Report, Case No. 2006, para. 427; and 326th Report, Case no. 2096, para. 428.)

194. In cases of repeated renewals of the state of emergency, the Committee has pointed out that the resolution concerning trade union rights and their relation to civil liberties, adopted by the International Labour Conference in 1970, states that "the rights conferred upon workers' and employers' organisations must be based on respect for (...) civil liberties (...) and that the absence of these civil liberties removes all meaning from the concept of trade union rights".

(See the 1996 *Digest*, para. 187.)

195. When a state of emergency has continued over a period of several years, entailing serious restrictions on trade union rights and civil liberties that are essential for the exercise of such rights, the Committee has considered that it is necessary to safeguard the exercise specifically of trade union rights such as the establishment of employers' and workers' organizations, the right to hold trade union meetings in trade union premises and the right to strike in non-essential services.

(See the 1996 *Digest*, para. 189.)

196. The enactment of emergency regulations which empower the government to place restrictions on the organization of public meetings and which are applicable not only to public trade union meetings, but also to all public meetings, and which are occasioned by events which the government considered so serious as to call for the declaration of a state of emergency, does not in itself constitute a violation of trade union rights.

(See the 1996 *Digest*, paras. 149 and 190; and 334th Report, Case No. 2279, para. 697.)

197. Where restrictions imposed by a revolutionary government on certain publications during a period of emergency appeared mainly to have been imposed for reasons of a general political character, the Committee, while taking account of the exceptional nature of these measures, drew the attention of the government to the importance of ensuring respect for the freedom of trade union publications.

(See the 1996 *Digest*, para. 191.)

198. Restrictions on the right to strike and on freedom of expression imposed in the context of an attempted coup d'état against the constitutional government, which gave rise to a state of emergency called in accordance with the constitution, do not violate freedom of association on the grounds that such restrictions are justified in the event of an acute national emergency.

(See the 1996 *Digest*, paras. 192 and 529.)

199. Any measures of suspension or dissolution by administrative authority, when taken during an emergency situation, should be accompanied by normal judicial safeguards, including the right of appeal to the courts against such dissolution or suspension.

(See the 1996 *Digest*, para. 193.)

200. In a case in which emergency measures had been extended over many years, the Committee pointed out that martial law was incompatible with the full exercise of trade union rights.

(See the 1996 *Digest*, para. 194.)

201. Emergency legislation aimed at anti-social disruptive elements should not be applied against workers for exercising their legitimate trade union rights.

(See the 1996 *Digest*, para. 196.)

202. As regards countries which are in a state of political crisis or have just undergone grave disturbances (civil war, revolution, etc.), the Committee has considered it necessary, when examining the various measures taken by governments, including some against trade union organizations, to take account of such exceptional circumstances when examining the merits of the allegations.

(See the 1996 *Digest*, para. 197.)

203. In cases in which martial law has been declared and special provisions adopted against terrorism, although the Committee is aware of the serious situation of violence which may affect a country, it has to point out that as far as possible recourse should be made to the provisions of the ordinary law rather than emergency measures which are liable, by their very nature, to involve certain restrictions on fundamental rights.

(See the 1996 *Digest*, paras. 188 and 198.)

204. If a revolutionary government suspends constitutional safeguards, this may constitute serious interference by the authorities in trade union affairs, contrary to Article 3 of Convention No. 87, except where such measures are necessary because the organizations concerned have diverged from their trade union objectives and have defied the law. In any case, such measures should be subject to appropriate judicial guarantees that may be invoked without delay.

(See the 1996 *Digest*, para. 199.)

Questions of a political nature affecting trade union rights

205. It is important to distinguish between the evolution of a country's political institutions and matters relating to the exercise of freedom of association, if, as was emphasized by the International Labour Conference in 1970 in the resolution concerning trade union rights and their relation to civil liberties, respect for freedom of association is closely bound up with respect for civil liberties. In general, workers' and employers' organizations nevertheless have their own specific functions to perform, irrespective of the country's political system.

(See the 1996 *Digest*, para. 201.)

206. Measures which, although of a political nature and not intended to restrict trade union rights as such, may nevertheless be applied in such a manner as to affect the exercise of such rights.

(See the 1996 *Digest*, para. 202.)

207. As stated by the International Labour Conference in 1970, although respect for freedom of association is closely bound up with respect for civil liberties in general, it is nevertheless important to distinguish between the recognition of freedom of association and questions relating to a country's political evolution.

(See the 1996 *Digest*, para. 203; and 326th Report, Case No. 2090, para. 240.)

208. Political matters which do not impair the exercise of freedom of association are outside the competence of the Committee. The Committee is not competent to deal with a complaint that is based on subversive acts, and it is likewise incompetent to deal with political matters that may be referred to in a government's reply.

(See the 1996 *Digest*, para. 204.)

Right of workers and employers, without distinction whatsoever, to establish and to join organizations

3

General principle

209. Article 2 of Convention No. 87 is designed to give expression to the principle of non-discrimination in trade union matters, and the words "without distinction whatsoever" used in this Article mean that freedom of association should be guaranteed without discrimination of any kind based on occupation, sex, colour, race, beliefs, nationality, political opinion, etc., not only to workers in the private sector of the economy, but also to civil servants and public service employees in general.

(See the 1996 *Digest*, para. 205; and 308th Report, Case No. 1900, para. 182.)

Distinctions based on race, political opinion or nationality

210. A law which prohibits African workers from establishing trade unions which can be registered and participate in industrial councils for the purpose of negotiating agreements and settling disputes constitutes a form of discrimination which is inconsistent with the principle accepted in the majority of countries, and embodied in Convention No. 87, that workers without distinction whatsoever should have the right to establish and, subject only to the rules of the organization concerned, to join organizations of their own choosing without previous authorization. It is also inconsistent with the principle that all workers' organizations should enjoy the right of collective bargaining.

(See the 1996 *Digest*, para. 208.)

211. The prohibition of registration of mixed trade unions (consisting of workers of different races) is not compatible with the generally accepted principle that workers, without distinction whatsoever, should have the right to establish and, subject only to the rules of the organizations concerned, to join organizations of their own choosing without previous authorization.

(See the 1996 *Digest*, para. 209.)

212. Workers should have the right, without distinction whatsoever, in particular without discrimination on the basis of political opinion, to join the organization of their own choosing.

(See the 1996 *Digest*, para. 210.)

213. Workers should have the right to establish the organizations that they consider necessary in a climate of complete security irrespective of whether or not they support the social and economic model of the Government, including the political model of the country.

(See 332nd Report, Case No. 2258, para. 515.)

214. With regard to the denial of the right to organize to migrant workers in an irregular situation, the Committee recalled that all workers, with the sole exception of the armed forces and the police, are covered by Convention No. 87, and it therefore requested the Government to take the terms of Article 2 of Convention No. 87 into account in the legislation in question.

(See 327th Report, Case No. 2121, para. 561.)

215. With regard to the granting of trade union rights to aliens, the requirement of reciprocity is not acceptable under Article 2 of Convention No. 87.

(See the 1996 *Digest*, para. 211.)

Distinctions based on occupational category

A. General principles

216. All workers, without distinction whatsoever, including without discrimination in regard to occupation, should have the right to establish and join organizations of their own choosing.

(See 326th Report, Case No. 2113, para. 372.)

217. To establish a limited list of occupations with a view to recognizing the right to associate would be contrary to the principle that workers, without distinction whatsoever, should have the right to establish and join organizations of their own choosing.

(See the 1996 *Digest*, para. 278.)

B. Public servants

218. The standards contained in Convention No. 87 apply to all workers "without distinction whatsoever", and are therefore applicable to employees of the State. It was indeed considered inequitable to draw any distinction in trade union matters between workers in the private sector and public servants, since workers in both categories should have the right to organize for the defence of their interests.

(See the 1996 *Digest*, para. 212; 300th Report, Case No. 1844, para. 240; and 334th Report, Case No. 2222, para. 206.)

219. Public servants, like all other workers, without distinction whatsoever, have the right to establish and join organizations of their own choosing, without previous authorization, for the promotion and defence of their occupational interests.

(See the 1996 *Digest*, para. 213; 300th Report, Case No. 1823, para. 438; 307th Report, Case No. 1865, para. 212; 316th Report, Case No. 1773, para. 616; 334th Report, Case No. 2222, para. 204; 335th Report, Case No. 1865, para. 816; and 338th Report, Case No. 2364, para. 979.)

220. Public employees (with the sole possible exception of the armed forces and the police, by virtue of Article 9 of Convention No. 87) should, like workers in the private sector, be able to establish organizations of their own choosing to further and defend the interests of their members.

(See the 1996 *Digest*, paras. 206 and 214; 308th Report, Case No. 1902, para. 701; 309th Report, Case No. 1865, para. 144; 320th Report, Case No. 1865, para. 509; 321st Report, Case No. 2066, para. 332; 323rd Report, Case No. 1874, para. 60; 327th Report, Case No. 1865, para. 484; 329th Report, Case No. 2177/2183, para. 633; 330th Report, Case No. 2200, para. 1096; 333rd Report, Case No. 2229, para. 108; and 338th Report, Case No. 2364, para. 979.)

221. In view of the importance of the right of employees of the State and local authorities to constitute and register trade unions, the prohibition of the right of association for workers in the service of the State is incompatible with the generally accepted principle that workers, without distinction whatsoever, should have the right to establish organizations of their own choosing without previous authorization.

(See the 1996 *Digest*, para. 215; and 328th Report, Case No. 1987/2085, para. 47.)

222. The denial of the right of workers in the public sector to set up trade unions, where this right is enjoyed by workers in the private sector, with the result that their "associations" do not enjoy the same advantages and privileges as "trade unions", involves discrimination as regards government-employed workers and their organizations as compared with private sector workers and their organizations. Such a situation gives rise to the question of compatibility of these distinctions with Article 2 of Convention No. 87, according to which workers "without distinction whatsoever" shall have the right to establish and join organizations of their own choosing without previous authorization, as well as with Articles 3 and 8, paragraph 2, of the Convention.

(See the 1996 *Digest*, para. 216; 307th Report, Case No. 1865, para. 212; 324th Report, Case No. 2083, para. 253; and 327th Report, Case No. 1865, para. 485.)

(a) Members of the armed forces and the police

223. The members of the armed forces who can be excluded from the application of Convention No. 87 should be defined in a restrictive manner.

(See the 1996 *Digest*, para. 219; 330th Report, Case No. 2229, para. 941; and 335th Report, Case No. 2257, para. 459.)

224. Article 9, paragraph 1, of Convention No. 87 provides that "the extent to which the guarantees provided for in this Convention shall apply to the armed forces and the police shall be determined by national laws or regulations"; under this provision, it is clear that the International Labour Conference intended to leave it to each State to decide on the extent to which it was desirable to grant members of the armed forces and of the police the rights covered by the Convention, which means that States having ratified the Convention are not required to grant these rights to the said categories of persons.

(See the 1996 *Digest*, para. 220; 332nd Report, Case No. 2240, para. 264; and 335th Report, Case No. 2325, para. 1257.)

225. The fact that Article 9, paragraph 1, of Convention No. 87 stipulates that the extent to which the guarantees provided for in the Convention shall apply to the armed forces and the police shall be determined by national laws and regulations cannot warrant the assumption that any limitations or exclusions imposed by the legislation of a State as regards the trade union rights of the armed forces and the police are contrary to the Convention; this is a matter which has been left to the discretion of the States Members of the ILO.

(See the 1996 *Digest*, para. 221; and 307th Report, Case No. 1898, para. 323.)

226. Article 2 of Convention No. 87 provides that workers and employers, without distinction whatsoever, shall have the right to establish and to join organizations of their own choosing. While Article 9 of the Convention does authorize exceptions to the scope of its provisions for the police and the armed forces, the Committee would recall that the members of the armed forces who can be excluded should be defined in a restrictive manner. Furthermore, the Committee of Experts on the Application of Conventions and Recommendations has observed that, since this Article of the Convention provides only for exceptions to the general principle, workers should be considered as civilians in case of doubt.

(See the 1996 *Digest*, para. 222; 321st Report, Case No. 2066, para. 332; and 333rd Report, Case No. 2288, para. 829.)

(b) Civilian staff in the armed forces

227. Civilian workers in the manufacturing establishments of the armed forces should have the right to establish organizations of their own choosing without previous authorization, in conformity with Convention No. 87.

(See the 1996 *Digest*, para. 223; and 330th Report, Case No. 2229, para. 941.)

228. The civilian staff working at the Army Bank should enjoy the right to establish and join trade union organizations, and adequate protection against acts of anti-union discrimination, in the same way as other trade union members and leaders in the country.

(See the 1996 *Digest*, para. 224.)

229. Civilians working in the services of the army should have the right to form trade unions.

(See 338th Report, Case No. 2387, para. 868.)

(c) Local public service employees

230. Local public service employees should be able effectively to establish organizations of their own choosing, and these organizations should enjoy the full right to further and defend the interests of the workers whom they represent.

(See the 1996 *Digest*, para. 217.)

(d) Firefighters

231. The functions exercised by firefighters do not justify their exclusion from the right to organize. They should therefore enjoy the right to organize.

(See 308th Report, Case No. 1902, para. 701; 329th Report, Case No. 2177/2183, para. 633; and 338th Report, Case No. 2187, para. 170.)

(e) Prison staff

232. Prison staff should enjoy the right to organize.

(See 329th Report, Case No. 2177/2183, para. 633.)

(f) Customs officials

233. Customs officials are covered by Convention No. 87 and therefore have the right to organize.

(See 333rd Report, Case no. 2288, para. 829.)

(g) Employees in the labour inspectorate

234. The denial of the right to organize to workers in the labour inspectorate constitutes a violation of Article 2 of Convention No. 87.

(See 302nd Report, Case No. 1823, para. 444.)

(h) Teachers

235. Teachers should have the right to establish and join organizations of their own choosing, without previous authorization, for the promotion and defence of their occupational interests.

(See 309th Report, Case No. 1865, para. 143.)

236. Instructors governed by contracts for the provision of services should be able to establish and join organizations of their own choosing.

(See 326th Report, Case No. 2013, para. 416.)

237. The Committee requested a government to take measures to repeal a provision of the Universities Act which empowered the employer to determine the persons who could be members of academic staff associations. The Committee also recommended that consideration be given to the possibility of introducing an independent system for the designation, where necessary, of academic staff members, either through third party arbitration or some form of informal machinery.

(See the 1996 *Digest*, para. 242.)

(i) Locally recruited personnel in embassies

238. Convention No. 87 is applicable to locally recruited personnel in embassies.

(See 334th Report, Case No. 2197, para. 130.)

C. Security agents

239. Private security agents should freely be able to establish trade union organizations of their own choosing.

(See 333rd Report, Case No. 2299, para. 562.)

240. A national constitution should not have the effect of denying the right to organize of workers who need to carry arms because of the nature of their work.

(See 333rd Report, Case No. 2299, para. 561.)

D. Agricultural workers

241. Agricultural workers should enjoy the right to organize.

(See the 1996 *Digest*, para. 225.)

242. Legislation which lays down that not less than 60 per cent of the members of a trade union must be literate is incompatible with the principle established in Convention No. 87 that workers, without distinction whatsoever, shall have the right to establish organizations of their choosing. Article 1 of Convention No. 11 confirms this principle and lays down that each Member of the International Labour Organization which ratifies this Convention undertakes to secure to all those engaged in agriculture the same rights of association and combination as to industrial workers.

(See the 1996 *Digest*, para. 226.)

E. Plantation workers

243. In the resolution adopted by the Plantations Committee at its First Session in 1950, it is provided that employers should remove existing hindrances, if any, in the way of the organization of free, independent and democratically controlled trade unions by plantation workers.

(See the 1996 *Digest*, para. 227.)

F. Employees of airlines

244. The prohibition of trade union activities in international airlines constitutes a serious violation of freedom of association.

(See the 1996 *Digest*, para. 228.)

G. Port workers

245. In one case where the port employees of a country were, by custom and agreement, classified as government officials and were therefore outside the coverage of the Trade Unions Act, and the government had considered that Convention No. 87 (ratified by the country concerned) did not apply to them, the Committee pointed out that the government had assumed an international obligation to apply the Convention to workers "without distinction whatsoever", and that in these circumstances the provisions of the Convention could not be modified as regards particular categories of workers because of any private or national agreement, custom or other arrangement between such categories of workers and the government.

(See the 1996 *Digest*, para. 218.)

H. Hospital personnel

246. The right to establish and to join organizations for the promotion and defence of workers' interests without previous authorization is a fundamental right which should be enjoyed by all workers without distinction whatsoever, including hospital personnel.

(See the 1996 *Digest*, para. 229.)

I. Managerial and supervisory staff

247. It is not necessarily incompatible with the requirements of Article 2 of Convention No. 87 to deny managerial or supervisory employees the right to belong to the same trade unions as other workers, on condition that two requirements are met: first, that such workers have the right to establish their own associations to defend their interests and, second, that the categories of such staff are not defined so broadly as to weaken the organizations of other workers in the enterprise or branch of activity by depriving them of a substantial proportion of their present or potential membership.

(See the 1996 *Digest*, para. 231; 307th Report, Case No. 1878, para. 453; 311th Report, Case No. 1951, para. 222; 313th Report, Case No. 1959, para. 217; 325th Report, Case No. 1951, para. 210; 329th Report, Case No. 2177/2183, para. 638; 330th Report, Case No. 2200, para. 1096; 332nd Report, Case No. 2242, para. 823; 335th Report, Case No. 2257, para. 460, and Case No. 1865, para. 816.)

248. As regards provisions which prohibit supervisory employees from joining workers' organizations, the Committee has taken the view that the expression "supervisors" should be limited to cover only those persons who genuinely represent the interests of employers.

(See the 1996 *Digest*, para. 232; 311th Report, Case No. 1951, para. 222; and 325th Report, Case No. 1951, para. 210.)

249. Limiting the definition of managerial staff to persons who have the authority to appoint or dismiss is sufficiently restrictive to meet the condition that these categories of staff are not defined too broadly.

(See 313th Report, Case No. 1959, para. 217.)

250. A reference in the definition of managerial staff to the exercise of disciplinary control over workers could give rise to an expansive interpretation which would exclude large numbers of workers from workers' rights.

(See 313th Report, Case No. 1959, para. 217.)

251. An excessively broad interpretation of the concept of "worker of confidence", which denies such workers their right of association, may seriously limit trade union rights and even, in small enterprises, prevent the establishment of trade unions, which is contrary to the principle of freedom of association.

(See the 1996 *Digest*, para. 233; 307th Report, Case No. 1878, para. 453; and 324th Report, Case No. 1880, para. 859.)

252. Legal provisions which permit employers to undermine workers' organizations through artificial promotions of workers constitute a violation of the principles of freedom of association.

(See the 1996 *Digest*, para. 234; 307th Report, Case No. 1878, para. 453; and 329th Report, Case No. 2177/2183, para. 638.)

253. As concerns persons exercising senior managerial or policy-making responsibilities, the Committee is of the opinion that while these public servants may be barred from joining trade unions which represent other workers, such restrictions should be strictly limited to this category of workers and they should be entitled to establish their own organizations.

(See the 1996 *Digest*, para. 230; and 327th Report, Case No. 1865, para. 484.)

J. Self-employed workers and the liberal professions

254. By virtue of the principles of freedom of association, all workers – with the sole exception of members of the armed forces and the police – should have the right to establish and join organizations of their own choosing. The criterion for determining the persons covered by that right, therefore, is not based on the existence of an employment relationship, which is often non-existent, for example in the case of agricultural workers, self-employed workers in general or those who practise liberal professions, who should nevertheless enjoy the right to organize.

(See the 1996 *Digest*, para. 235; 304th Report, Case No. 1796, para. 464; 323rd Report, Case No. 2059, para. 475; 326th Report, Case No. 2013, para. 416; 332nd Report, Case No. 2221, para. 222; and 336th Report, Case No. 2347, para. 628.)

K. Temporary workers

255. All workers, without distinction whatsoever, whether they are employed on a permanent basis, for a fixed term or as contract employees, should have the right to establish and join organizations of their own choosing.

(See the 1996 *Digest*, para. 236; 324th Report, Case No. 2083, para. 253; and 330th Report, Case No. 2158, para. 846.)

L. Workers undergoing a period of work probation

256. Workers undergoing a period of work probation should be able to establish and join organizations of their choosing, if they so wish.

(See the 1996 *Digest*, para. 237; 304th Report, Case No. 1796, para. 467; 327th Report, Case No. 2138, para. 544; and 330th Report, Case No. 2158, para. 846.)

257. The denial of the right to organize to workers undergoing a period of work probation could raise problems with regard to the application of Convention No. 87.

(See the 1996 *Digest*, para. 238.)

M. Workers hired under training contracts

258. Persons hired under training agreements should have the right to organize.

(See 304th Report, Case No. 1796, para. 464; and 323rd Report, Case No. 2059, para. 475.)

259. The status under which workers are engaged with the employer, as apprentices or otherwise, should not have any effect on their right to join workers' organizations and participate in their activities.

(See 330th Report, Case No. 2158, para. 846.)

N. Persons working under community participation programmes intended to combat unemployment

260. Persons working under community participation programmes intended to combat unemployment are workers within the meaning of Convention No. 87 and they must have the right to organize, given that they undeniably have collective interests which must be promoted and defended.

(See 316th Report, Case No. 1975, para. 270; and 324th Report, Case No. 2022, para. 765.)

O. Workers in cooperatives

261. The Promotion of Cooperatives Recommendation, 2002 (No. 193), calls on governments to ensure that cooperatives are not set up or used for non-compliance with labour law or used to establish disguised employment relationships.

(See 338th Report, Case No. 2239, para. 144.)

262. Mindful of the particular characteristics of cooperatives, the Committee considers that associated labour cooperatives (whose members are their own bosses) cannot be considered, in law or in fact, as "workers' organizations" within the meaning of Convention No. 87, that is organizations that have as their objective to promote and defend workers' interests. That being so, referring to Article 2 of Convention No. 87 and recalling that the concept of worker means not only salaried worker, but also independent or autonomous worker, the Committee has considered that workers associated in cooperatives should have the right to establish and join organizations of their own choosing.

(See 335th Report, Case No. 2237, para. 72; 336th Report, Case No. 2239, para. 353; 337th Report, Case No. 2362, para. 757; and 338th Report, Case No. 2239, para. 144.)

P. Distributors and sales agents

263. The Committee does not have the competence to express an opinion concerning the legal relationship (labour or commercial) of certain distributors and sales agents of an enterprise including on the question of whether the absence of a recognized employment relationship implies that they are not covered by the Labour Act. Nevertheless, in view of the fact that Convention No. 87 permits the exclusion only of the armed forces and the police, the sales agents in question should be able to establish organizations of their own choosing (Convention No. 87, Article 2).

(See the 1996 *Digest*, para. 239.)

Q. Workers in export processing zones

264. Workers in export processing zones – despite the economic arguments often put forward – like other workers, without distinction whatsoever, should enjoy the trade union rights provided for by the freedom of association Conventions.

(See the 1996 *Digest*, para. 240; 302nd Report, Case No. 1826, para. 411; and 337th Report, Case No. 2327, para. 195.)

265. In a case relating to violations of trade union rights in export processing zones, the Committee recalled that the standards contained in Convention No. 87 apply to all workers "without distinction whatsoever" and requested the government to amend the legislation in order to guarantee the workers concerned the right of association and collective bargaining in accordance with Conventions Nos. 87 and 98.

(See the 1996 *Digest*, para. 241; and 335th Report, Case No. 2228, para. 905.)

266. The ILO Tripartite Declaration of Principles concerning Multinational Enterprises and Social Policy provides that special incentives to attract foreign investment should not include any limitation of the workers' freedom of association or the right to organize and bargain collectively. The Committee considers that legal provisions on export processing zones should ensure the right to organize and bargain collectively for workers.

(See the 1996 *Digest*, para. 801; and 333rd Report, Case No. 2281, para. 636.)

R. Domestic workers

267. Domestic workers are not excluded from the application of Convention No. 87 and should therefore be governed by the guarantees it affords and have the right to establish and join occupational organizations.

(See 308th Report, Case No. 1900, para. 182.)

S. Workers who have been dismissed

268. A provision depriving dismissed workers of the right to union membership is incompatible with the principles of freedom of association since it deprives the persons concerned of joining the organization of their choice. Such a provision entails the risk of acts of anti-union discrimination being carried out to the extent that the dismissal of trade union activists would prevent them from continuing their trade union activities within their organization.

(See 336th Report, Case No. 1865, para. 333.)

269. The loss of a person's trade union status as a result of dismissal for strike activities is contrary to the principles of freedom of association.

(See 309th Report, Case No. 1851/1922, para. 238.)

T. Retired workers

270. The right to decide whether or not a trade union should represent retired workers for the defence of their specific interests is a question pertaining to the internal autonomy of all trade unions.

(See 336th Report, Case No. 2347, para. 627.)

Other distinctions

271. The requirement for the establishment of a trade union that workers need to be employees of only one employer is a violation of the principles of freedom of association.

(See the 1996 *Digest*, para. 243.)

Right of workers and employers to establish organizations without previous authorization

4

Requirement of previous authorization

(See also para. 377)

272. The principle of freedom of association would often remain a dead letter if workers and employers were required to obtain any kind of previous authorization to enable them to establish an organization. Such authorization could concern the formation of the trade union organization itself, the need to obtain discretionary approval of the constitution or rules of the organization, or, again, authorization for taking steps prior to the establishment of the organization. This does not mean that the founders of an organization are freed from the duty of observing formalities concerning publicity or other similar formalities which may be prescribed by law. However, such requirements must not be such as to be equivalent in practice to previous authorization, or as to constitute such an obstacle to the establishment of an organization that they amount in practice to outright prohibition. Even in cases where registration is optional but where such registration confers on the organization the basic rights enabling it to "further and defend the interests of its members", the fact that the authority competent to effect registration has discretionary power to refuse this formality is not very different from cases in which previous authorization is required.

(See the 1996 *Digest*, paras. 207 and 244; and, for example, 308th Report, Case No. 1894, para. 536; 313th Report, Case No. 1987, para. 111; 318th Report, Case No. 2038, para. 530; 324th Report, Case No. 2090, para. 200, and Case No. 2053, para. 231; 329th Report, Case No. 2140, para. 295, and Case No. 2133, para. 545; 332nd Report, Case No. 2225, para. 377; 333rd Report, Case No. 2268, para. 733; and 334th Report, Case No. 2282, para. 638.)

273. A law providing that the right of association is subject to authorization granted by a government department purely in its discretion is incompatible with the principle of freedom of association.

(See the 1996 *Digest*, para. 245; and 332nd Report, Case No. 2225, para. 380.)

274. The absence of recourse to a judicial authority against any refusal by the Ministry to grant an authorization to establish a trade union violates the principles of freedom of association.

(See the 1996 *Digest*, para. 246; and 308th Report, Case No. 1894, para. 537.)

Legal formalities for the establishment of organizations

275. In its report to the 1948 International Labour Conference, the Committee on Freedom of Association and Industrial Relations declared that "the States would remain free to provide such formalities in their legislation as appeared appropriate to ensure the normal functioning of occupational organizations". Consequently, the formalities prescribed by national regulations concerning the constitution and functioning of workers' and employers' organizations are compatible with the provisions of that Convention provided, of course, that the provisions in such regulations do not impair the guarantees laid down in Convention No. 87.

(See the 1996 *Digest*, para. 247; and 313th Report, Case No. 1977, para. 237.)

276. Although the founders of a trade union should comply with the formalities prescribed by legislation, these formalities should not be of such a nature as to impair the free establishment of organizations.

(See the 1996 *Digest*, para. 248; and, for example, 308th Report, Case No. 1894, para. 536; 316th Report, Case No. 1773, para. 615; 323rd Report, Case No. 2085, para. 172, and Case No. 2079, para. 540; 329th Report, Case No. 2075, para. 151; 334th Report, Case No. 2222, para. 208; 336th Report, Case No. 2046, para. 312; 337th Report, Case No. 2327, para. 200, and Case No. 2346, para. 1056; and 338th Report, Case No. 2046, para. 106.)

277. A provision stating that workers will not be allowed to establish workers' associations until the expiry of a period of three months following the commencement of commercial production in the concerned unit is contrary to Article 2 of Convention No. 87 and should be amended to ensure that the workers in question may establish workers' associations from the beginning of their contractual relationship.

(See 337th Report, Case No. 2327, para. 197.)

278. If there is grave suspicion that trade union leaders have committed acts which are punishable by law, they should be subject to normal judicial proceedings in order to determine their responsibilities, and their detention should not in itself constitute an obstacle to the granting of legal personality to the organization concerned.

(See the 1996 *Digest*, para. 250.)

Requirements for the establishment of organizations (minimum number of members, etc.)

(See also para. 681)

279. The formalities prescribed by law for the establishment of a trade union should not be applied in such a manner as to delay or prevent the establishment of trade union organizations. Any delay caused by authorities in registering a trade union constitutes an infringement of Article 2 of Convention No. 87.

(See the 1996 *Digest*, paras. 249 and 251; 308th Report, Case No. 1894, para. 536; 316th Report, Case No. 1773, para. 615; 324th Report, Case No. 2053, para. 231; 332nd Report, Case No. 2225, para. 377; and 334th Report, Case No. 2282, para. 638.)

280. National legislation providing that an organization must deposit its rules is compatible with Article 2 of Convention No. 87 if it is merely a formality to ensure that those rules are made public. However, problems may arise when the competent authorities are obliged by law to request the founders of organizations to incorporate in their constitution certain provisions which are not in accord with the principles of freedom of association.

(See 318th Report, Case No. 2038, para. 530.)

281. Employers' occupational associations should not be restricted by excessively detailed provisions which discourage their establishment, contrary to Article 2 of Convention No. 87, which provides that employers, as well as workers, shall have the right to establish organizations of their own choosing without previous authorization.

(See the 1996 *Digest*, para. 252; and 333rd Report, Case No. 2133, para. 59.)

282. The requirement that a trade union shall have a registered office is a normal requirement in a large number of countries.

(See the 1996 *Digest*, para. 253; and 318th Report, Case No. 2038, para. 530.)

283. A minimum requirement of 100 workers to establish unions by branch of activity, occupation or for various occupations must be reduced in consultation with the workers' and employers' organizations.

(See the 1996 *Digest*, para. 254; and 325th Report, Case No. 2098, para. 543.)

284. The establishment of a trade union may be considerably hindered, or even rendered impossible, when legislation fixes the minimum number of members of a trade union at obviously too high a figure, as is the case, for example, where legislation requires that a union must have at least 50 founder members.

(See the 1996 *Digest*, para. 255; 316th Report, Case No. 1996, para. 662; and 336th Report, Case No. 2153, para. 166.)

285. Even though the minimum number of 30 workers would be acceptable in the case of sectoral trade unions, this minimum number should be reduced in the case of works councils so as not to hinder the establishment of such bodies, particularly when it is taken into account that the country has a very large proportion of small enterprises and that the trade union structure is based on enterprise unions.

(See the 1996 *Digest*, para. 257.)

286. The legal requirement laid down in the Labour Code for a minimum of 30 workers to establish a trade union should be reduced in order not to hinder the establishment of trade unions at enterprises, especially taking into account the very significant proportion of small enterprises in the country.

(See 327th Report, Case No. 2138, para. 539.)

287. While a minimum membership requirement is not in itself incompatible with Convention No. 87, the number should be fixed in a reasonable manner so that the establishment of organizations is not hindered. What constitutes a reasonable number may vary according to the particular conditions in which a restriction is imposed.

(See 336th Report, Case No. 2332, para. 703.)

288. A minimum membership requirement of 30 per cent of the workers concerned to establish an organization is too high.

(See 306th Report, Case No. 1862, para. 102; and 337th Report, Case no. 2327, para. 200.)

289. Provisions which impose a membership requirement of 30 per cent of the total number of workers employed in the establishment concerned for a union to be registered and which permit dissolution if membership falls below that level are not in conformity with Article 2 of Convention No. 87.

(See 306th Report, Case No. 1862, para. 102.)

290. Where the legislation provided that a trade union should consist of more than 50 per cent of the workers, if it was a workers' union; more than 50 per cent of the salaried employees, if it was a union of salaried employees; and more than 50 per cent of both categories if it was a mixed union, the Committee recalled that such a provision was not in conformity with Article 2 of Convention No. 87, and that it placed a major obstacle in the way of the establishment of trade unions capable of "furthering and defending the interests" of their members; moreover, the provision had the indirect result of prohibiting the establishment of a new trade union whenever a trade union already existed in the undertaking or establishment concerned.

(See the 1996 *Digest*, para. 294.)

291. The minimum membership requirement of 10,000 members for the registration of trade unions at the federal level could influence unduly the workers' free choice of union to which they wish to belong, even when federal registration is only one of the alternatives available for protecting their rights.

(See the 1996 *Digest*, para. 270.)

292. The legal requirement that there be a minimum number of 20 members to form a union does not seem excessive and, therefore, does not in itself constitute an obstacle to the formation of a trade union.

(See the 1996 *Digest*, para. 256; and 316th Report, Case No. 1996, para. 662.)

293. A provision which requires ten or more employers engaged in the same industry or activity, or similar or related industries or activities, to establish an employers' association imposes an excessively high minimum number and violates the right of employers to establish organizations of their own choosing.

(See the 1996 *Digest*, para. 258.)

Registration of organizations

294. If the conditions for the granting of registration are tantamount to obtaining previous authorization from the public authorities for the establishment or functioning of a trade union, this would undeniably constitute an infringement of Convention No. 87. This, however, would not seem to be the case when the registration of trade unions consists solely of a formality where the conditions are not such as to impair the guarantees laid down by the Convention.

(See the 1996 *Digest*, para. 259; 307th Report, Case No. 1918, para. 250; and 325th Report, Case No. 2100, para. 429.)

295. The right to official recognition through legal registration is an essential facet of the right to organize since that is the first step that workers' or employers' organizations must take in order to be able to function efficiently, and represent their members adequately.

(See 324th Report, Case No. 2053, para. 232.)

296. Although the registration procedure very often consists in a mere formality, there are a number of countries in which the law confers on the relevant authorities more or less discretionary powers in deciding whether or not an organization meets all the conditions required for registration, thus creating a situation which is similar to that in which previous authorization is required. Similar situations can arise where a complicated and lengthy registration procedure exists, or where the competent administrative authorities may exercise their powers with great latitude; these factors are such as to create a serious obstacle for the establishment of a trade union and lead to a denial of the right to organize without previous authorization.

(See the 1996 *Digest*, para. 260; 327th Report, Case No. 1581, para. 110; and 328th Report, Case No. 2158, para. 321.)

297. The administrative authorities should not be able to refuse registration of an organization simply because they consider that the organization could exceed normal union activities or that it might not be able to exercise its functions. Such a system would be tantamount to subjecting the compulsory registration of trade unions to the previous authorization of the administrative authorities.

(See the 1996 *Digest*, para. 261.)

298. A provision whereby registration of a trade union may be refused if the union "is about to engage" in activities likely to cause a serious threat to public safety or public order could give rise to abuse, and it should therefore be applied with the greatest caution. The refusal to register should only take place under the supervision of the competent judicial authorities where serious acts have been committed, and have been duly proven.

(See the 1996 *Digest*, para. 262.)

299. The obligation for trade unions to obtain the consent of a central trade union organization in order to be registered must be removed.

(See the 1996 *Digest*, para. 263.)

300. An appeal should lie to the courts against any administrative decision concerning the registration of a trade union. Such a right of appeal constitutes a necessary safeguard against unlawful or ill-founded decisions by the authorities responsible for registration.

(See the 1996 *Digest*, para. 264; 307th Report, Case No. 1918, para. 251; 308th Report, Case No. 1894, para. 537; and 334th Report, Case No. 2222, para. 208.)

301. A decision to prohibit the registration of a trade union which has received legal recognition should not become effective until the statutory period of lodging an appeal against this decision has expired without an appeal having been lodged, or until it has been confirmed by the courts following an appeal.

(See the 1996 *Digest*, para. 265; and 333rd Report, Case No. 2301, para. 594.)

302. Where a registrar has to form his or her own judgement as to whether the conditions for the registration of a trade union have been fulfilled, although an appeal lies against the registrar's decisions to the courts, the Committee has considered that the existence of a procedure of appeal to the courts does not appear to be a sufficient guarantee; in effect, this does not alter the nature of the powers conferred on the authorities responsible for effecting registration, and the judges hearing such an appeal would only be able to ensure that the legislation has been correctly applied. The Committee has drawn attention to the desirability of defining clearly in the legislation the precise conditions which trade unions must fulfil in order to be entitled to registration and on the basis of which the registrar may refuse or cancel registration, and of prescribing specific statutory criteria for the purpose of deciding whether such conditions are fulfilled or not.

(See the 1996 *Digest*, para. 266; and 333rd Report, Case No. 2301, para. 594.)

303. Where the difficulties with regard to the interpretation of standards concerning the inclusion of trade unions in the appropriate state registers create situations where competent authorities make excessive use of their powers, problems of compatibility with Convention No. 87 may arise.

(See 330th Report, Case No. 2038, para. 156.)

304. Judges should be able to deal with the substance of a case concerning a refusal to register so that they can determine whether the provisions on which the administrative measures in question are based constitute a violation of the rights accorded to occupational organizations by Convention No. 87.

(See the 1996 *Digest*, para. 267; 307th Report, Case No. 1918, para. 251; and 333rd Report, Case No. 2301, para. 594.)

305. Normal control of the activities of trade unions should be effected a posteriori and by the judicial authorities; and the fact that an organization which seeks to enjoy the status of an occupational organization might in certain cases engage in activities unconnected with trade union activities would not appear to constitute a sufficient reason for subjecting trade union organizations a priori to control with respect to their composition and with respect to the composition of their management committees. The refusal to register a union because the authorities, in advance and in their own judgement, consider that this would be politically undesirable, would be tantamount to submitting the compulsory registration of trade unions to previous authorization on the part of the authorities, which is not compatible with the principles of freedom of association.

(See the 1996 *Digest*, para. 268; 307th Report, Case No. 1918, para. 251; and 333rd Report, Case No. 2301, para. 591.)

306. In a legal system where registration of a workers' organization is optional, the act of registration may confer on an organization a number of important advantages such as special immunities, tax exemption, the right to obtain recognition as exclusive bargaining agent, etc. In order to obtain such recognition, an organization may be required to fulfil certain formalities which do not amount to previous authorization and which do not normally pose any problem as regards the requirements of Convention No. 87.

(See the 1996 *Digest*, para. 269.)

307. A long registration procedure constitutes a serious obstacle to the establishment of organizations and amounts to a denial of the right of workers to establish organizations without previous authorization.

(See 338th Report, case No. 2273, para. 294.)

308. A period of one month envisaged by the legislation to register an organization is reasonable.

(See 337th Report, Case No. 2244, para. 1261.)

5 Right of workers and employers to establish and join organizations of their own choosing

General principles

309. The right of workers to establish and join organizations of their own choosing in full freedom cannot be said to exist unless such freedom is fully established and respected in law and in fact.

(See the 1996 *Digest*, para. 271; 302nd Report, Case No. 1825, para. 491; 304th Report, Case No. 1712, para. 376; 318th Report, Case No. 1978, para. 217; 325th Report, Case No. 2109, para. 460; 333rd Report, Case No. 2133, para. 59, and Case No. 2301, para. 592; and 337th Report, Case No. 2388, para. 1353.)

310. The Committee has emphasized the importance that it attaches to the fact that workers and employers should in practice be able to establish and join organizations of their own choosing in full freedom.

(See the 1996 *Digest*, para. 274; 302nd Report, Case No. 1840, para. 351; 304th Report, Case No. 1819, para. 156; 316th Report, Case No. 1989, para. 194; 325th Report, Case No. 2109, para. 460; 328th Report, Case No. 2160, para. 658; 332nd Report, Case No. 2262, para. 398, and Case No. 2233, para. 638.)

Trade union unity and pluralism

311. The right of workers to establish organizations of their own choosing implies, in particular, the effective possibility of forming, in a climate of full security, organizations independent both of those which exist already and of any political party.

(See the 1996 *Digest*, para. 273; 304th Report, Case No. 1819, para. 156; 310th Report, Case No. 1930, para. 366; 321st Report, Case No. 2031, para. 169; 325th Report, Case No. 1888, para. 397; 328th Report, Case No. 1961, para. 41; and 330th Report, Case No. 2189, para. 465.)

312. The free choice of workers to establish and join organizations is so fundamental to freedom of association as a whole that it cannot be compromised by delays.

(See 306th Report, Case No. 1865, para. 329.)

313. The existence of an organization in a specific occupation should not constitute an obstacle to the establishment of another organization, if the workers so wish.

(See the 1996 *Digest*, para. 276; 306th Report, Case No. 1884, para. 691; and 315th Report, Case No. 1935, para. 21.)

314. The provisions contained in a national constitution concerning the prohibition of creating more than one trade union for a given occupational or economic category, regardless of the level of organization, in a given territorial area which in no case may be smaller than a municipality, are not compatible with the principles of freedom of association.

(See the 1996 *Digest*, para. 277.)

315. The right of workers to establish organizations of their own choosing implies, in particular, the effective possibility to create – if the workers so choose – more than one workers' organization per enterprise.

(See the 1996 *Digest*, para. 280; 302nd Report, Case No. 1840, para. 351; 327th Report, Case No. 1581, para. 109; and 337th Report, Case No. 2327, para. 198.)

316. A provision of the law which does not authorize the establishment of a second union in an enterprise fails to comply with Article 2 of Convention No. 87, which guarantees workers the right to establish and join organizations of their own choosing without previous authorization.

(See the 1996 *Digest*, para. 281; and 337th Report, Case No. 2327, para. 198.)

317. Provisions which require a single union for each enterprise, trade or occupation are not in accordance with Article 2 of Convention No. 87.

(See the 1996 *Digest*, para. 282; and 333rd Report, Case No. 2301, para. 592.)

318. The Committee has pointed out that the International Labour Conference, by including the words "organizations of their own choosing" in Convention No. 87, made allowance for the fact that, in certain countries, there are a number of different workers' and employers' organizations which an individual may choose to join for occupational, denominational or political reasons; it did not pronounce, however, as to whether, in the interests of workers and employers, a unified trade union movement is preferable to trade union pluralism. The Conference thereby recognized the right of any group of workers (or employers) to establish organizations in addition to the existing organization if they think this desirable to safeguard their material or moral interests.

(See the 1996 *Digest*, para. 286; 332nd Report, Case No. 2046, para. 453; and 334th Report, Case No. 2258, para. 448.)

319. While it may generally be to the advantage of workers to avoid a multiplicity of trade union organizations, unification of the trade union movement imposed through state intervention by legislative means runs counter to the principle embodied in Articles 2 and 11 of Convention No. 87. The Committee of Experts of the ILO on the Application of Conventions and Recommendations has emphasized on this question that "there is a fundamental difference, with respect to the guarantees of freedom of association and protection of the right to organize, between a situation in which a trade union monopoly is instituted or maintained by legislation and the factual situations which are found to exist in certain countries in which all the trade union organizations join together voluntarily in a single federation or confederation, without this being the direct or indirect result of legislative provisions applicable to trade unions and to the establishment of trade union organizations. The fact that workers and employers generally find it in their interests to avoid a multiplication of the number of competing organizations does not, in fact, appear sufficient to justify direct or indirect intervention by the State, and especially, intervention by the State by means of legislation". While fully appreciating the desire of any government to promote a strong trade union movement by avoiding the defects resulting from an undue multiplicity of small and competing trade unions, whose independence may be endangered by their weakness, the Committee has drawn attention to the fact that it is more desirable in such cases for a government to seek to encourage trade unions to join together voluntarily to form strong and united organizations than to impose upon them by legislation a compulsory unification which deprives the workers of the free exercise of their right of association and thus runs counter to the principles which are embodied in the international labour Conventions relating to freedom of association.

(See the 1996 *Digest*, para. 287.)

320. While it is generally to the advantage of workers and employers to avoid the proliferation of competing organizations, a monopoly situation imposed by law is at variance with the principle of free choice of workers' and employers' organizations.

(See the 1996 *Digest*, para. 288; and 338th Report, Case No. 2348, para. 995.)

321. Unity within the trade union movement should not be imposed by the State through legislation because this would be contrary to the principles of freedom of association.

(See the 1996 *Digest*, para. 289; 320th Report, Case No. 1963, para. 220; and 324th Report, Case No. 2067, para. 988.)

322. The government should neither support nor obstruct a legal attempt by a trade union to displace an existing organization. Workers should be free to choose the union which, in their opinion, will best promote their occupational interests without interference by the authorities. It may be to the advantage of workers to avoid a multiplicity of trade unions, but this choice should be made freely and voluntarily. By including the words “organizations of their own choosing” in Convention No. 87, the International Labour Conference recognized that individuals may choose between several workers’ or employers’ organizations for occupational, denominational or political reasons. It did not pronounce as to whether, in the interests of workers and employers, a unified trade union movement is preferable to trade union pluralism.

(See the 1996 *Digest*, para. 290.)

323. Where one government stated that it was not prepared to “tolerate” a trade union movement split into several tendencies and that it was determined to impose unity on the whole movement, the Committee recalled that Article 2 of Convention No. 87 provides that workers and employers shall have the right to establish and to join organizations “of their own choosing”. This provision of the Convention is in no way intended as an expression of support either for the idea of trade union unity or for that of trade union diversity. It is intended to convey, on the one hand, that in many countries there are several organizations among which the workers or the employers may wish to choose freely and, on the other hand, that workers and employers may wish to establish new organizations in a country where no such diversity has hitherto been found. In other words, although the Convention is evidently not intended to make trade union diversity an obligation, it does at least require this diversity to remain possible in all cases. Accordingly, any governmental attitude involving the “imposition” of a single trade union organization would be contrary to Article 2 of Convention No. 87.

(See the 1996 Digest, para. 291; 337th Report, Case No. 2258, para. 836; and 338th Report, Case No. 2348. para. 995.)

324. A situation in which an individual is denied any possibility of choice between different organizations, by reason of the fact that the legislation permits the existence of only one organization in the area in which that individual carries on his or her occupation, is incompatible with the principles embodied in Convention No. 87; in fact, such provisions establish, by legislation, a trade union monopoly which must be distinguished both from union security clauses and practices and from situations in which the workers voluntarily form a single organization.

(See the 1996 *Digest*, para. 292; and 320th Report, Case No. 1963, para. 220.)

325. The power to impose an obligation on all the workers in the category concerned to pay contributions to the single national trade union, the establishment of which is permitted by branch of industry and by region, is not compatible with the principle that workers should have the right to join organizations “of their own choosing”. In these circumstances, it would seem that a legal obligation to pay contributions to that monopoly trade union, whether workers are members or not, represents a further consecration and strengthening of that monopoly.

(See the 1996 *Digest*, para. 293.)

326. The Committee has suggested that a State should amend its legislation so as to make it clear that when a trade union already exists for the same employees as those whom a new union seeking registration is organizing or is proposing to organize, or the fact that the existing union holds a bargaining certificate in respect of such class of employees, this cannot give rise to objections of sufficient substance to justify the registrar in refusing to register the new union.

(See the 1996 *Digest*, para. 295.)

327. The Committee has endorsed the position of the Committee of Experts on the Application of Conventions and Recommendations in taking exception to legislation designed to set up and maintain a single trade union system by expressly mentioning the national trade union confederation. The Committee of Experts has considered that this constitutes an obstacle to the creation of another confederation if the workers so wish.

(See the 1996 *Digest*, para. 296.)

328. A provision authorizing the refusal of an application for registration if another union, already registered, is sufficiently representative of the interests which the union seeking registration proposes to defend, means that, in certain cases, workers may be denied the right to join the organization of their own choosing, contrary to the principles of freedom of association.

(See the 1996 *Digest*, para. 297; 304th Report, Case No. 1865, para. 249; and 305th Report, Case No. 1883, para. 393.)

329. Where workers' organizations have themselves requested the unification of the trade unions, and this desire has been confirmed in such a way as to make it equivalent to a legal obligation, the Committee has pointed out that, when a unified trade union movement results solely from the will of the workers, this situation does not require to be sanctioned by legal texts, the existence of which might give the impression that the unified trade union movement is merely the result of existing legislation or is maintained only through such legislation.

(See the 1996 *Digest*, para. 298.)

330. Even in a situation where, historically speaking, the trade union movement has been organized on a unitary basis, the law should not institutionalize this situation by referring, for example, to the single federation by name, even if it is referring to the will of an existing trade union organization. In fact, the right of workers who do not wish to join the federation or the existing trade unions should be protected, and such workers should have the right to form organizations of their own choosing, which is not the case in a situation where the law has imposed the system of the single trade union.

(See the 1996 *Digest*, para. 299; and 315th Report, Case No. 1935, para. 21.)

331. The requirement that a trade union is obliged to obtain the recommendation of a specific central organization in order to be duly recognized constitutes an obstacle for workers to establish freely the organization of their own choosing and is therefore contrary to freedom of association.

(See 302nd Report, Case No. 1773, para. 472.)

332. Trade union unity voluntarily achieved should not be prohibited and should be respected by the public authorities.

(See 320th Report, Case No. 1963, para. 220.)

Freedom of choice of trade union structure

333. The free exercise of the right to establish and join unions implies the free determination of the structure and composition of unions.

(See the 1996 *Digest*, para. 275; 306th Report, Case No. 1862, para. 103; 321st Report, Case No. 1978, para. 34; 325th Report, Case No. 2100, para. 430; 327th Report, Case No. 2115, para. 681; 330th Report, Case No. 2207, para. 907; 332nd Report, Case No. 2115, para. 114, and Case No. 2207, para. 119; 333rd Report, Case No. 2301, para. 592; and 335th Report, Case No. 2308, para. 1041.)

334. Workers should be free to decide whether they prefer to establish, at the primary level, a works union or another form of basic organization, such as an industrial or craft union.

(See the 1996 *Digest*, para. 279; 305th Report, Case No. 1874, para. 268; and 325th Report, Case No. 2100, para. 430.)

335. Under Article 2 of Convention No. 87, workers have the right to establish organizations of their own choosing, including organizations grouping together workers from different workplaces and different cities.

(See the 1996 *Digest*, para. 283; and 306th Report, Case No. 1862, para. 103.)

336. The restriction established under a local public service law that negotiation must take place at the regional level, and that the negotiating organization must therefore only exist at the regional level, constitutes a limitation of the right of workers to establish and join organizations of their own choosing and to elect their representatives in full freedom.

(See the 1996 *Digest*, para. 284.)

337. With regard to restrictions limiting all public servants to membership of unions confined to that category of workers, it is admissible for first-level organizations of public servants to be limited to that category of workers on condition that their organizations are not also restricted to employees of any particular ministry, department or service, and that the first-level organizations may freely join the federations and confederations of their own choosing.

(See the 1996 *Digest*, para. 285.)

Sanctions imposed for attempting to establish organizations

338. Measures taken against workers because they attempt to constitute organizations or to reconstitute organizations of workers outside the official trade union organization would be incompatible with the principle that workers should have the right to establish and join organizations of their own choosing without previous authorization.

(See the 1996 *Digest*, para. 301; 327th Report, Case No. 1581, para. 109; 328th Report, Case No. 2160, para. 658; 332nd Report, Case No. 2046, para. 454; and 338th Report, Case No. 2348, para. 995.)

Favouritism or discrimination in respect of particular organizations

339. Considering the limited functions which, in one case, were by law open to certain categories of trade unions, the Committee felt that the distinction made between trade unions under the national legislation could have the indirect consequence of restricting the freedom of workers to belong to the organizations of their choosing. The reasons which led the Committee to adopt this position are as follows. As a general rule, when a government can grant an advantage to one particular organization or withdraw that advantage from one organization in favour of another, there is a risk, even if such is not the government's intention, that one trade union will be placed at an unfair advantage or disadvantage in relation to the others, which would thereby constitute an act of discrimination. More precisely, by placing one organization at an advantage or at a disadvantage in relation to the others, a government may either directly or indirectly influence the choice of workers regarding the organization to which they intend to belong, since they will undeniably want to belong to the union best able to serve them, even if their natural preference would have led them to join another organization for occupational, religious, political or other reasons. The freedom of the parties to choose is a right expressly laid down in Convention No. 87.

(See the 1996 *Digest*, para. 303; and 328th Report, Case No. 2139, para. 445.)

340. By according favourable or unfavourable treatment to a given organization as compared with others, a government may be able to influence the choice of workers as to the organization which they intend to join. In addition, a government which deliberately acts in this manner violates the principle laid down in Convention No. 87 that the public authorities shall refrain from any interference which would restrict the rights provided for in the Convention or impede their lawful exercise; more indirectly, it would also violate the principle that the law of the land shall not be such as to impair, nor shall it be so applied as to impair, the guarantees provided for in the Convention. It would seem desirable that, if a government wishes to make certain facilities available to trade union organizations, these organizations should enjoy equal treatment in this respect.

(See the 1996 *Digest*, para. 304; 324th Report, Case No. 2067, para. 988; 325th Report, Case No. 1888, para. 397; 328th Report, Case No. 2139, para. 445; 330th Report, Case No. 2200, para. 1100; 331st Report, Case No. 2090, para. 164; 334th Report, Case No. 2200, para. 750; 337th Report, Case No. 2244, para. 1272; and 338th Report, Case No. 2200, para. 325.)

341. In a case in which there was at the very least a close working relationship between a trade union and the labour and other authorities, the Committee emphasized the importance it attaches to the resolution of 1952 concerning the independence of the trade union movement and urged the government to refrain from showing favouritism towards, or discriminating against, any given trade union, and requested it to adopt a neutral attitude in its dealings with all workers' and employers' organizations, so that they are all placed on an equal footing.

(See the 1996 *Digest*, para. 305; 309th Report, Case No. 1851/1922, para. 242; and 323rd Report, Case No. 1888, para. 192.)

342. On more than one occasion, the Committee has examined cases in which allegations were made that the public authorities had, by their attitude, favoured or discriminated against one or more trade union organizations:
(1) pressure exerted on workers by means of public statements made by the authorities;
(2) unequal distribution of subsidies among unions or the granting to one union, rather than to the others, of premises for holding its meetings or carrying on its activities;
(3) refusal to recognize the leaders of certain organizations in the performance of their legitimate activities.

Discrimination by such methods, or by others, may be an informal way of influencing the trade union membership of workers. It is therefore sometimes difficult to prove. The fact, nevertheless, remains that any discrimination of this kind jeopardizes the right of workers set out in Convention No. 87, Article 2, to establish and join organizations of their own choosing.

(See the 1996 *Digest*, para. 306; 311th Report, Case No. 1969, para. 146; 334th Report, Case No. 2200, para. 750, and Case No. 2249, para. 871; and 338th Report, Case No. 2200, para. 325.)

343. Both the government authorities and employers should refrain from any discrimination between trade union organizations, especially as regards recognition of their leaders who seek to perform legitimate trade union activities.

(See the 1996 *Digest*, para. 307; 311th Report, Case No. 1969, para. 146; 324th Report, Case No. 2055, para. 683; and 338th Report, Case No. 2374, para. 509.)

344. Situations in which the local authorities interfere in the activities of a freely constituted trade union by establishing alternative workers' organizations and inciting workers using unfair means to change their membership violate the right of workers to establish and join organizations of their own choosing.

(See 330th Report, Case No. 2144, para. 719.)

345. Generally, the fact that a government is able to offer the use of premises to a particular organization, or to evict a given organization from premises which it has been occupying in order to offer them to another organization, may, even if this is not intended, lead to the favourable or unfavourable treatment of a particular trade union as compared with others, and thereby constitute an act of discrimination.

(See the 1996 *Digest*, para. 308.)

Admissible privileges for most representative unions

(See also paras. 339 and 949 to 980)

346. The Committee has pointed out on several occasions, and particularly during discussion on the draft of the Right to Organize and Collective Bargaining Convention, that the International Labour Conference referred to the question of the representative character of trade unions, and, to a certain extent, it agreed to the distinction that is sometimes made between the various unions concerned according to how representative they are. Article 3, paragraph 5, of the Constitution of the ILO includes the concept of "most representative" organizations. Accordingly, the Committee felt that the mere fact that the law of a country draws a distinction between the most representative trade union organizations and other trade union organizations is not in itself a matter for criticism. Such a distinction, however, should not result in the most representative organizations being granted privileges extending beyond that of priority in representation, on the ground of their having the largest membership, for such purposes as collective bargaining or consultation by governments, or for the purpose of nominating delegates to international bodies. In other words, this distinction should not have the effect of depriving trade union organizations that are not recognized as being among the most representative of the essential means for defending the occupational interests of their members, for organizing their administration and activities and formulating their programmes, as provided for in Convention No. 87.

(See the 1996 *Digest*, para. 309; 332nd Report, Case No. 2216, para. 908; and 337th Report, Case No. 2334, para. 1219.)

347. The determination of the most representative trade union should always be based on objective and pre-established criteria so as to avoid any opportunity for partiality or abuse.

(See the 1996 *Digest*, para. 314; 305th Report, Case No. 1871, para. 79, and Case No. 1765, para. 98; 327th Report, Case No. 2132, para. 661; 331st Report, Case No. 2132, para. 588; and 333rd Report, Case No. 2288, para. 827.)

348. Pre-established, precise and objective criteria for the determination of the representativity of workers' and employers' organizations should exist in the legislation and such a determination should not be left to the discretion of governments.

(See the 1996 *Digest*, para. 315; 302nd Report, Case No. 1817, para. 325; 331st Report, Case No. 2132, para. 588; 333rd Report, Case No. 2288, para. 827; and 337th Report, Case No. 2334, para. 1220.)

349. Conventions Nos. 87 and 98 are compatible with systems which envisage union representation for the exercise of collective trade union rights based on the degree of actual union membership, as well as those envisaging union representation on the basis of general ballots of workers or officials, or a combination of both systems.

(See 320th Report, Case No. 2040, para. 669.)

350. A system under which the apportioning of the number of union stewards for joint organizations is determined by a committee responsible for verifying the trade union membership of the different organizations is compatible with the principles of freedom of association, as long as it offers certain guarantees. Clearly, the protection of data regarding union membership is a fundamental aspect of human rights and, in particular, with regard to the right to privacy; however, inasmuch as the verification of union membership is subject to strict guarantees, there is no reason why it should not be compatible with the observance of such rights or guarantee confidentiality in respect of members' identities. It is also important for the bodies responsible for verifying the membership levels of union organizations to enjoy the confidence of all such organizations.

(See 320th Report, Case No. 2040, para. 669.)

351. The determination to ascertain or verify the representative character of trade unions can best be ensured when strong guarantees of secrecy and impartiality are offered. Thus, verification of the representative character of a union should a priori be carried out by an independent and impartial body.

(See 302nd Report, Case No. 1817, para. 325.)

352. It is unnecessary to draw up a list of trade union members in order to determine the number of members; this will be evident from the record of trade union membership dues, and there is no need for a list of names which could make acts of anti-union discrimination easier.

(See 327th Report, Case No. 2132, para. 661.)

353. The requirement that the authorities make in practice of obtaining a list of the names of all the members of an organization and a copy of their membership card to determine the most representative organization poses a problem with regard to the principles of freedom of association. There is a risk of reprisals and anti-union discrimination inherent in this type of requirement

(See 336th Report, Case No. 2153, para. 166.)

354. Recognizing the possibility of trade union pluralism does not preclude granting certain rights and advantages to the most representative organizations. However, the determination of the most representative organization must be based on objective, pre-established and precise criteria so as to avoid any possibility of bias or abuse, and the distinction should generally be limited to the recognition of certain preferential rights, for example for such purposes as collective bargaining, consultation by the authorities or the designation of delegates to international organizations.

(See 300th Report, Case No. 1844, para. 241.)

355. The Committee has considered that certain advantages, especially with regard to representation, might be accorded to trade unions by reason of the extent of their representativeness. But it has taken the view that the intervention of the public authorities as regards such advantages should not be of such a nature as to influence unduly the choice of the workers in respect of the organization to which they wish to belong.

(See the 1996 *Digest*, para. 311; 327th Report, Case No. 2132, para. 661; and 335th Report, Case No. 2317, para. 1083.)

356. The fact of establishing in the legislation a percentage in order to determine the threshold for the representativeness of organizations and grant certain privileges to the most representative organizations (in particular for collective bargaining purposes) does not raise any difficulty provided that the criteria are objective, precise and pre-established, in order to avoid any possibility of bias or abuse.

(See 336th Report, Case No. 2153, para. 166.)

357. The Committee has considered, with regard to legislation establishing a system for determining representitivity, that granting the right to sit on the Economic and Social Council only to those trade union organizations deemed to be the most representative would not appear to influence workers unduly in the choice of organization that they wish to join, nor to prevent less representative organizations from defending the interests of their members, organizing their activities and formulating their programmes.

(See 311th Report, Case No. 1968, para. 502.)

358. The Committee has considered that a registration system set up by law which grants exclusive negotiation rights to registered unions would not be incompatible with the principles of freedom of association provided that the registration is based on objective and predetermined criteria. However, the granting of exclusive rights to the most representative organization should not mean that the existence of other unions to which certain involved workers might wish to belong is prohibited.

(See the 1996 *Digest*, para. 312.)

359. Minority trade unions that have been denied the right to negotiate collectively should be permitted to perform their activities and at least to speak on behalf of their members and represent them in the case of an individual claim.

(See the 1996 *Digest*, para. 313; and 336th Report, Case No. 2153, para. 168.)

Right to join organizations freely

360. Workers should be able, if they so wish, to join trade unions at the branch level as well as the enterprise level at the same time.

(See the 1996 *Digest*, para. 317; and 325th Report, Case No. 2100, para. 430.)

361. In one case where any member of a trade union who wished to resign from the union could only do so in the presence of a notary who had to verify the identity of the person concerned and attest his or her signature, the Committee considered that this requirement in itself did not constitute an infringement of trade union rights provided that this was a formality which, in practice, could be carried out easily and without delay. However, if such a requirement could, in certain circumstances, present practical difficulties for workers wishing to withdraw from a union, it might restrict the free exercise of their right to join organizations of their own choosing. In order to avoid such a situation, the Committee considered that the government should examine the possibility of introducing an alternative method of resigning from a union which would involve no practical or financial difficulties for the workers concerned.

(See the 1996 *Digest*, para. 319.)

362. The Committee urged a government to withdraw the requirement by the Seamen Employment Control Division that seafarers must sign an affidavit before leaving the country restricting their right to affiliate with or contact an international trade union organization for assistance to protect their occupational interests.

(See the 1996 *Digest*, para. 320.)

Union security clauses

(See also paras. 324 and 480)

363. A distinction should be made between union security clauses allowed by law and those imposed by law, only the latter of which appear to result in a trade union monopoly system contrary to the principles of freedom of association.

(See the 1996 *Digest*, para. 321; and 320th Report, Case No. 1963, para. 220.)

364. The admissibility of union security clauses under collective agreements was left to the discretion of ratifying States, as evidenced by the preparatory work for Convention No. 98.

(See the 1996 *Digest*, para. 322.)

365. Problems related to union security clauses should be resolved at the national level, in conformity with national practice and the industrial relations system in each country. In other words, both situations where union security clauses are authorized and those where they are prohibited can be considered to be in conformity with ILO principles and standards on freedom of association.

(See the 1996 *Digest*, para. 323; 329th Report, Case No. 2136, para. 102; and 332nd Report, Case No. 2187, para. 721.)

366. In certain cases where the deduction of union contributions and other forms of union protection were instituted, not in virtue of the legislation in force, but as a result of collective agreements or established practice existing between both parties, the Committee has declined to examine the allegations made, basing its reasoning on the statement of the Committee on Industrial Relations appointed by the International Labour Conference in 1949, according to which Convention No. 87 can in no way be interpreted as authorizing or prohibiting union security arrangements, such questions being matters for regulation in accordance with national practice. According to this statement, those countries – and more particularly those countries having trade union pluralism – would in no way be bound under the provisions of the Convention to permit union security clauses either by law or as a matter of custom, while other countries which allow such clauses would not be placed in the position of being unable to ratify the Convention.

(See the 1996 *Digest*, para. 324.)

367. Basing its reasoning on the declaration made in 1949 by the Committee on Industrial Relations of the International Labour Conference, the Committee has considered that legislation which provides that no one shall be compelled to join or not to join a trade union does not in itself infringe Conventions Nos. 87 and 98.

(See the 1996 *Digest*, para. 329.)

368. Where union security arrangements exist requiring membership of a given organization as a condition of employment, there might be discrimination if unreasonable conditions were to be imposed upon persons seeking such membership.

(See the 1996 *Digest*, para. 330.)

Right of organizations to draw up their constitutions and rules 6

Legislation on the subject and interference by the authorities

(See also paras. 392, 401, 405, 427, 430 and 473)

369. Legislative provisions which regulate in detail the internal functioning of workers' and employers' organizations pose a serious risk of interference by the public authorities. Where such provisions are deemed necessary by the public authorities, they should simply establish an overall framework in which the greatest possible autonomy is left to the organizations in their functioning and administration. Restrictions on this principle should have the sole objective of protecting the interests of members and guaranteeing the democratic functioning of organizations. Furthermore, there should be a procedure for appeal to an impartial and independent judicial body so as to avoid any risk of excessive or arbitrary interference in the free functioning of organizations.

(See the 1996 *Digest*, para. 331; and 321st Report, Case No. 2011, para. 215.)

370. In the Committee's opinion, the mere existence of legislation concerning trade unions in itself does not constitute a violation of trade union rights, since the State may legitimately take measures to ensure that the constitutions and rules of trade unions are drawn up in accordance with the law. On the other hand, any legislation adopted in this area should not undermine the rights of workers as defined by the principles of freedom of association. Overly detailed or restrictive legal provisions in this area may in practice hinder the creation and development of trade union organizations.

(See the 1996 *Digest*, para. 332; and 302nd Report, Case No. 1817, para. 326.)

371. To guarantee the right of workers' organizations to draw up their constitutions and rules in full freedom, national legislation should only lay down formal requirements as regards trade union constitutions, and the constitutions and rules should not be subject to prior approval by the public authorities.

(See the 1996 *Digest*, para. 333; 302nd Report, Case No. 1817, para. 323; 321st Report, Case No. 2011, para. 215; 327th Report, Case No. 2115, para. 681; 330th Report, Case No. 2207, para. 907; 332nd Report, Case No. 2115, para. 114, and Case No. 2207, para. 119; and 335th Report, Case No. 2308, para. 1041.)

372. Requirements regarding territorial competence and number of union members should be left for trade unions to determine in their own by-laws. In fact, any legislative provisions that go beyond formal requirements may hinder the establishment and development of organizations and constitute interference contrary to Article 3, paragraph 2, of the Convention.

(See 318th Report, Case No. 2038, para. 529.)

373. A provision that union rules shall comply with national statutory requirements is not in violation of the principle that workers' organizations shall have the right to draw up their constitutions and rules in full freedom, provided that such statutory requirements in themselves do not infringe the principle of freedom of association and provided that approval of the rules by the competent authority is not within the discretionary powers of such authorities.

(See the 1996 *Digest*, para. 334.)

374. The drafting by the public authorities themselves of the constitutions of central workers' organizations constitutes a violation of the principles of freedom of association.

(See the 1996 *Digest*, para. 335; and 299th Report, Case No. 1772, para. 132.)

375. Where the approval of trade union rules is within the discretionary powers of a competent authority, this is not compatible with the generally accepted principle that workers' organizations shall have the right to draw up their constitutions and rules in full freedom.

(See the 1996 *Digest*, para. 336.)

376. The existence of a right to appeal to the courts in connection with the approval of by-laws does not in itself constitute a sufficient guarantee. This would not change the nature of the powers conferred on the administrative authorities and the courts would only be able to ensure that the legislation had been correctly applied. The courts should, therefore, be entitled to re-examine the substance of the case, as well as the grounds on which an administrative decision is based.

(See the 1996 *Digest*, para. 337.)

377. A legal provision which authorizes the government in certain circumstances to object to the setting up of a trade union within a period of three months from the date of registration of its by-laws is in contradiction with the basic principle that employers and workers should have the right to establish organizations of their own choosing without previous authorization.

(See the 1996 *Digest*, para. 338.)

378. The existence of legislation which is designed to promote democratic principles within trade union organizations is acceptable. Secret and direct voting is certainly a democratic process and cannot be criticized as such.

(See the 1996 *Digest*, para. 339.)

379. The listing in the legislation of the particulars that must be contained in a union's constitution is not in itself an infringement of the right of workers' organizations to draw up their internal rules in full freedom.

(See the 1996 *Digest*, para. 340; and 306th Report, Case No. 1884, para. 690.)

380. A mandatory list of functions and aims that associations must have that is excessively extensive and detailed may in practice hinder the establishment and development of organizations.

(See the 1996 *Digest*, para. 341.)

381. Amendments to the constitution of a trade union should be debated and adopted by the union members themselves.

(See the 1996 *Digest*, para. 342; and 302nd Report, Case No. 1817, para. 323.)

382. In some countries the law requires that the majority of the members of a trade union – at least at a first vote – decide on certain questions which affect the very existence or structure of the organization (adoption and amendments of the constitution, dissolution, etc.). In such cases involving basic matters relating to the existence and structure of a union or the fundamental rights of its members, the regulation by law of majority votes for the adoption of the decisions involved does not imply interference contrary to the Convention, provided that this regulation is not such as to seriously impede the running of a trade union, thereby making it practically impossible to adopt the required decisions in the prevailing circumstances, and provided that the purpose is to guarantee the members' right to participate democratically in the organization.

(See the 1996 *Digest*, para. 343.)

383. The insertion in the constitution of a trade union, on the decision of the public authorities, of a clause whereby the trade union must forward annually to the ministry a series of documents – namely a copy of the minutes of the last general assembly indicating precisely the names of the members present, a copy of the general secretary's report, as approved by the assembly, a copy of the treasurer's report, etc. – and where failure to do so within a prescribed period will result in the union being considered as having ceased to exist – is incompatible with the principles of freedom of association.

(See the 1996 *Digest*, para. 345.)

Model constitutions

384. Any obligation on a trade union to base its constitution on a compulsory model (apart from certain purely formal clauses) would infringe the rules which ensure freedom of association. The case is quite different, however, when a government merely makes model constitutions available to organizations that are being established without requiring them to accept such a model. The preparation of model constitutions and rules for the guidance of trade unions, provided that there is no compulsion or pressure on the unions to accept them in practice, does not necessarily involve any interference with the right of organizations to draw up their constitutions and rules in full freedom.

(See the 1996 *Digest*, para. 346.)

Racial discrimination

385. Laws providing for the organization, in registered mixed trade unions, of separate branches for workers of different races, and the holding of separate meetings by the separate branches, are not compatible with the generally accepted principle that workers' and employers' organizations shall have the right to draw up their constitutions and rules and to organize their administration and activities.

(See the 1996 *Digest*, para. 347.)

Relations between first-level trade unions and higher-level organizations

386. As a rule, the autonomy of trade unions and higher-level organizations, including as regards their various relationships, should be respected by public authorities. Legal provisions impinging on this autonomy should therefore remain an exception and, where deemed necessary by reason of unusual circumstances, should be accompanied by all possible guarantees against undue interference.

(See the 1996 *Digest*, para. 348.)

387. The subjection of grass-roots organizations to the control of trade union organizations at a higher level, the approval of their establishment by the latter, and the establishment by the National Congress of Trade Union Members of the constitutions of trade unions constitute major constraints on the right of the unions to establish their own constitutions, organize their activities and formulate their programmes.

(See the 1996 *Digest*, para. 349; and 310th Report, Case No. 1930, para. 343.)

Right of organizations to elect their representatives in full freedom 7

General principles

(See also para. 417)

388. Freedom of association implies the right of workers and employers to elect their representatives in full freedom.

(See the 1996 *Digest*, para. 350; 305th Report, Case No. 1874, para. 268; 329th Report, Case No. 2177/2183, para. 639; and 333rd Report, Case No. 2301, para. 591.)

389. Workers and their organizations should have the right to elect their representatives in full freedom and the latter should have the right to put forward claims on their behalf.

(See the 1996 *Digest*, para. 352.)

390. It is the prerogative of workers' and employers' organizations to determine the conditions for electing their leaders and the authorities should refrain from any undue interference in the exercise of the right of workers' and employers' organizations freely to elect their representatives, which is guaranteed by Convention No. 87.

(See the 1996 *Digest*, para. 351; 306th Report, Case No. 1884, para. 692; 333rd Report, Case No. 2301, para. 591; and 335th Report, Case No. 2276, para. 404.)

391. The right of workers' organizations to elect their own representatives freely is an indispensable condition for them to be able to act in full freedom and to promote effectively the interests of their members. For this right to be fully acknowledged, it is essential that the public authorities refrain from any intervention which might impair the exercise of this right, whether it be in determining the conditions of eligibility of leaders or in the conduct of the elections themselves.

(See the 1996 *Digest*, para. 353; 302nd Report, Case No. 1817, para. 322; 304th Report, Case No. 1865, para. 251; 328th Report, Case No. 2128, para. 262; 329th Report, Case No. 2090, para. 273; 333rd Report, Case No. 2301, para. 591; and 337th Report, Case No. 2327, para. 210.)

Electoral procedures

(See also para. 955)

392. The regulation of procedures and methods for the election of trade union officials is primarily to be governed by the trade unions' rules themselves. The fundamental idea of Article 3 of Convention No. 87 is that workers and employers may decide for themselves the rules which should govern the administration of their organizations and the elections which are held therein.

(See the 1996 *Digest*, para. 354; 307th Report, Case No. 1905, para. 154; 308th Report, Case No. 1920, para. 520; 326th Report, Case No. 2067, para. 512; and 335th Report, Case No. 2276, para. 404.)

393. An excessively meticulous and detailed regulation of the trade union electoral process is an infringement of the right of such organizations to elect their representatives in full freedom, as established in Article 3 of Convention No. 87.

(See the 1996 *Digest*, para. 355.)

394. Legislation which minutely regulates the internal election procedures of a trade union and the composition of its executive committees, fixes the days on which meetings will take place, the precise date for the annual general assembly and the date on which the mandates of trade union officers shall expire, is incompatible with the rights afforded to trade unions by Convention No. 87.

(See the 1996 *Digest*, para. 356.)

395. A provision which gives a broad discretionary power to the minister to regulate minutely the internal election procedures of trade unions, the composition and the date of elections of their various committees, and even the way in which they should function, is incompatible with the principles of freedom of association.

(See the 1996 *Digest*, para. 357.)

396. If a government regulates trade union elections too closely, this may be considered as a limitation of the right of trade unions to elect their own representatives freely. However, in general, laws governing the frequency of elections and fixing a maximum period for the terms of office of executive bodies do not affect the principles of freedom of association.

(See the 1996 *Digest*, para. 358; and 308th Report, Case No. 1920, para. 520.)

397. It should be left to the unions themselves to set the period of terms of office.

(See the 1996 *Digest*, para. 359; 308th Report, Case No. 1920, para. 520; and 329th Report, Case No. 2177/2183, para. 639.)

398. The imposition by legislative means of a direct, secret and universal vote for the election of trade union leaders does not raise any problems regarding the principles of freedom of association.

(See the 1996 *Digest*, para. 360.)

399. No violation of the principles of freedom of association is involved where the legislation contains certain rules intended to promote democratic principles within trade union organizations or to ensure that the electoral procedure is conducted in a normal manner and with due respect for the rights of members in order to avoid any dispute as to the election results.

(See the 1996 *Digest*, para. 361.)

400. Provisions requiring registered organizations to elect their officers by postal vote do not appear to infringe the freedom to elect trade union leaders.

(See the 1996 *Digest*, para. 362.)

401. It should be left to the workers' organizations themselves to make provision, in their constitutions or rules, as to the majority of votes required for the election of trade union leaders.

(See the 1996 *Digest*, para. 363.)

402. The number of leaders of an organization should be a matter for decision by the trade union organizations themselves.

(See the 1996 *Digest*, para. 364.)

403. The registration of the executive boards of trade union organizations should take place automatically when reported by the trade union, and should be contested only at the request of the members of the trade union in question.

(See the 1996 *Digest*, para. 365; 318th Report, Case No. 2003, para. 390; and 325th Report, Case No. 2068, para. 311.)

404. Since the creation of works councils and councils of employers can constitute a preliminary step towards the setting up of independent and freely established workers' and employers' organizations, all official positions in such councils should, without exception, be occupied by persons who are freely elected by the workers or employers concerned.

(See the 1996 *Digest*, para. 367; and 332nd Report, Case No. 2255, para. 947.)

Eligibility conditions

405. The determination of conditions of eligibility for union membership or union office is a matter that should be left to the discretion of union by-laws and the public authorities should refrain from any intervention which might impair the exercise of this right by trade union organizations.

(See 309th Report, Case No. 1865, para. 153; and 311th Report, Case No. 1942, para. 263.)

A. Racial discrimination

406. Legislative provisions which reserve to Europeans the right to be members of the executive committees of mixed trade unions (made up of workers of different races), are incompatible with the principle that workers' and employers' organizations shall have the right to elect their representatives in full freedom.

(See the 1996 *Digest*, para. 368.)

B. Employment in the occupation or enterprise

407. The requirement of membership of an occupation or establishment as a condition of eligibility for union office are not consistent with the right of workers to elect their representatives in full freedom.

(See 318th Report, Case No. 2003, para. 390.)

408. If the national legislation provides that all trade union leaders must belong to the occupation in which the organization functions, there is a danger that the guarantees provided for in Convention No. 87 may be jeopardized. In fact, in such cases, the laying off of a worker who is a trade union official can, as well as making him forfeit his position as a trade union official, affect the freedom of action of the organization and its right to elect its representatives in full freedom, and even encourage acts of interference by employers.

(See the 1996 *Digest*, para. 369; 307th Report, Case No. 1905, para. 154; and 326th Report, Case No. 2096, para. 427.)

409. For the purpose of bringing legislation which restricts union office to persons actually employed in the occupation or establishment concerned into conformity with the principle of the free election of representatives, it is necessary at least to make these provisions more flexible by admitting as candidates persons who have previously been employed in the occupation concerned and by exempting from the occupational requirement a reasonable proportion of the officers of an organization.

(See the 1996 *Digest*, para. 371; 326th Report, Case No. 2096, para. 427; and 335th Report, Case No. 1865, para. 829.)

410. Provisions which require that all trade union leaders shall, at the time of their election, have been engaged in the occupation or trade for more than one year are not in harmony with Convention No. 87.

(See the 1996 *Digest*, para. 372.)

411. Given that workers' organizations are entitled to elect their representatives in full freedom, the dismissal of a trade union leader, or simply the fact that a trade union leader leaves the work that he or she was carrying out in a given undertaking, should not affect his or her trade union status or functions unless stipulated otherwise by the constitution of the trade union in question.

(See the 1996 *Digest*, para. 373; 304th Report, Case No. 1865, para. 251; and 326th Report, Case No. 2105, para. 447.)

412. A requirement that trade union leaders shall continue to carry out their employment during their term of office prevents the existence of full-time officers. Such a provision may be highly detrimental to the interests of trade unions, in particular those whose size or geographical extent require the contribution of a considerable amount of time by the officers. Such a provision impedes the free functioning of trade unions and is not in conformity with the requirements of Article 3 of Convention No. 87.

(See the 1996 *Digest*, para. 374.)

C. Duration of membership of the organization

413. A provision laying down as one of the eligibility requirements for trade union office that the candidate must have belonged to the organization for at least one year could be interpreted as meaning that all trade union leaders must belong to the occupation or work in the undertaking in which the trade union represents the workers. In this event, if the requirement were applied to all office-holders in trade union organizations, it would be incompatible with the principles of freedom of association.

(See the 1996 *Digest*, para. 375.)

414. A provision requiring any trade union leader to have been a member of the trade union for not less than six months implies an important restriction on the right of workers' organizations to elect their representatives in full freedom.

(See the 1996 *Digest*, para. 376.)

D. Political opinions or activities

415. Legislation which disqualifies persons from trade union office because of their political beliefs or affiliations is not in conformity with the right of trade unionists to elect their representatives in full freedom.

(See the 1996 *Digest*, para. 377.)

416. Where a body representing the workers in a dispute is elected by those workers, the right to elect their representatives in full freedom is restricted if some only of those representatives, on the basis of their political opinions, are considered by a government to be capable of participating in conciliation proceedings. Where the law of the land provides that the government may only deal with those who appear to be the representatives of the workers of an undertaking and, in effect, choose those with whom it will deal, any selection based on the political opinions of those concerned in such a way as to eliminate from negotiations, even indirectly, the leaders of the organization that is the most representative of the category of workers concerned would appear to result in the law of the land being so applied as to impair the right of the workers to choose their representatives freely.

(See the 1996 *Digest*, para. 378.)

417. Legislation which debars from trade union office for a period of ten years "any person taking part in political activities of a Communist character" and which lists a number of "legal presumptions" whereby any person can be held to be responsible for such activities, may involve a violation of the principle laid down in Convention No. 87, which states that workers' and employers' organizations shall have the right "to elect their representatives in full freedom, to organise their administration and activities" and that the "public authorities shall refrain from any interference which would restrict this right or impede the lawful exercise thereof".

(See the 1996 *Digest*, para. 379.)

418. The Committee has taken the view that a law is contrary to the principles of freedom of association when a trade unionist can be barred from union office and membership because, in the view of the minister, his or her activities might further the interests of Communism.

(See the 1996 *Digest*, para. 380.)

E. Moral standing of candidates for office

419. A legal requirement that candidates for trade union office must be subjected to a background investigation conducted by the ministry of the interior and the department of justice amounts to prior approval by the authorities of candidates, which is incompatible with Convention No. 87.

(See the 1996 *Digest*, para. 381.)

F. Nationality

420. Legislation should be made flexible so as to permit the organizations to elect their leaders freely and without hindrance, and to permit foreign workers access to trade union posts, at least after a reasonable period of residence in the host country.

(See the 1996 *Digest*, para. 382.)

G. Criminal record

421. A law which generally prohibits access to trade union office because of any conviction is incompatible with the principles of freedom of association, when the activity condemned is not prejudicial to the aptitude and integrity required to exercise trade union office.

(See the 1996 *Digest*, para. 383.)

422. Conviction on account of offences the nature of which is not such as to call into question the integrity of the person concerned and is not such as to be prejudicial to the exercise of trade union functions should not constitute grounds for disqualification from holding trade union office, and any legislation providing for disqualification on the basis of any offence is incompatible with the principles of freedom of association.

(See the 1996 *Digest*, para. 384.)

423. As regards legislation which provides that a sentence by any court whatsoever, except for political offences, to a term of imprisonment of one month or more, constitutes grounds that are incompatible with, or which disqualify from the holding of executive or administrative posts in a trade union, the Committee has taken the view that such a general provision could be interpreted in such a way as to exclude from responsible trade union posts any individuals convicted for activities involving the exercise of trade union rights, such as a violation of the laws governing the press, thereby restricting unduly the right of trade unionists to elect their representatives in full freedom.

(See the 1996 *Digest*, para. 385.)

424. Ineligibility for trade union office based on "any crime involving fraud, dishonesty or extortion" could run counter to the right to elect representatives in full freedom since "dishonesty" could cover a wide range of conduct not necessarily making it inappropriate for persons convicted of this crime to hold positions of trust such as trade union office.

(See the 1996 *Digest*, para. 387.)

H. Re-election

425. A ban on the re-election of trade union officials is not compatible with Convention No. 87. Such a ban, moreover, may have serious repercussions on the normal development of a trade union movement which does not have a sufficient number of persons capable of adequately carrying out the functions of trade union office.

(See the 1996 *Digest*, para. 388.)

426. Legislation which fixes the maximum length of the terms of trade union officers and which at the same time limits their right of re-election violates the right of organizations to elect their representatives in full freedom.

(See the 1996 *Digest*, para. 389.)

Obligation to participate in ballots

427. The obligation for the organization's members to vote should be left to the unions' rules and not imposed by law.

(See the 1996 *Digest*, para. 390.)

428. A law which imposes fines on workers who do not participate in trade union elections is not in conformity with the provisions of Convention No. 87.

(See the 1996 *Digest*, para. 391.)

Intervention by the authorities in trade union elections

429. Any intervention by the public authorities in trade union elections runs the risk of appearing to be arbitrary and thus constituting interference in the functioning of workers' organizations, which is incompatible with Convention No. 87, Article 3, which recognizes their right to elect their representatives in full freedom.

(See the 1996 *Digest*, para. 392.)

430. The right of workers to elect their representatives in full freedom should be exercised in accordance with the statutes of their occupational associations and should not be subject to the convening of elections by ministerial resolution.

(See the 1996 *Digest*, para. 393; and 308th Report, Case No. 1915, para. 271.)

431. With regard to an internal dispute within the trade union organization between two rival administrations, the Committee considered that, with a view to guaranteeing the impartiality and objectivity of the procedure, the supervision of trade union elections should be entrusted to the competent judicial authorities.

(See the 1996 *Digest*, para. 394; and 308th Report, Case No. 1920, para. 524.)

432. Any interference by the authorities and the political party in power concerning the presidency of the central trade union organization in a country is incompatible with the principle that organizations shall have the right to elect their representatives in full freedom.

(See the 1996 *Digest*, para. 395; 324th Report, Case No. 2090, para. 203; 329th Report, Case No. 2090, para. 271; and 330th Report, Case No. 2144, para. 711.)

433. The nomination by the authorities of members of executive committees of trade unions constitutes direct interference in the internal affairs of trade unions and is incompatible with Convention No. 87.

(See the 1996 *Digest*, para. 396; and 306th Report, Case No. 1908, para. 459.)

434. When the authorities intervene during the election proceedings of a union, expressing their opinion of the candidates and the consequences of the election, this seriously challenges the principle that trade union organizations have the right to elect their representatives in full freedom.

(See the 1996 *Digest*, para. 397; 324th Report, Case No. 2090, para. 203; and 329th Report, Case No. 2090, para. 271.)

435. Where trade union leaders were removed from office, not by decision of the members of the trade unions concerned but by the administrative authority, and not because of infringement of specific provisions of the trade union constitution or of the law, but because the administrative authorities considered these trade union leaders incapable of maintaining "discipline" in their unions, the Committee was of the view that such measures were obviously incompatible with the principle that trade union organizations have the right to elect their representatives in full freedom and to organize their administration and activities.

(See the 1996 *Digest*, para. 398.)

436. Legislation which requires candidates for trade union office to have obtained the approval of the Provincial Governor, which is given on the basis of a report from the police, is incompatible with the principle that employers' and workers' organizations should have the right to elect their representatives in full freedom.

(See the 1996 *Digest*, para. 399.)

437. The following provisions are incompatible with the right to hold free elections, namely those which involve interference by the public authorities in various stages of the electoral process, beginning with the obligation to submit the candidates' names in advance to the ministry of labour, together with personal particulars, the presence of a representative of the ministry of labour or the civil or military authorities at the elections, including the approval of the election of the executive committee by ministerial decision, without which they are invalid.

(See the 1996 *Digest*, para. 400; and 308th Report, Case No. 1920, para. 523.)

438. The presence during trade union elections of the authorities is liable to infringe freedom of association and, in particular, to be incompatible with the principle that workers' organizations shall have the right to elect their representatives in full freedom, and that the public authorities should refrain from any interference which would restrict this right or impede the lawful exercise thereof.

(See the 1996 *Digest*, para. 401; and 330th Report, Case No. 2144, para. 711.)

439. The Committee has observed that, in a number of countries, legal provisions exist whereby an official who is independent of the public authorities – such as a trade union registrar – may take action, subject to an appeal to the courts, if a complaint is made or if there are reasonable grounds for supposing that irregularities have taken place in a trade union election, contrary to the law or the constitution of the organization concerned. The situation, however, is different when the elections can be valid only after being approved by the administrative authorities. The Committee has considered that the requirement of approval by the authorities of the results of trade union elections is not compatible with the principle of freedom of election.

(See the 1996 *Digest*, para. 402.)

Challenges to trade union elections

440. Measures taken by the administrative authorities when election results are challenged run the risk of being arbitrary. Hence, and in order to ensure an impartial and objective procedure, matters of this kind should be examined by the judicial authorities.

(See the 1996 *Digest*, para. 403.)

441. In order to avoid the danger of serious limitation on the right of workers to elect their representatives in full freedom, complaints brought before labour courts by an administrative authority challenging the results of trade union elections should not – pending the final outcome of the judicial proceedings – have the effect of suspending the validity of such elections.

(See the 1996 *Digest*, para. 404; 330th Report, Case No. 2067, para. 173, and Case No. 2046, para. 526.)

442. In cases where the results of trade union elections are challenged, such questions should be referred to the judicial authorities in order to guarantee an impartial, objective and expeditious procedure.

(See the 1996 *Digest*, para. 405; 306th Report, Case No. 1908, para. 459; and 335th Report, Case No. 2294, para. 383.)

443. In order to avoid the danger of serious limitations on the right of workers to elect their representatives in full freedom, cases brought before the courts by the administrative authorities involving a challenge to the results of trade union elections should not – pending the final outcome of the proceedings – have the effect of paralysing the operations of trade unions.

(See the 1996 *Digest*, para. 406.)

Removal of executive committees and the placing of trade unions under control

444. The removal by the Government of trade union leaders from office is a serious infringement of the free exercise of trade union rights.

(See 299th Report, Case No. 1772, para. 131.)

445. The appointment by the government of persons to administer the central national trade union on the ground that such a measure was rendered necessary by the corrupt administration of the unions would seem to be incompatible with freedom of association in a normal period.

(See the 1996 *Digest*, para. 407.)

446. In a case where an administrator of trade union affairs had been appointed by the government so as to ensure, on behalf of the trade unions, the functions normally carried out by a central workers' organization, the Committee considered that any reorganization of the trade union movement should be left to the trade union organizations themselves and that the administrator should confine himself to coordinating the efforts made by the unions to bring this about. The prerogatives conferred on the administrator should not be such as to restrict the rights guaranteed by Article 3, paragraph 1, of Convention No. 87.

(See the 1996 *Digest*, para. 408.)

447. Legislation which confers on the public authorities the power to remove the management committee of a union whenever, in their discretion, they consider that they have "serious and justified reasons", and which empowers the government to appoint executive committees to replace the elected committees of trade unions, is not compatible with the principle of freedom of association. Such provisions can in no way be compared with those which, in some countries, make it possible for the courts to declare an election invalid for specific reasons defined by law.

(See the 1996 *Digest*, para. 409.)

448. The setting up by the government, following a change of regime, of a provisional consultative committee of a trade union confederation and the refusal to recognize the executive committee which has been elected at the congress of that organization constitutes a breach of the principle that the public authorities should refrain from any interference which would restrict the right of workers' organizations to elect their representatives in full freedom and to organize their administration and activities.

(See the 1996 *Digest*, para. 410.)

449. With regard to the placing of certain unions under control, the Committee has drawn attention to the importance which it attaches to the principle that the public authorities should refrain from any interference which would restrict the right of workers' organizations to elect their representatives in full freedom and to organize their administration and activities.

(See the 1996 *Digest*, para. 411; and 300th Report, Case No. 1793, para. 270.)

450. The placing of trade union organizations under control involves a serious danger of restricting the rights of workers' organizations to elect their representatives in full freedom and to organize their administration and activities.

(See the 1996 *Digest*, para. 412.)

451. While recognizing that certain events were of an exceptional kind and may have warranted intervention by the authorities, the Committee considered that, in order to be admissible, the taking over of a trade union must be temporary and aimed solely at permitting the organization of free elections.

(See the 1996 *Digest*, para. 413.)

452. Measures taken by the administrative authorities, such as the placing of organizations under control, are liable to appear arbitrary, even if they are temporary and may be challenged before the courts.

(See the 1996 *Digest*, para. 414.)

453. The power conferred on a person with a view to facilitating the normal functioning of a trade union organization should not be such as to lead to limitations on the right of trade union organizations to draw up their constitutions, elect their representatives, organize their administration and formulate their programmes.

(See the 1996 *Digest*, para. 415.)

Right of organizations to organize their administration 8

General principles

454. Freedom of association implies the right of workers and employers to elect their representatives in full freedom and to organize their administration and activities without any interference by the public authorities.

(See the 1996 *Digest*, para. 416; and 331st Report, Case No. 2132, para. 589.)

455. The fundamental idea of Article 3 of Convention No. 87 is that workers and employers may decide for themselves the rules which should govern the administration of their organizations and the elections which are held therein.

(See the 1996 *Digest*, para. 417.)

Internal administration of organizations

456. In view of the fact that in every democratic trade union movement the congress of members is the supreme trade union authority which determines the regulations governing the administration and activities of trade unions and which establishes their programme, the prohibition of such congresses would seem to constitute an infringement of trade union rights.

(See the 1996 *Digest*, para. 418.)

457. When legislation is applied in such a manner as to prevent trade union organizations from using the services of experts who are not necessarily elected officers, such as industrial advisers, lawyers or agents able to represent them in judicial or administrative proceedings, there would be serious doubt as to the compatibility of such provisions with Article 3 of Convention No. 87, according to which workers' organizations shall have the right, inter alia, to organize their administration and activities.

(See the 1996 *Digest*, para. 420.)

458. A provision prohibiting a trade union leader from receiving remuneration of any kind is not in conformity with the requirements of Article 3 of Convention No. 87.

(See the 1996 *Digest*, para. 421.)

459. With regard to legislation which had just been adopted prohibiting the payment of the wages of full-time union officials by employers, the Committee considered that abandoning such a widespread, long-standing practice may lead to financial difficulties for unions and entail the risk of considerably hindering their functioning.

(See 307th Report, Case No. 1865, para. 225.)

460. Freedom of association implies the right of workers' and employers' organizations to resolve any disputes by themselves and without interference by the authorities; it is for the government to create an atmosphere conducive to the resolution of such disputes.

(See the 1996 *Digest*, para. 422.)

Control over the internal activities of organizations

461. Legislation which accords to the minister the discretionary right to investigate the internal affairs of a trade union merely if he or she considers it necessary in the public interest is not in conformity with the principles that workers' organizations should have the right to organize their administration and activities without any interference by the public authorities which would restrict this right or impede the lawful exercise thereof.

(See the 1996 *Digest*, para. 423.)

462. Events of an exceptional nature may warrant direct intervention by a government in internal trade union matters in order to re-establish a situation in which trade union rights are fully respected.

(See the 1996 *Digest*, para. 424.)

463. The only limitation on the rights set out in Article 3 of Convention No. 87 which might possibly be acceptable should aim solely at ensuring respect for democratic rules within the trade union movement.

(See the 1996 *Digest*, para. 425.)

464. The principles established in Article 3 of Convention No. 87 do not prevent the control of the internal acts of a trade union if those internal acts violate legal provisions or rules. Nevertheless, it is important that control over the internal acts of a trade union and the power to take measures for its suspension or dissolution should be exercised by the judicial authorities, not only to guarantee an impartial and objective procedure and to ensure the right of defence (which normal judicial procedure alone can guarantee), but also to avoid the risk that measures taken by the administrative authorities may appear to be arbitrary.

(See the 1996 *Digest*, para. 426.)

465. There should be outside control only in exceptional cases, when there are serious circumstances justifying such action, since otherwise there would be a risk of limiting the right that workers' organizations have, by virtue of Article 3 of Convention No. 87, to organize their administration and activities without interference by the public authorities which would restrict this right or impede its lawful exercise. The Committee has considered that a law which confers the power to intervene on an official of the judiciary, against whose decisions an appeal may be made to the Supreme Court, and which lays down that a request for intervention must be supported by a substantial number of those in the occupational category in question, does not violate these principles.

(See the 1996 *Digest*, para. 427.)

Financial administration of organizations

A. Financial independence in respect of the public authorities

466. The right of workers to establish organizations of their own choosing and the right of such organizations to draw up their own constitutions and internal rules and to organize their administration and activities presuppose financial independence. Such independence implies that workers' organizations should not be financed in such a way as to allow the public authorities to enjoy discretionary powers over them.

(See the 1996 *Digest*, para. 428; 300th Report, Case No. 1793, para. 267; and 304th Report, Case No. 1865, para. 248.)

467. With regard to systems of financing the trade union movement which made trade unions financially dependent on a public body, the Committee considered that any form of state control is incompatible with the principles of freedom of association and should be abolished since it permitted interference by the authorities in the financial management of trade unions.

(See the 1996 *Digest*, para. 429.)

468. Provisions governing the financial operations of workers' organizations should not be such as to give the public authorities discretionary powers over them.

(See the 1996 *Digest*, para. 430; 304th Report, Case No. 1865, para. 248; and 306th Report, Case No. 1865, para. 326.)

469. Provisions which restrict the freedom of trade unions to administer and utilize their funds as they wish for normal and lawful trade union purposes are incompatible with principles of freedom of association.

(See 324th Report, Case No. 1942, para. 41.)

470. A system in which workers are bound to pay contributions to a public organization which, in turn, finances trade union organizations, constitutes a serious threat to the independence of these organizations.

(See the 1996 *Digest*, para. 431.)

471. While trade union training is to be encouraged, it should be provided by the unions themselves; the unions can, of course, take advantage of any material or moral assistance which the government may offer to them.

(See the 1996 *Digest*, para. 432.)

472. Various systems of subsidizing workers' organizations have very different consequences according to the form which they assume, the spirit in which they are conceived and applied and the extent to which the subsidies are granted as a matter of right, by virtue of statutory provisions, or at the discretion of a public authority. The repercussions which financial aid may have on the autonomy of trade union organizations will depend essentially on circumstances; they cannot be assessed by applying general principles: they are questions of fact which must be examined in the light of the circumstances of each case.

(See the 1996 *Digest*, para. 433.)

B. Union dues

(See also para. 325)

473. Questions concerning the financing of trade union and employers' organizations, as regards both their own budgets and those of federations and confederations, should be governed by the by-laws of the organizations, federations and confederations themselves, and therefore, constitutional or legal provisions which require contributions are incompatible with the principles of freedom of association.

(See the 1996 *Digest*, para. 434; 326th Report, Case No. 2090, para. 237; and 327th Report, Case No. 2146, para. 895.)

474. The repartition of trade union dues among various trade union structures is a matter to be determined solely by the trade unions concerned.

(See 326th Report, Case No. 2090, para. 237.)

475. The withdrawal of the check-off facility, which could lead to financial difficulties for trade union organizations, is not conducive to the development of harmonious industrial relations and should therefore be avoided.

(See the 1996 *Digest*, para. 435; and, for example, 315th Report, Case No. 1935, para. 23; 318th Report, Case No. 2016, para. 101; 324th Report, Case No. 2055, para. 683; 325th Report, Case No. 2090, para. 165; 329th Report, Case No. 2163, para. 705; 330th Report, Case No. 2206, para. 915; 332nd Report, Case No. 2187, para. 723; 335th Report, Case No. 2330, para. 876; 337th Report, Case No. 2395, para. 1188; and 338th Report, Case No. 2386, para. 1253.)

476. The requirement that workers confirm their trade union membership in writing in order to have their union dues deducted from their wages does not violate the principles of freedom of association.

(See 304th Report, Case No. 1832, para. 36.)

477. The Committee has requested a Government to take the necessary steps to amended the legislation so that workers can opt for deductions from their wages under the check-off system to be paid to trade union organizations of their choice, even if they are not the most representative.

(See 304th Report, Case No. 1832, para. 38.)

478. In a case in which the requirements for the deduction of trade union dues from wages included the provision of the worker's identity document and her/his membership card, a list of members, an affidavit by the General-Secretary of the union stating the veracity of the list of members and the posting of the list on the employer's website, the Committee considered that all these requirements combined to violate the principles of freedom of association and emphasizes that, for the deduction of trade union dues from wages, the enterprise should confine itself to requesting evidence of members' affiliation and disaffiliation. Furthermore, the annual publication of the list of trade union members on the employer's website is particularly unacceptable as it has nothing to do with the deduction of trade union dues and violates the privacy of union members.

(See 337th Report, Case No. 2293, para. 1135.)

479. In a case in which the authorities had not transferred to the trade union concerned the dues that had been deducted from the wages of public officials, the Committee considered that trade union dues do not belong to the authorities, nor are they public funds, but rather they are an amount on deposit that the authorities may not use for any reason other than to remit them to the organization concerned without delay.

(See 334th Report, Case No. 2224, para. 143.)

480. When legislation admits trade union security clauses, such as the withholding of trade union dues from the wages of non-members benefiting from the conclusion of a collective agreement, those clauses should only take effect through collective agreements.

(See the 1996 Digest, para. 325.)

481. The deduction of trade union dues by employers and their transfer to trade unions is a matter which should be dealt with through collective bargaining between employers and all trade unions without legislative obstruction.

(See the 1996 *Digest*, para. 326; 300th Report, Case No. 1744, para. 99; and 323rd Report, Case No. 2043, para. 502.)

482. A considerable delay in the administration of justice with regard to the remittance of trade union dues withheld by an enterprise is tantamount in practice to a denial of justice.

(See the 1996 *Digest*, para. 328; and 323rd Report, Case No. 2043, para. 504.)

483. A legal restriction on the amount which a federation may receive from the unions affiliated to it would appear to be contrary to the generally accepted principle that workers' organizations shall have the right to organize their administration and activities and those of the federations which they form.

(See the 1996 *Digest*, para. 437.)

484. Particularly in transition countries, special measures, including tax deductions for trade union dues and membership dues of employers' organizations, should be considered in order to ease the development of employers' and workers' organizations.

(See 338th Report, Case No. 2350, para. 1084.)

C. Control and restrictions on the use of trade union funds

(See also para. 702)

485. Provisions which give the authorities the right to restrict the freedom of a trade union to administer and utilize its funds as it wishes for normal and lawful trade union purposes are incompatible with the principles of freedom of association.

(See the 1996 *Digest*, para. 438; and 311th Report, Case No. 1942, para. 264.)

486. The freezing of union bank accounts may constitute serious interference by the authorities in trade union activities.

(See the 1996 *Digest*, para. 439; 308th Report, Case No. 1888, para. 341; 323rd Report, Case No. 2075, para. 522; 324th Report, Case No. 2090, para. 207; and 333rd Report, Case No. 2246, para. 937.)

487. While the legislation in many countries requires that trade union accounts be audited, either by an auditor appointed by the trade union or, less frequently, appointed by the registrar of trade unions, it is generally accepted that such an auditor shall possess the required professional qualifications and be an independent person. A provision which reserves to the government the right to audit trade union funds is therefore not consistent with the generally accepted principle that trade unions should have the right to organize their administration and that the public authorities should refrain from any interference which would restrict this right or impede the lawful exercise thereof.

(See the 1996 *Digest*, para. 440.)

488. Legislation obliging a trade union to have its books of account stamped and the pages numbered by the ministry of labour before they are opened for use appears only to be aimed at preventing fraud. The Committee has taken the view that such a requirement does not constitute a breach of trade union rights.

(See the 1996 *Digest*, para. 441.)

489. The Committee has observed that, in general, trade union organizations appear to agree that legislative provisions requiring, for instance, financial statements to be presented annually to the authorities in the prescribed form and the submission of other data on points which may not seem clear in the said statements, do not per se infringe trade union autonomy. Measures of supervision over the administration of trade unions may be useful if they are employed only to prevent abuses and to protect the members of the trade union themselves against mismanagement of their funds. However, it would seem that measures of this kind may, in certain cases, entail a danger of interference by the public authorities in the administration of trade unions and that this interference may be of such a nature as to restrict the rights of organizations or impede the lawful exercise thereof, contrary to Article 3 of Convention No. 87. It may be considered, however, to some extent, that a guarantee exists against such interference where the official appointed to exercise supervision enjoys some degree of independence of the administrative authorities and where that official is subject to the control of the judicial authorities.

(See the 1996 *Digest*, para. 442; 323rd Report, Case No. 2081, para. 573; and 334th Report, Case No. 2259, para. 564.)

490. The control exercised by the public authorities over trade union finances should not normally exceed the obligation to submit periodic reports. The discretionary right of the authorities to carry out inspections and request information at any time entails a danger of interference in the internal administration of trade unions.

(See the 1996 *Digest*, para. 443; 308th Report, Case No. 1911, para. 254; 323rd Report, Case No. 2081, para. 569; 327th Report, Case No. 1581, para. 110; 330th Report, Case No. 2229, para. 944; and 331st Report, Case No. 2081, para. 110.)

491. As regards certain measures of administrative control over trade union assets, such as financial audits and investigations, the Committee has considered that these should be applied only in exceptional cases, when justified by grave circumstances (for instance, presumed irregularities in the annual statement or irregularities reported by members of the organization), in order to avoid any discrimination between one trade union and another and to preclude the danger of excessive intervention by the authorities which might hamper a union's exercise of the right to organize its administration freely, and also to avoid harmful and perhaps unjustified publicity or the disclosure of information which might be confidential.

(See the 1996 *Digest*, para. 444; 308th Report, Case No. 1911, para. 254; 323rd Report, Case No. 2081, para. 569; 330th Report, Case No. 2229, para. 944; 331st Report, Case No. 2081, para. 110; and 338th Report, Case No. 2387, para. 865.)

492. The general principle that there should be judicial control of the internal management of an occupational organization in order to ensure an impartial and objective procedure is particularly important in regard to the administration of trade union property and finances.

(See the 1996 *Digest*, para. 445.)

493. Where the bank accounts of trade union leaders accused of embezzlement of trade union funds are frozen, the Committee has pointed out that if, following investigation, no evidence of misappropriation of trade union funds has been found, it would be unreasonable for the accounts of the trade unionists, whether or not they have remained in the country, to remain frozen.

(See the 1996 *Digest*, para. 446.)

494. It is for the organizations themselves to decide whether they shall receive funding for legitimate activities to promote and defend human rights and trade union rights.

(See 332nd Report, Case No. 2258, para. 515.)

Right of organizations freely to organize their activities and to formulate their programmes

9

General principles

495. Freedom of association implies not only the right of workers and employers to form freely organizations of their own choosing, but also the right for the organizations themselves to pursue lawful activities for the defence of their occupational interests.

(See the 1996 *Digest*, para. 447; 308th Report, Case No. 1934, para. 127; 323rd Report, Case No. 2075, para. 523; 329th Report, Case No. 2140, para. 295; 330th Report, Case No. 1888, para. 658; 334th Report, Case No. 2313, para. 1119; and 335th Report, Case No. 2236, para. 970.)

496. Any provision which gives the authorities, for example, the right to restrict the activities and objects pursued by trade unions for the furtherance and defence of the interests of their members would be incompatible with the principles of freedom of association.

(See the 1996 *Digest*, para. 448.)

Political activities and relations

(See also paras. 13, 29, 157, 165, 169 to 171, 205 to 208, 305, 528 and 529)

497. In order that trade unions may be sheltered from political vicissitudes, and in order that they may avoid being dependent on the public authorities, it is desirable that, without prejudice to the freedom of opinion of their members, they should limit the field of their activities to the occupational and trade union fields; the government, on the other hand, should refrain from interfering in the functioning of trade unions.

(See the 1996 *Digest*, para. 449.)

498. In the interests of the normal development of the trade union movement, it would be desirable to have regard to the principles enunciated in the resolution concerning the independence of the trade union movement adopted by the International Labour Conference at its 35th Session (1952) that the fundamental and permanent mission of the trade union movement is the economic and social advancement of the workers and that when trade unions, in accordance with the national law and practice of their respective countries and at the decision of their members, decide to establish relations with a political party or to undertake constitutional political action as a means towards the advancement of their economic and social objectives, such political relations or actions should not be of such a nature as to compromise the continuance of the trade union movement or its social or economic functions irrespective of political changes in the country.

(See the 1996 *Digest*, para. 450; 318th Report, Case No. 2005, para. 180; and 328th Report, Case No. 2129, para. 604.)

499. The Committee has reaffirmed the principle expressed by the International Labour Conference in the resolution concerning the independence of the trade union movement that governments should not attempt to transform the trade union movement into an instrument for the pursuance of political aims, nor should they attempt to interfere with the normal functions of a trade union movement because of its freely established relationship with a political party.

(See the 1996 Digest, para. 451; 299th Report, Case No. 1772, para. 133; 318th Report, Case No. 2005, para. 180; and 323rd Report, Case No. 2081, para. 572.)

500. Provisions imposing a general prohibition on political activities by trade unions for the promotion of their specific objectives are contrary to the principles of freedom of association.

(See the 1996 *Digest*, para. 452; 311th Report, Case No. 1942, para. 264; 321st Report, Case No. 2031, para. 167; and 323rd Report, Case No. 2081, para. 572.)

501. If trade unions are prohibited in general terms from engaging in any political activities, this may raise difficulties by reason of the fact that the interpretation given to the relevant provisions may, in practice, change at any moment and considerably restrict the possibility of action of the organizations. It would, therefore, seem that States, without prohibiting in general terms political activities of occupational organizations, should be able to entrust to the judicial authorities the task of repressing abuses which might, in certain cases, be committed by organizations which have lost sight of the fact that their fundamental objective should be the economic and social advancement of their members.

(See the 1996 *Digest*, para. 453.)

502. Trade union organizations should not engage in political activities in an abusive manner and go beyond their true functions by promoting essentially political interests.

(See the 1996 *Digest*, para. 454; 311th Report, Case No. 1942, para. 264; 332nd Report, Case No. 2238, para. 967; 334th Report, Case No. 2313, para. 1116; 336th Report, Case No. 2365, para. 910; and 337th Report, Case No. 2365, para. 1661.)

503. A general prohibition on trade unions from engaging in any political activities would not only be incompatible with the principles of freedom of association, but also unrealistic in practice. Trade union organizations may wish, for example, to express publicly their opinion regarding the government's economic and social policy.

(See the 1996 *Digest*, para. 455; 321st Report, Case No. 2031, para. 167; 328th Report, Case No. 2129, para. 604; 332nd Report, case No. 2238, para. 967; 334th Report, Case No. 2313, para. 1116; 336th Report, Case No. 2365, para. 910; and 337th Report, Case No. 2365, para. 1661.)

504. There should be no confusion between the performance of their specific functions by trade unions and employers' organizations, i.e. the defence and promotion of the occupational interests of workers and employers, and the possible pursuit by certain of their members of other activities that are unconnected with trade union functions. The penal responsibility which such persons may incur as a result of such acts should in no way lead to measures being taken to deprive the organizations themselves or their leaders of their means of action.

(See the 1996 *Digest*, para. 456; and 334th Report, Case No. 2254, para. 1083.)

505. It is only in so far as trade union organizations do not allow their occupational demands to assume a clearly political aspect that they can legitimately claim that there should be no interference in their activities. On the other hand, it is difficult to draw a clear distinction between what is political and what is, properly speaking, trade union in character. These two notions overlap and it is inevitable, and sometimes usual, for trade union publications to take a stand on questions having political aspects, as well as on strictly economic and social questions.

(See the 1996 *Digest*, paras. 164 and 457; 305th Report, Case No. 1893, para. 458; and 306th Report, Case No. 1884, para. 684.)

506. With regard to legal provisions under which "the trade unions shall mobilize and educate workers and employees so that they ... respect work discipline", they "shall organize workers and employees by conducting socialist emulation campaigns at the workplace" and "the trade unions shall educate workers and employees ... in order to strengthen their ideological convictions", the Committee has considered that the functions assigned to the trade unions by this body of provisions must necessarily limit their right to organize their activities, contrary to the principles of freedom of association. It has considered that the obligations thus defined, which the unions must observe, prevent the establishment of trade union organizations that are independent of the public authorities and of the ruling party, and whose mission should be to defend and promote the interests of their constituents and not to reinforce the country's political and economic systems.

(See the 1996 *Digest*, para. 300.)

507. A law obliging leaders of occupational associations to make a declaration "to uphold democracy" could lead to abuses, since such a provision does not include any precise criteria on which a judicial decision could be based were a trade union leader to be accused of not having respected the terms of the declaration.

(See the 1996 *Digest*, para. 458.)

Other activities of trade union organizations (protest activities, sit-ins, public demonstrations, etc.)

508. The right of petition is a legitimate activity of trade union organizations, and persons who sign such trade union petitions should not be reprimanded or punished for this type of activity.

(See the 1996 *Digest*, paras. 460 and 719; 325th Report, Case No. 2068, para. 319; 329th Report, case No. 2188, para. 215; and 331st Report, Case No. 2217, para. 210.)

509. The fact of having presented a list of dispute grievances is a legitimate trade union activity.

(See the 1996 *Digest*, para. 461.)

510. Trade unions should be free to determine the procedure for submitting claims to the employer and the legislation should not impede the functioning of a trade union by obliging a trade union to call a general meeting every time there is a claim to be made to an employer.

(See 332nd Report, Case No. 2216, para. 911.)

511. If a government takes reprisals, directly or indirectly, against trade unionists or the leaders of workers' or employers' organizations for the simple reason that they protest against the appointment of workers' or employers' delegates to a national or international meeting, this constitutes an infringement of trade union rights.

(See the 1996 *Digest*, para. 462.)

512. Legislation which permits the competent authorities to ban any organization which carries on any normal trade union activity, such as campaigning for a minimum wage, is incompatible with the generally accepted principle that the public authorities should refrain from any interference which would restrict the right of workers' organizations to organize their activities and to formulate their programmes, or which would impede the lawful exercise of this right.

(See the 1996 *Digest*, para. 463.)

513. The expression of an opinion by a trade union organization concerning a court decision relative to the killing of trade union members is in fact a legitimate trade union activity.

(See the 1996 *Digest*, para. 465.)

514. By threatening retaliatory measures against workers who had merely expressed their intention to hold a sit-in in pursuance of their legitimate economic and social interests, the employer interfered in the workers' basic right to organize their administration and activities and to formulate their programmes, contrary to Article 3 of Convention No. 87.

(See the 1996 *Digest*, para. 466.)

515. The extent to which the part played by the trade unions in organizing work competition and undertaking propaganda for production or the carrying out of economic plans is consistent with the fulfilment by the trade unions of their responsibility for protecting the interests of the workers depends on the degree of freedom enjoyed by the trade unions in other respects.

(See the 1996 *Digest*, para. 468.)

516. The Committee has considered that, while it is not called upon to express an opinion as to the desirability of entrusting the administration of social insurance and the supervision of the application of social legislation to occupational associations rather than to administrative state organs, in so far as such a measure might restrict the free exercise of trade union rights, such questions might be within its mandate: (1) if the trade unions exercise discrimination in administering the social insurance funds made available to them for the purpose of exercising pressure on unorganized workers; (2) if the independence of the trade union movement should thereby be compromised.

(See the 1996 *Digest*, para. 469.)

517. The right of workers to be represented by an official of their union in any proceedings involving their working conditions, in accordance with procedures prescribed by laws or regulations, is a right that is generally recognized in a large number of countries. It is particularly important that this right should be respected when workers whose level of education does not enable them to defend themselves adequately without the assistance of a more experienced person, are not permitted to be represented by a lawyer and so can rely only on their union officers for assistance.

(See the 1996 *Digest*, para. 470.)

518. The boycott is a very special form of action which, in some cases, may involve a trade union whose members continue their work and are not directly involved in the dispute with the employer against whom the boycott is imposed. In these circumstances, the prohibition of boycotts by law does not necessarily appear to involve an interference with trade union rights.

(See the 1996 *Digest*, para. 471.)

519. The choice of unionists to take part in purely union-organized training courses, wherever held, should be left to the workers' organization or educational institution responsible for such activities and not be dictated by any political parties.

(See the 1996 *Digest*, para. 472.)

Right to strike 10

Importance of the right to strike and its legitimate exercise

(See also para. 131)

520. While the Committee has always regarded the right to strike as constituting a fundamental right of workers and of their organizations, it has regarded it as such only in so far as it is utilized as a means of defending their economic interests.

(See the 1996 *Digest*, para. 473; 336th Report, Case No. 2324, para. 282; and 338th Report, Case No. 2407, para. 491.)

521. The Committee has always recognized the right to strike by workers and their organizations as a legitimate means of defending their economic and social interests.

(See the 1996 *Digest*, para. 474; and, for example, 302nd Report, Case No. 1809, para. 381; 304th Report, Case No. 1863, para. 356; 307th Report, Case No. 1850, para. 120; 308th Report, Case No. 1900, para. 183; 311th Report, Case No. 1934, para. 126; 324th Report, Case No. 2072, para. 587; 327th Report, Case No. 1581, para. 111; 328th Report, Case No. 2116, para. 368; 332nd Report, Case No. 2258, para. 522; and 335th Report, Case No. 2305, para. 505.)

522. The right to strike is one of the essential means through which workers and their organizations may promote and defend their economic and social interests.

(See the 1996 *Digest*, para. 475; and, for example, 299th Report, Case No. 1687, para. 457; 300th Report, Case No. 1799, para. 207; 306th Report, Case No. 1884, para. 695; 308th Report, Case No. 1934, para. 131; 310th Report, Case No. 1928, para. 176; 316th Report, Case No. 1930, para. 365; 327th Report, Case No. 1581, para. 111; 330th Report, Case No. 2196, para. 304; 335th Report, Case No. 2257, para. 466; 336th Report, Case No. 2340, para. 645; and 337th Report, Case No. 2365, para. 1665.)

523. The right to strike is an intrinsic corollary to the right to organize protected by Convention No. 87.

(See 311th Report, Case No. 1954, para. 405.)

524. It does not appear that making the right to call a strike the sole preserve of trade union organizations is incompatible with the standards of Convention No. 87. Workers, and especially their leaders in undertakings, should however be protected against any discrimination which might be exercised because of a strike and they should be able to form trade unions without being exposed to anti-union discrimination.

(See the 1996 *Digest*, para. 477; 334th Report, Case No. 2258, para. 454; and 336th Report, Case No. 2153, para. 173.)

525. The prohibition on the calling of strikes by federations and confederations is not compatible with Convention No. 87.

(See the 1996 *Digest*, para. 478; and 306th Report, Case No. 1884, para. 686.)

Objective of the strike (strikes on economic and social issues, political strikes, solidarity strikes, etc.)

526. The occupational and economic interests which workers defend through the exercise of the right to strike do not only concern better working conditions or collective claims of an occupational nature, but also the seeking of solutions to economic and social policy questions and problems facing the undertaking which are of direct concern to the workers.

(See the 1996 *Digest*, para. 479; 304th Report, Case No. 1851, para. 280; 314th Report, Case No. 1787, para. 31; 320th Report, Case No. 1865, para. 526; 326th Report, Case No. 2094, para. 491; 329th Report, Case No. 2094, para. 135; and 331st Report, Case No. 1937/2027, para. 104.)

527. Organizations responsible for defending workers' socio-economic and occupational interests should be able to use strike action to support their position in the search for solutions to problems posed by major social and economic policy trends which have a direct impact on their members and on workers in general, in particular as regards employment, social protection and standards of living.

(See the 1996 *Digest*, para. 480; 305th Report, Case No. 1870, para. 143; 320th Report, Case No. 1865, para. 526, and Case No. 2027, para. 876; 336th Report, Case No. 2354, para. 682; and 337th Report, Case No. 2323, para. 1039.)

528. Strikes of a purely political nature and strikes decided systematically long before negotiations take place do not fall within the scope of the principles of freedom of association.

(See the 1996 *Digest*, para. 481; 303rd Report, Case No. 1810/1830, para. 61; and 329th Report, Case No. 2094, para. 135.)

529. While purely political strikes do not fall within the scope of the principles of freedom of association, trade unions should be able to have recourse to protest strikes, in particular where aimed at criticizing a government's economic and social policies.

(See the 1996 *Digest*, para. 482; 300th Report, Case No. 1777, para. 71; 304th Report, Case No. 1851, para. 280, and Case No 1863, para. 356; 314th Report, Case No. 1787, para. 31; 320th Report, Case No. 1865, para. 526; and 333rd Report, Case No. 2251, para. 985.)

530. In one case where a general strike against an ordinance concerning conciliation and arbitration was certainly one against the government's policy, the Committee considered that it seemed doubtful whether allegations relating to it could be dismissed at the outset on the ground that it was not in furtherance of a trade dispute, since the trade unions were in dispute with the government in its capacity as an important employer following the initiation of a measure dealing with industrial relations which, in the view of the trade unions, restricted the exercise of trade union rights.

(See the 1996 *Digest*, para. 483.)

531. The right to strike should not be limited solely to industrial disputes that are likely to be resolved through the signing of a collective agreement; workers and their organizations should be able to express in a broader context, if necessary, their dissatisfaction as regards economic and social matters affecting their members' interests.

(See the 1996 *Digest*, para. 484; 300th Report, Case No. 1777, para. 71; and 320th Report, Case No. 1865, para. 526.)

532. The solution to a legal conflict as a result of a difference in interpretation of a legal text should be left to the competent courts. The prohibition of strikes in such a situation does not constitute a breach of freedom of association.

(See the 1996 *Digest*, para. 485.)

533. If strikes are prohibited while a collective agreement is in force, this restriction must be compensated for by the right to have recourse to impartial and rapid mechanisms, within which individual or collective complaints about the interpretation or application of collective agreements can be examined; this type of mechanism not only allows the inevitable difficulties which may occur regarding the interpretation or application of collective agreements to be resolved while the agreements are in force, but also has the advantage of preparing the ground for future rounds of negotiations, given that it allows problems which have arisen during the period of validity of the collective agreement in question to be identified.

(See 330th Report, Case No. 2208, para. 601.)

534. A general prohibition of sympathy strikes could lead to abuse and workers should be able to take such action provided the initial strike they are supporting is itself lawful.

(See the 1996 *Digest*, para. 486; 303rd Report, Case No. 1810/1830, para. 61; 307th Report, Case No. 1898, para. 325; 320th Report, Case No. 1963, para. 235; 333rd Report, Case No. 2251, para. 985; and 338th Report, Case No. 2326, para. 445.)

535. The fact that a strike is called for recognition of a union is a legitimate interest which may be defended by workers and their organizations.

(See the 1996 *Digest*, para. 487; and 302nd Report, Case No. 1809, para. 381.)

536. A ban on strikes related to recognition disputes (for collective bargaining) is not in conformity with the principles of freedom of association.

(See the 1996 *Digest*, para. 488; and 321st Report, Case No. 2066, para. 336.)

537. Protest strikes in a situation where workers have for many months not been paid their salaries by the Government are legitimate trade union activities.

(See 304th Report, Case No. 1850, para. 216.)

538. A ban on strike action not linked to a collective dispute to which the employee or union is a party is contrary to the principles of freedom of association.

(See the 1996 *Digest*, para. 489; and 307th Report, Case No. 1898, para. 325.)

539. Provisions which prohibit strikes if they are concerned with the issue of whether a collective employment contract will bind more than one employer are contrary to the principles of freedom of association on the right to strike; workers and their organizations should be able to call for industrial action in support of multi-employer contracts.

(See the 1996 *Digest*, para. 490.)

540. Workers and their organizations should be able to call for industrial action (strikes) in support of multi-employer contracts (collective agreements).

(See the 1996 *Digest*, para. 491.)

541. The Committee has stated on many occasions that strikes at the national level are legitimate in so far as they have economic and social objectives and not purely political ones; the prohibition of strikes could only be acceptable in the case of public servants exercising authority in the name of the State or of workers in essential services in the strict sense of the term, i.e. services whose interruption could endanger the life, personal safety or health of the whole or part of the population.

(See the 1996 *Digest*, para. 492.)

542. A declaration of the illegality of a national strike protesting against the social and labour consequences of the government's economic policy and the banning of the strike constitute a serious violation of freedom of association.

(See the 1996 *Digest*, para. 493.)

543. As regards a general strike, the Committee has considered that strike action is one of the means of action which should be available to workers' organizations. A 24-hour general strike seeking an increase in the minimum wage, respect of collective agreements in force and a change in economic policy (to decrease prices and unemployment) is legitimate and within the normal field of activity of trade union organizations.

(See the 1996 *Digest*, para. 494.)

544. A general protest strike demanding that an end be brought to the hundreds of murders of trade union leaders and unionists during the past few years is a legitimate trade union activity and its prohibition therefore constitutes a serious violation of freedom of association.

(See the 1996 *Digest*, para. 495.)

Types of strike action

545. Regarding various types of strike action denied to workers (wild-cat strikes, tools-down, go-slow, working to rule and sit-down strikes), the Committee considers that these restrictions may be justified only if the strike ceases to be peaceful.

(See the 1996 *Digest*, paras. 496 and 497; and 306th Report, Case No. 1865, para. 337.)

546. The Committee has considered that the occupation of plantations by workers and by other persons, particularly when acts of violence are committed, is contrary to Article 8 of Convention No. 87. It therefore requested the Government, in future, to enforce the evacuation orders pronounced by the judicial authorities whenever criminal acts are committed on plantations or at places of work in connection with industrial disputes.

(See 323rd Report, Case No. 2021, paras. 324 and 325.)

Prerequisites

547. The conditions that have to be fulfilled under the law in order to render a strike lawful should be reasonable and in any event not such as to place a substantial limitation on the means of action open to trade union organizations.

(See the 1996 *Digest*, para. 498; 300th Report, Case No. 1799, para. 207; 318th Report, Case No. 2018, para. 514; 325th Report, Case No. 2049, para. 520; 327th Report, Case No. 2118, para. 635; and 333rd Report, Case No. 2251, para. 995.)

548. The legal procedures for declaring a strike should not be so complicated as to make it practically impossible to declare a legal strike.

(See the 1996 *Digest*, para. 499; and 316th Report, Case No. 1989, para. 189.)

549. Legislation which provides for voluntary conciliation and arbitration in industrial disputes before a strike may be called cannot be regarded as an infringement of freedom of association, provided recourse to arbitration is not compulsory and does not, in practice, prevent the calling of the strike.

(See the 1996 *Digest*, para. 500; 307th Report, Case No. 1899, para. 83, and Case No. 1898, para. 324; 309th Report, Case No. 1912, para. 364; 324th Report, Case No. 2092/2101, para. 731; and 336th Report, Case No. 2369, para. 212.)

550. In general, a decision to suspend a strike for a reasonable period so as to allow the parties to seek a negotiated solution through mediation or conciliation efforts, does not in itself constitute a violation of the principles of freedom of association.

(See 338th Report, Case No. 2329, para. 1274.)

551. The Committee has emphasized that, although a strike may be temporarily restricted by law until all procedures available for negotiation, conciliation and arbitration have been exhausted, such a restriction should be accompanied by adequate, impartial and speedy conciliation and arbitration proceedings in which the parties concerned can take part at every stage.

(See the 1996 *Digest*, para. 501.)

552. The obligation to give prior notice to the employer before calling a strike may be considered acceptable.

(See the 1996 *Digest*, para. 502; 325th Report, Case No. 2049, para. 520; and 333rd Report, Case No. 2251, para. 996.)

553. The requirement that a 20-day period of notice be given in services of social or public interest does not undermine the principles of freedom of association.

(See the 1996 *Digest*, para. 504; and 309th Report, Case No. 1912, para. 365.)

554. The legal requirement of a cooling-off period of 40 days before a strike is declared in an essential service, in so far as it is designed to provide the parties with a period of reflection, is not contrary to the principles of freedom of association. This clause which defers action may enable both parties to come once again to the bargaining table and possibly to reach an agreement without having recourse to a strike.

(See the 1996 *Digest*, para. 505.)

555. With regard to the majority vote required by one law for the calling of a legal strike (two-thirds of the total number of members of the union or branch concerned), non-compliance with which might entail a penalty by the administrative authorities, including the dissolution of the union, the Committee recalled the conclusions of the Committee of Experts on the Application of Conventions and Recommendations that such legal provisions constitute an intervention by the public authorities in the activities of trade unions which is of such a nature as to restrict the rights of these organizations, contrary to Article 3 of the Convention.

(See the 1996 *Digest*, para. 506.)

556. The requirement of a decision by over half of all the workers involved in order to declare a strike is excessive and could excessively hinder the possibility of carrying out a strike, particularly in large enterprises.

(See the 1996 *Digest*, para. 507.)

557. The requirement that an absolute majority of workers should be obtained for the calling of a strike may be difficult, especially in the case of unions which group together a large number of members. A provision requiring an absolute majority may, therefore, involve the risk of seriously limiting the right to strike.

(See the 1996 *Digest*, para. 508; and 316th Report, Case No. 1989, para. 190.)

558. The Committee requested a government to take measures to amend the legal requirement that a decision to call a strike be adopted by more than half of the workers to which it applies, in particular in enterprises with a large union membership.

(See the 1996 *Digest*, para. 509.)

559. The obligation to observe a certain quorum and to take strike decisions by secret ballot may be considered acceptable.

(See the 1996 *Digest*, para. 510; 316th Report, Case No. 1989, para. 190; and 332nd Report, Case No. 2216, para. 912.)

560. The observance of a quorum of two-thirds of the members may be difficult to reach, in particular where trade unions have large numbers of members covering a large area.

(See the 1996 *Digest*, para. 511; 332nd Report, Case No. 2216, para. 912; and 333rd Report, Case No. 2251, para. 987.)

561. A provision requiring the agreement of the majority of the members of federations and confederations, or the approval by the absolute majority of the workers of the undertaking concerned for the calling of a strike, may constitute a serious limitation on the activities of trade union organizations.

(See the 1996 *Digest*, para. 512.)

562. The Committee has considered to be in conformity with the principles of freedom of association a situation where the decision to call a strike in the local branches of a trade union organization may be taken by the general assembly of the local branches, when the reason for the strike is of a local nature and where, in the higher-level trade union organizations, the decision to call a strike may be taken by the executive committee of these organizations by an absolute majority of all the members of the committee.

(See the 1996 *Digest*, para. 513.)

563. The obligation to hold a second strike vote if a strike has not taken place within three months of the first vote does not constitute an infringement of freedom of association.

(See the 1996 *Digest*, para. 514.)

Recourse to compulsory arbitration

564. Compulsory arbitration to end a collective labour dispute and a strike is acceptable if it is at the request of both parties involved in a dispute, or if the strike in question may be restricted, even banned, i.e. in the case of disputes in the public service involving public servants exercising authority in the name of the State or in essential services in the strict sense of the term, namely those services whose interruption would endanger the life, personal safety or health of the whole or part of the population.

(See the 1996 *Digest*, paras. 515 and 553; 302nd Report, Case No. 1845, para. 512; 303rd Report, Case No. 1810/1830, para. 62; 307th Report, Case No. 1890, para. 372; 310th Report, Case No. 1931, para. 506; 314th Report, Case No. 1948/1955, para. 75; 333rd Report, Case No. 2281, para. 631; 335th Report, Case No. 2303, para. 1376; and 338th Report, Case No. 2329, para. 1275.)

565. In as far as compulsory arbitration prevents strike action, it is contrary to the right of trade unions to organize freely their activities and could only be justified in the public service or in essential services in the strict sense of the term.

(See the 1996 *Digest*, para. 518.)

566. A provision which permits either party unilaterally to request the intervention of the labour authority to resolve a dispute may effectively undermine the right of workers to call a strike and does not promote voluntary collective bargaining.

(See the 1996 Digest, paras. 519 and 863; 300th Report, Case No. 1839, para. 86; and 310th Report, Case No. 1930, para. 348.)

567. The right to strike would be affected if a legal provision were to permit employers to submit in every case for compulsory arbitral decision disputes resulting from the failure to reach agreement during collective bargaining, thereby preventing recourse to strike action.

(See the 1996 *Digest*, para. 520.)

568. The Committee considers that a system of compulsory arbitration through the labour authorities, if a dispute is not settled by other means, can result in a considerable restriction of the right of workers' organizations to organize their activities and may even involve an absolute prohibition of strikes, contrary to the principles of freedom of association.

(See the 1996 *Digest*, para. 521.)

569. In order to gain and retain the parties' confidence, any arbitration system should be truly independent and the outcomes of arbitration should not be predetermined by legislative criteria.

(See 299th Report, Case No. 1768, para. 110.)

Cases in which strikes may be restricted or even prohibited, and compensatory guarantees

A. Acute national emergency

(See also paras. 198, 606, 609, 620, 636 and 637)

570. A general prohibition of strikes can only be justified in the event of an acute national emergency and for a limited period of time.

(See the 1996 *Digest*, para. 527; 316th Report, Case No. 1985, para. 320; 327th Report, Case No. 1581, para. 111; 333rd Report, Case No. 2288, para. 829, and Case No. 2251, para. 993; 336th Report, Case No. 2340, para. 645; and 337th Report, Case No. 2244, para. 1268.)

571. Responsibility for suspending a strike on the grounds of national security or public health should not lie with the Government, but with an independent body which has the confidence of all parties concerned.

(See 335th Report, Case No. 2303, para. 1377; and 338th Report, Case No. 2366, para. 1279.)

B. Public service

(See also paras. 588, 589 and 590)

572. Recognition of the principle of freedom of association in the case of public servants does not necessarily imply the right to strike.

(See the 1996 *Digest*, para. 531; and 304th Report, Case No. 1719, para. 413.)

573. The Committee has acknowledged that the right to strike can be restricted or even prohibited in the public service or in essential services in so far as a strike there could cause serious hardship to the national community and provided that the limitations are accompanied by certain compensatory guarantees.

(See the 1996 *Digest*, para. 533; 300th Report, Case No. 1791, para. 345; 302nd Report, Case No. 1849, para. 203; and 318th Report, Case No. 2020, para. 318.)

574. The right to strike may be restricted or prohibited only for public servants exercising authority in the name of the State.

(See the 1996 *Digest*, para. 534; 304th Report, Case No. 1719, para. 413; 338th Report, Case No. 2363, para. 731, and Case No. 2364, para. 975.)

575. Too broad a definition of the concept of public servant is likely to result in a very wide restriction or even a prohibition of the right to strike for these workers. The prohibition of the right to strike in the public service should be limited to public servants exercising authority in the name of the State.

(See the 1996 *Digest*, para. 535.)

576. The right to strike may be restricted or prohibited: (1) in the public service only for public servants exercising authority in the name of the State; or (2) in essential services in the strict sense of the term (that is, services the interruption of which would endanger the life, personal safety or health of the whole or part of the population).

(See the 1996 *Digest*, paras. 526 and 536; and, for example, 306th Report, Case No. 1882, para. 427; 309th Report, Case No. 1913, para. 305; 316th Report, Case No. 1934, para. 210; 320th Report, Case No. 2025, para. 405; 326th Report, Case No. 2135, para. 266; 329th Report, Case No. 2157, para. 191; 330th Report, Case No. 2212, para. 749; 333rd Report, Case No. 2251, para. 993; 335th Report, Case No. 2257, para. 466; 336th Report, Case No. 2383, para. 759; and 337th Report, Case No 2244, para. 1268.)

577. Public servants in state-owned commercial or industrial enterprises should have the right to negotiate collective agreements, enjoy suitable protection against acts of anti-union discrimination and enjoy the right to strike, provided that the interruption of services does not endanger the life, personal safety or health of the whole or part of the population.

(See the 1996 *Digest*, para. 532; and 338th Report, Case No. 2348, para. 997.)

578. Officials working in the administration of justice and the judiciary are officials who exercise authority in the name of the State and whose right to strike could thus be subject to restrictions, such as its suspension or even prohibition.

(See the 1996 *Digest*, paras. 537 and 538; and 336th Report, Case No. 2383, para. 763.)

579. The prohibition of the right to strike of customs officers, who are public servants exercising authority in the name of the State, is not contrary to the principles of freedom of association.

(See 304th Report, Case No. 1719, para. 413.)

580. Action taken by a government to obtain a court injunction to put a temporary end to a strike in the public sector does not constitute an infringement of trade union rights.

(See the 1996 *Digest*, para. 539.)

C. Essential services

(See also para. 576)

581. To determine situations in which a strike could be prohibited, the criterion which has to be established is the existence of a clear and imminent threat to the life, personal safety or health of the whole or part of the population.

(See the 1996 *Digest*, para. 540; 320th Report, Case No. 1989, para. 324; 324th Report, Case No. 2060, para. 517; 329th Report, Case No. 2195, para. 737; 332nd Report, Case No. 2252, para. 883; 336th Report, Case No. 2383, para. 766; 338th Report, Case No. 2326, para. 446, and Case No. 2329, para. 1275.)

582. What is meant by essential services in the strict sense of the term depends to a large extent on the particular circumstances prevailing in a country. Moreover, this concept is not absolute, in the sense that a non-essential service may become essential if a strike lasts beyond a certain time or extends beyond a certain scope, thus endangering the life, personal safety or health of the whole or part of the population.

(See the 1996 *Digest*, para. 541; 320th Report, Case No. 1963, para. 229; 321st Report, Case No. 2066, para. 340; 330th Report, Case No. 2212, para. 749; 335th Report, Case No. 2305, para. 505; and 338th Report, Case No. 2373, para. 382.)

583. The principle regarding the prohibition of strikes in essential services might lose its meaning if a strike were declared illegal in one or more undertakings which were not performing an "essential service" in the strict sense of the term, i.e. services whose interruption would endanger the life, personal safety or health of the whole or part of the population.

(See the 1996 *Digest*, para. 542; 308th Report, Case No. 1923, para. 221; 314th Report, Case No. 1787, para. 32; 320th Report, Case No. 1963, para. 229; 328th Report, Case No. 2120, para. 540; and 336th Report, Case No. 2340, para. 645.)

584. It would not appear to be appropriate for all state-owned undertakings to be treated on the same basis in respect of limitations of the right to strike, without distinguishing in the relevant legislation between those which are genuinely essential and those which are not.

(See the 1996 *Digest*, para. 543.)

585. The following may be considered to be essential services:

- the hospital sector (see the 1996 *Digest*, para. 544; 300th Report, Case No. 1818, para. 366; 306th Report, Case No. 1882, para. 427; 308th Report, Case No. 1897, para. 477; 324th Report, Case No. 2060, para. 517, and Case No. 2077, para. 551; 329th Report, Case No. 2174, para. 795; 330th Report, Case No. 2166, para. 292; and 338th Report, Case No. 2399, para. 1171);
- electricity services (see the 1996 *Digest*, para. 544; 308th Report, Case No. 1921, para. 573; 309th Report, Case No. 1912, para. 365; 318th Report, Case No. 1999, para. 165; and Case No. 1994, para. 458);
- water supply services (see the 1996 *Digest*, para. 544; and 326th Report, Case No. 2135, para. 267);
- the telephone service (see the 1996 *Digest*, para. 544; 314th Report, Case No. 1948/1955, para. 72; and 318th Report, Case No. 2020, para. 318);
- the police and the armed forces (see 307th Report, Case No. 1898, para. 323);
- the fire-fighting services (see 309th Report, Case No. 1865, para. 145; and 321st Report, Case No. 2066, para. 336);
- public or private prison services (see 336th Report, Case No. 2383, para. 767);
- the provision of food to pupils of school age and the cleaning of schools (see 324th Report, Case No. 2037, para. 102);
- air traffic control (see the 1996 *Digest*, para. 544; and 327th Report, Case No. 2127, para. 191).

586. The principle that air traffic control is an essential service applies to all strikes, whatever their form – go-slow, work-to-rule, sick-out, etc. – as these may be just as dangerous as a regular strike for the life, personal safety or health of the whole or part of the population.

(See 327th Report, Case No. 2127, para. 191.)

587. The following do not constitute essential services in the strict sense of the term:

- radio and television (see the 1996 *Digest*, para. 545; 302nd Report, Case No. 1849, para. 204; 306th Report, Case No. 1865, para. 332, and Case No. 1884, para. 688);
- the petroleum sector (see the 1996 *Digest*, para. 545; 302nd Report, Case No. 1849, para. 204; 306th Report, Case No. 1865, para. 332; 337th Report, Case No. 2355, para. 630, and Case No. 2249, para. 1478);
- ports (see the 1996 *Digest*, para. 545; 318th Report, Case No. 2018, para. 514; 320th Report, Case No. 1963, para. 229; and 321st Report, Case No. 2066, para. 340);
- banking (see the 1996 *Digest*, para. 545; 303rd Report, Case No. 1810/1830, para. 62; and 309th Report, Case No. 1937, para. 450);
- computer services for the collection of excise duties and taxes (see the 1996 *Digest*, para. 545);

- department stores and pleasure parks (see the 1996 *Digest*, para. 545);
- the metal and mining sectors (see the 1996 *Digest*, para. 545);
- transport generally (see the 1996 *Digest*, para. 545; 302nd Report, Case No. 1849, para. 203, and Case No. 1695, para. 248; 303rd Report, Case No. 1810/1830, para. 62; 316th Report, Case No. 1989, para. 191; 317th Report, Case No. 1971, para. 56);
- airline pilots (see 329th Report, Case No. 2195, para. 737);
- production, transport and distribution of fuel (see 307th Report, Case No. 1898, para. 325);
- railway services (see 308th Report, Case No. 1923, para. 221);
- metropolitan transport (see the 1996 *Digest*, para. 545);
- postal services (see the 1996 *Digest*, para. 545; 307th Report, Case No. 1898, para 325; 316th Report, Case No. 1985, para. 321; and 318th Report, Case No. 2020, para. 318);
- refuse collection services (see 309th Report, Case No. 1916, para. 100; and 338th Report, Case No. 2373, para. 382);
- refrigeration enterprises (see the 1996 *Digest*, para. 545);
- hotel services (see the 1996 *Digest*, para. 545; 324th Report, Case No. 1890, para. 58; 326th Report, Case No. 2116, para. 356; and 328th Report, Case No. 2120, para. 540);
- construction (see the 1996 *Digest*, para. 545; and 338th Report, Case No. 2326, para. 446);
- automobile manufacturing (see the 1996 *Digest*, para. 545);
- agricultural activities, the supply and distribution of foodstuffs (see the 1996 *Digest*, para. 545; and 308th Report, Case No. 1900, para. 183);
- the Mint (see the 1996 *Digest*, para. 545; and 306th Report, Case No. 1865, para. 332);
- the government printing service and the state alcohol, salt and tobacco monopolies (see the 1996 *Digest*, para. 545);
- the education sector (see the 1996 *Digest*, para. 545; 310th Report, Case No. 1928, para. 172, and Case No. 1943, para. 226; 311th Report, Case No. 1950, para. 457; 320th Report, Case No. 2025, para. 405; 327th Report, Case No. 2145, para. 302, and Case No. 2148, para. 800; 329th Report, Case No. 2157, para. 191; and 330th Report, Case No. 2173, para. 297);
- mineral water bottling company (see 328th Report, Case No. 2028, para. 475.)

588. While the Committee has found that the education sector does not constitute an essential service, it has held that principals and vice-principals can have their right to strike restricted or even prohibited.

(See 311th Report, Case No. 1951, para. 227.)

589. Arguments that civil servants do not traditionally enjoy the right to strike because the State as their employer has a greater obligation of protection towards them have not persuaded the Committee to change its position on the right to strike of teachers.

(See 277th Report, Case No. 1528, para. 288; and 311th Report, Case No. 1950, para. 458.)

590. The possible long-term consequences of strikes in the teaching sector do not justify their prohibition.

(See 262nd Report, Case No. 1448, para. 117; and 327th Report, Case No. 2145, para. 303.)

591. The refuse collection service might become essential if the strike affecting it exceeds a certain duration or extent so as to endanger the life, personal safety or health of the population.

(See 309th Report, Case No. 1916, para. 100.)

592. By linking restrictions on strike action to interference with trade and commerce, a broad range of legitimate strike action could be impeded. While the economic impact of industrial action and its effect on trade and commerce may be regrettable, such consequences in and of themselves do not render a service "essential", and thus the right to strike should be maintained.

(See 320th Report, Case No. 1963, para. 230.)

593. Within essential services, certain categories of employees, such as hospital labourers and gardeners, should not be deprived of the right to strike.

(See 333rd Report, Case No. 2277, para. 274; and 338th Report, Case No. 2403, para. 601.)

594. The exclusion from the right to strike of wage-earners in the private sector who are on probation is incompatible with the principles of freedom of association.

(See the 1996 *Digest*, para. 476.)

D. Compensatory guarantees in the event of the prohibition of strikes in the public service or in essential services

595. Where the right to strike is restricted or prohibited in certain essential undertakings or services, adequate protection should be given to the workers to compensate for the limitation thereby placed on their freedom of action with regard to disputes affecting such undertakings and services.

(See the 1996 *Digest*, para. 546; and, for example, 300th Report, Case No. 1818, para. 367; 306th Report, Case No. 1882, para. 429; 310th Report, Case No. 1943, para. 227; 318th Report, Case No. 1999, para. 166; 324th Report, Case No. 2060, para. 518; 327th Report, Case No. 2127, para. 192; 330th Report, Case No. 2166, para. 292; 333rd Report, Case No. 2277, para. 274; 336th Report, Case No. 2340, para. 649; and 337th Report, Case No. 2244, para. 1269.)

596. As regards the nature of appropriate guarantees in cases where restrictions are placed on the right to strike in essential services and the public service, restrictions on the right to strike should be accompanied by adequate, impartial and speedy conciliation and arbitration proceedings in which the parties concerned can take part at every stage and in which the awards, once made, are fully and promptly implemented.

(See the 1996 *Digest*, para. 547; and, for example, 300th Report, Case No. 1818, para. 367; 306th Report, Case No. 1882, para. 429; 308th Report, Case No. 1897, para. 478; 310th Report, Case No. 1943, para. 227; 318th Report, Case No. 2020, para. 318; 324th Report, Case No. 2060, para. 518; 330th Report, Case No. 2166, para. 292; 333rd Report, Case No. 2277, para. 274; 336th Report, Case No. 2340, para. 649; and 337th Report, Case No. 2244, para. 1269.)

597. The reservation of budgetary powers to the legislative authority should not have the effect of preventing compliance with the terms of awards handed down by the compulsory arbitration tribunal. Any departure from this practice would detract from the effective application of the principle that, where strikes by workers in essential services are prohibited or restricted, such prohibition should be accompanied by the existence of conciliation procedures and of impartial arbitration machinery, the awards of which are binding on both parties.

(See the 1996 *Digest*, para. 548.)

598. In mediation and arbitration proceedings it is essential that all the members of the bodies entrusted with such functions should not only be strictly impartial but, if the confidence of both sides, on which the successful outcome even of compulsory arbitration really depends, is to be gained and maintained, they should also appear to be impartial both to the employers and to the workers concerned.

(See the 1996 *Digest*, para. 549; 310th Report, Case No. 1928, para. 182, and Case No. 1943, para. 240; 318th Report, Case No. 1943, para. 117; 324th Report, Case No. 1943, para. 26; 327th Report, Case No. 2145, para. 306; 328th Report, Case No. 2114, para. 406; 333rd Report, Case No. 2288, para. 829; 335th Report, Case No. 2305, para. 507; and 336th Report, Case No. 2383, para. 773.)

599. The appointment by the minister of all five members of the Essential Services Arbitration Tribunal calls into question the independence and impartiality of such a tribunal, as well as the confidence of the concerned parties in such a system. The representative organizations of workers and employers should, respectively, be able to select members of the Essential Services Arbitration Tribunal who represent them.

(See the 1996 *Digest*, para. 550; and 328th Report, Case No. 2114, para. 406.)

600. Employees deprived of the right to strike because they perform essential services must have appropriate guarantees to safeguard their interests; a corresponding denial of the right of lockout, provision of joint conciliation procedures and where, and only where, conciliation fails, the provision of joint arbitration machinery.

(See the 1996 *Digest*, para. 551; 306th Report, Case No. 1882, para. 428; 308th Report, Case No. 1902, para. 703; and 309th Report, Case No. 1913, para. 306.)

601. Referring to its recommendation that restrictions on the right to strike would be acceptable if accompanied by conciliation and arbitration procedures, the Committee has made it clear that this recommendation does not refer to the absolute prohibition of the right to strike, but to the restriction of that right in essential services or in the public service, in relation to which adequate guarantees should be provided to safeguard the workers' interests.

(See the 1996 *Digest*, para. 552.)

602. Regarding the requirement that the parties pay for the conciliation and mediation/arbitration services, the Committee has concluded that, provided the costs are reasonable and do not inhibit the ability of the parties, in particular those with inadequate resources, to make use of the services, there has not been a violation of freedom of association on this basis.

(See 310th Report, Case No. 1928, para. 182.)

603. The Committee takes no position as to the desirability of conciliation over mediation as both are means of assisting the parties in voluntarily reaching an agreement. Nor does the Committee take a position as to the desirability of a separated conciliation and arbitration system over a combined mediation-arbitration system, as long as the members of the bodies entrusted with such functions are impartial and are seen to be impartial.

(See 310th Report, Case No. 1928, para. 182.)

Situations in which a minimum service may be imposed to guarantee the safety of persons and equipment (minimum safety service)

(See also para. 607)

604. Restrictions on the right to strike in certain sectors to the extent necessary to comply with statutory safety requirements are normal restrictions.

(See the 1996 *Digest*, para. 554; and 310th Report, Case No. 1931, para. 496.)

605. In one case, the legislation provided that occupational organizations in all branches of activity were obliged to ensure that the staff necessary for the safety of machinery and equipment and the prevention of accidents continued to work, and that disagreements as to the definition of "necessary staff" would be settled by an administrative arbitration tribunal. These restrictions on the right to strike were considered to be acceptable.

(See the 1996 *Digest*, para. 555.)

Situations and conditions under which a minimum operational service could be required

606. The establishment of minimum services in the case of strike action should only be possible in: (1) services the interruption of which would endanger the life, personal safety or health of the whole or part of the population (essential services in the strict sense of the term); (2) services which are not essential in the strict sense of the term but where the extent and duration of a strike might be such as to result in an acute national crisis endangering the normal living conditions of the population; and (3) in public services of fundamental importance.

(See the 1996 *Digest*, para. 556; 316th Report, Case No. 1985, para. 324; 320th Report, Case No. 2057, para. 780; 329th Report, Case No. 2174, para. 795; 333rd Report, Case No. 2251, para. 990; 336th Report, Case No. 2300, para. 383; 337th Report, Case No. 2355, para. 630; and 338th Report, Case No. 2364, para. 975.)

607. A minimum service could be appropriate as a possible alternative in situations in which a substantial restriction or total prohibition of strike action would not appear to be justified and where, without calling into question the right to strike of the large majority of workers, one might consider ensuring that users' basic needs are met or that facilities operate safely or without interruption.

(See 299th Report, Case No. 1782, para. 324; and 300th Report, Case No. 1791, para. 346.)

608. Measures should be taken to guarantee that the minimum services avoid danger to public health and safety.

(See 309th Report, Case No. 1916, para. 100.)

609. A certain minimum service may be requested in the event of strikes whose scope and duration would cause an acute national crisis, but in this case, the trade union organizations should be able to participate, along with employers and the public authorities, in defining the minimum service.

(See the 1996 *Digest*, para. 557; 308th Report, Case No. 1923, para. 222; 316th Report, Case No. 1985, para. 324; 337th Report, Case No. 2249, para. 1478; and 338th Report, Case No. 2364, para. 975.)

610. A minimum service may be set up in the event of a strike, the extent and duration of which might be such as to result in an acute national crisis endangering the normal living conditions of the population. Such a minimum service should be confined to operations that are strictly necessary to avoid endangering the life or normal living conditions of the whole or part of the population; in addition, workers' organizations should be able to participate in defining such a service in the same way as employers and the public authorities.

(See the 1996 *Digest*, para. 558; 308th Report, Case No. 1923, para. 222; 317th Report, Case No. 1971, para. 57; and 330th Report, Case No. 2212, para. 751.)

611. The Committee has pointed out that it is important that the provisions regarding the minimum service to be maintained in the event of a strike in an essential service are established clearly, applied strictly and made known to those concerned in due time.

(See the 1996 *Digest*, para. 559; 308th Report, Case No. 1921, para. 573; and 330th Report, Case No. 2212, para. 751.)

612. The determination of minimum services and the minimum number of workers providing them should involve not only the public authorities, but also the relevant employers' and workers' organizations. This not only allows a careful exchange of viewpoints on what in a given situation can be considered to be the minimum services that are strictly necessary, but also contributes to guaranteeing that the scope of the minimum service does not result in the strike becoming ineffective in practice because of its limited impact, and to dissipating possible impressions in the trade union organizations that a strike has come to nothing because of over-generous and unilaterally fixed minimum services.

(See the 1996 *Digest*, para. 560; 299th Report, Case No. 1782, para. 325; 302nd Report, Case No. 1856, para. 436; 308th Report, Case No. 1923, para. 222; 320th Report, Case No. 1963, para. 231, and Case No. 2044, para. 453; 324th Report, Case No. 2078, para. 617; 325th Report, Case No. 2018, para. 88; and 338th Report, Case No. 2373, para. 381.)

613. As regards the legal requirement that a minimum service must be maintained in the event of a strike in essential public services, and that any disagreement as to the number and duties of the workers concerned shall be settled by the labour authority, the Committee is of the opinion that the legislation should provide for any such disagreement to be settled by an independent body and not by the ministry of labour or the ministry or public enterprise concerned.

(See the 1996 *Digest*, para. 561; 299th Report, Case No. 1782, para. 325; 308th Report, Case No. 1923, para. 222; 320th Report, Case No. 2044, para. 453; and 330th Report, Case No. 2212, para. 751.)

614. A definitive ruling on whether the level of minimum services was indispensable or not – made in full knowledge of the facts – can be pronounced only by the judicial authorities, in so far as it depends, in particular, upon a thorough knowledge of the structure and functioning of the enterprises and establishments concerned and of the real impact of the strike action.

(See the 1996 *Digest*, para. 562; 302nd Report, Case No. 1856, para. 437; and 304th Report, Case No. 1866, para. 114.)

Examples of when the Committee has considered that the conditions were met for requiring a minimum operational service

615. The ferry service is not an essential service. However, in view of the difficulties and inconveniences that the population living on islands along the coast could be subjected to following a stoppage in ferry services, an agreement may be concluded on minimum services to be maintained in the event of a strike.

(See the 1996 *Digest*, para. 563; 330th Report, Case No. 2212, para. 749; and 336th Report, Case No. 2324, para. 282.)

616. The services provided by the National Ports Enterprise and ports themselves do not constitute essential services, although they are an important public service in which a minimum service could be required in case of a strike.

(See the 1996 *Digest*, para. 564; 318th Report, Case No. 2018, para. 514; 320th Report, Case No. 1963, para. 231; and 321st Report, Case No. 2066, para. 340.)

617. Respect for the obligation to maintain a minimum service of the underground railway's activities to meet the minimal needs of the local communities is not an infringement of the principles of freedom of association.

(See 320th Report, Case No. 2057, para. 780.)

618. In relation to strike action taken by workers in the underground transport enterprise, the establishment of minimum services in the absence of agreement between the parties should be handled by an independent body.

(See the 1996 *Digest*, para. 565; and 320th Report, Case No. 2057, para. 780.)

619. It is legitimate for a minimum service to be maintained in the event of a strike in the rail transport sector.

(See the 1996 *Digest*, para. 567.)

620. In view of the particular situation of the railway services of one country, a total and prolonged stoppage could lead to a situation of acute national emergency endangering the well-being of the population, which may in certain circumstances justify government intervention, for instance by establishing a minimum service.

(See 308th Report, Case No. 1923, para. 221.)

621. The transportation of passengers and commercial goods is not an essential service in the strict sense of the term; however, this is a public service of primary importance where the requirement of a minimum service in the event of a strike can be justified.

(See the 1996 *Digest*, para. 566; 320th Report, Case No. 2044, para. 453; 324th Report, Case No. 2078, para. 616; 325th Report, Case No. 2018, para. 88; and 330th Report, Case No. 2212, para. 749.)

622. The maintenance of a minimum service could be foreseen in the postal services.

(See the 1996 *Digest*, para. 568; 304th Report, Case No. 1866, para. 113; and 316th Report, Case No. 1985, para. 324.)

623. The imposition of a minimum service is permissible in the refuse collection service.

(See 309th Report, Case No. 1916, para. 100.)

624. The Mint, banking services and the petroleum sector are services where a minimum negotiated service could be maintained in the event of a strike so as to ensure that the basic needs of the users of these services are satisfied.

(See 309th Report, Case No. 1865, para. 149; and 337th Report, Case No. 2355, para. 630.)

625. Minimum services may be established in the education sector, in full consultation with the social partners, in cases of strikes of long duration.

(See 330th Report, Case No. 2173, para. 297.)

626. The decision adopted by a government to require a minimum service in the Animal Health Division, in the face of an outbreak of a highly contagious disease, does not violate the principles of freedom of association.

(See 331st Report, Case No. 2209, para. 734.)

Non-compliance with a minimum service

627. Even though the final decision to suspend or revoke a trade union's legal status is made by an independent judicial body, such measures should not be adopted in the case of non-compliance with a minimum service.

(See the 1996 Digest, para. 569.)

Responsibility for declaring a strike illegal

628. Responsibility for declaring a strike illegal should not lie with the government, but with an independent body which has the confidence of the parties involved.

(See the 1996 *Digest*, para. 522; and, for example, 304th Report, Case No. 1851, para. 280; 309th Report, Case No. 1916, para. 102; 311th Report, Case No. 1954, para. 405; 314th Report, Case No. 1948/1955, para. 72; 320th Report, Case No. 2007, para. 282; 326th Report, Case No. 2111, para. 474; 329th Report, Case No. 2195, para. 736; 330th Report, Case No. 2208, para. 599; 333rd Report, Case No. 2281, para. 634; and 337th Report, Case No. 2355, para. 631.)

629. Final decisions concerning the illegality of strikes should not be made by the government, especially in those cases in which the government is a party to the dispute.

(See the 1996 *Digest*, para. 523; 305th Report, Case No. 1870, para. 143; 307th Report, Case No. 1899, para. 83; and 316th Report, Case No. 1934, para. 210.)

630. It is contrary to freedom of association that the right to declare a strike in the public service illegal should lie with the heads of public institutions, which are thus judges and parties to a dispute.

(See the 1996 *Digest*, para. 524.)

631. With reference to an official circular concerning the illegality of any strike in the public sector, the Committee has considered that such matters are not within the competence of the administrative authority.

(See the 1996 *Digest*, para. 525.)

Back-to-work orders, the hiring of workers during a strike, requisitioning orders

632. The hiring of workers to break a strike in a sector which cannot be regarded as an essential sector in the strict sense of the term, and hence one in which strikes might be forbidden, constitutes a serious violation of freedom of association.

(See the 1996 *Digest*, para. 570; 302nd Report, Case No. 1849, para. 217; 306th Report, Case No. 1865, para. 336; 307th Report, Case No. 1899, para. 81; 311th Report, Case No. 1954, para. 406; 327th Report, Case No. 2141, para. 322; 333rd Report, Case No. 2251, para. 998; and 335th Report, Case No. 1865, para. 826.)

633. If a strike is legal, recourse to the use of labour drawn from outside the undertaking to replace the strikers for an indeterminate period entails a risk of derogation from the right to strike, which may affect the free exercise of trade union rights.

(See the 1996 *Digest*, para. 571; 306th Report, Case No. 1865, para. 336; 318th Report, Case No. 2005, para. 183; and 333rd Report, Case No. 2251, para. 998.)

634. Whenever a total and prolonged strike in a vital sector of the economy might cause a situation in which the life, health or personal safety of the population might be endangered, a back-to-work order might be lawful, if applied to a specific category of staff in the event of a strike whose scope and duration could cause such a situation. However, a back-to-work requirement outside such cases is contrary to the principles of freedom of association.

(See the 1996 *Digest*, para. 572; 320th Report, Case No. 2044, para. 452; 329th Report, Case No. 2195, para. 737; 332nd Report, Case No. 2252, para. 883; and 333rd Report, Case No. 2281, para. 634.)

635. The use of the military and requisitioning orders to break a strike over occupational claims, unless these actions aim at maintaining essential services in circumstances of the utmost gravity, constitutes a serious violation of freedom of association.

(See the 1996 *Digest*, para. 573; 308th Report, Case No. 1921, para. 575; 320th Report, Case No. 2044, para. 452; and 333rd Report, Case No. 2288, para. 831.)

636. The employment of the armed forces or of another group of persons to perform duties which have been suspended as a result of a labour dispute can, if the strike is lawful, be justified only by the need to ensure the operation of services or industries whose suspension would lead to an acute crisis.

(See the 1996 *Digest*, paras. 528 and 574; 321st Report, Case No. 2066, para. 340; 324th Report, Case No. 2077, para. 551; and 328th Report, Case No. 2082, para. 475.)

637. Although it is recognized that a stoppage in services or undertakings such as transport companies, railways and the oil sector might disturb the normal life of the community, it can hardly be admitted that the stoppage of such services could cause a state of acute national emergency. The Committee has therefore considered that measures taken to mobilize workers at the time of disputes in services of this kind are such as to restrict the workers' right to strike as a means of defending their occupational and economic interests.

(See the 1996 *Digest*, paras. 530 and 575; 317th Report, Case No. 1971, para. 56; 335th Report, Case No. 1865, para. 826; and 337th Report, Case No. 2249, para. 1478.)

638. The requisitioning of railway workers in the case of strikes, the threat of dismissal of strike pickets, the recruitment of underpaid workers and a ban on the joining of a trade union in order to break up lawful and peaceful strikes in services which are not essential in the strict sense of the term are not in accordance with freedom of association.

(See the 1996 *Digest*, para. 576.)

639. Where an essential public service, such as the telephone service, is interrupted by an unlawful strike, a government may have to assume the responsibility of ensuring its functioning in the interests of the community and, for this purpose, may consider it expedient to call in the armed forces or other persons to perform the duties which have been suspended and to take the necessary steps to enable such persons to be installed in the premises where such duties are performed.

(See the 1996 *Digest*, para. 577.)

Interference by the authorities during the course of the strike

640. In one case where the government had consulted the workers in order to determine whether they wished the strike to continue or be called off, and where the organization of the ballot had been entrusted to a permanent, independent body, with the workers enjoying the safeguard of a secret ballot, the Committee emphasized the desirability of consulting the representative organizations with a view to ensuring freedom from any influence or pressure by the authorities which might affect the exercise of the right to strike in practice.

(See the 1996 *Digest*, para. 578.)

641. The intervention of the army in relation to labour disputes is not conducive to the climate free from violence, pressure or threats that is essential to the exercise of freedom of association.

(See 333rd Report, Case No. 2268, para. 765.)

Police intervention during the course of the strike

642. The Committee has recommended the dismissal of allegations of intervention by the police when the facts showed that such intervention was limited to the maintenance of public order and did not restrict the legitimate exercise of the right to strike.

(See the 1996 *Digest*, para. 579.)

643. The use of police for strike-breaking purposes is an infringement of trade union rights.

(See 304th Report, Case No. 1863, para. 361.)

644. In cases of strike movements, the authorities should resort to the use of force only in grave situations where law and order is seriously threatened.

(See the 1996 *Digest*, para. 580; and, for example, 299th Report, Case No. 1687, para. 456; 302nd Report, Case No. 1825, para. 492; 304th Report, Case No. 1863, para. 361; 306th Report, Case No. 1884, para. 695; 308th Report, Case No. 1773, para. 446, and Case No. 1914, para. 669; 311th Report, Case No. 1954, para. 407; 324th Report, Case No. 1865, para. 412; 332nd Report, Case No. 2252, para. 888; and 333rd Report, Case No. 2153, para. 211.)

645. While workers and their organizations have an obligation to respect the law of the land, the intervention by security forces in strike situations should be limited strictly to the maintenance of public order.

(See the 1996 *Digest*, para. 581; 302nd Report, Case No. 1849, para. 211; and 324th Report, Case No. 2093, para. 437.)

646. While workers and their organizations are obliged to respect the law of the land, police intervention to enforce the execution of a court decision affecting strikers should observe the elementary guarantees applicable in any system that respects fundamental public freedoms.

(See 306th Report, Case No. 1891, para. 571.)

647. The authorities should resort to calling in the police in a strike situation only if there is a genuine threat to public order. The intervention of the police should be in proportion to the threat to public order and governments should take measures to ensure that the competent authorities receive adequate instructions so as to avoid the danger of excessive violence in trying to control demonstrations that might undermine public order.

(See the 1996 *Digest*, para. 582; 320th Report, Case No. 1865, para. 524; 324th Report, Case No. 2093, para. 437; 325th Report, Case No. 2068, para. 314; 335th Report, Case No. 2228, para. 901; 336th Report, Case No. 2153, para. 175; and 338th Report, Case No. 2364, para. 976.)

Pickets

648. The action of pickets organized in accordance with the law should not be subject to interference by the public authorities.

(See the 1996 *Digest*, para. 583.)

649. The prohibition of strike pickets is justified only if the strike ceases to be peaceful.

(See the 1996 *Digest*, para. 584.)

650. The Committee has considered legitimate a legal provision that prohibited pickets from disturbing public order and threatening workers who continued work.

(See the 1996 *Digest*, para. 585; and 320th Report, Case No. 1963, para. 232.)

651. Taking part in picketing and firmly but peacefully inciting other workers to keep away from their workplace cannot be considered unlawful. The case is different, however, when picketing is accompanied by violence or coercion of non-strikers in an attempt to interfere with their freedom to work; such acts constitute criminal offences in many countries.

(See the 1996 *Digest*, para. 586; and, for example, 299th Report, Case No. 1640/1646, para. 152, and Case No. 1687, para. 456; 304th Report, Case No. 1851, para. 282; 305th Report, Case No. 1879, para. 204; 306th Report, Case No. 1865, para. 337; 307th Report, Case No. 1863, para. 344; 310th Report, Case No. 1931, para. 496; 314th Report, Case No. 1787, para. 33; 316th Report, Case No. 2000, para. 638; and 320th Report, Case No. 1963, para. 232.)

652. The exercise of the right to strike should respect the freedom to work of non-strikers, as established by the legislation, as well as the right of the management to enter the premises of the enterprise.

(See 300th Report, Case No. 1811/1816, para. 307.)

653. The requirement that strike pickets can only be set up near an enterprise does not infringe the principles of freedom of association.

(See the 1996 *Digest*, para. 587.)

Wage deductions

654. Salary deductions for days of strike give rise to no objection from the point of view of freedom of association principles.

(See the 1996 *Digest*, para. 588; 304th Report, Case No. 1863, para. 363; and 307th Report, Case No. 1899, para. 83.)

655. In a case in which the deductions of pay were higher than the amount corresponding to the period of the strike, the Committee recalled that the imposition of sanctions for strike action was not conducive to harmonious labour relations.

(See the 1996 *Digest*, paras. 589 and 595.)

656. Obliging the employer to pay wages in respect of strike days in cases where the employer is declared "responsible" for the strike, apart from potentially disrupting the balance in industrial relations and proving costly for the employer, raises problems of conformity with the principles of freedom of association, as such payment should be neither required nor prohibited. It should consequently be a matter for resolution between the parties.

(See 318th Report, Case No. 1931, para. 366.)

657. Failure to reply to a statement of claims may be deemed an unfair practice contrary to the principle of good faith in collective bargaining, which may entail certain penalties as foreseen by law, without resulting in a legal obligation upon the employer to pay strike days, which is a matter to be left to the parties concerned.

(See 318th Report, Case No. 1931, para. 369.)

Sanctions

A. In the event of a legitimate strike

(See also paras. 57, 77, 269 and 853)

658. Imposing sanctions on unions for leading a legitimate strike is a grave violation of the principles of freedom of association.

(See 302nd Report, Case No. 1849, para. 207.)

659. The closure of trade union offices, as a consequence of a legitimate strike, is a violation of the principles of freedom of association.

(See 302nd Report, Case No. 1849, para. 215.)

660. No one should be penalized for carrying out or attempting to carry out a legitimate strike.

(See the 1996 *Digest*, para. 590; and, for example, 302nd Report, Case No. 1849, para. 211; 307th Report, Case No. 1890, para. 372; 310th Report, Case No. 1932, para. 515; 311th Report, Case No. 1934, para. 127; 316th Report, Case No. 1934, para. 211; 318th Report, Case No. 1978, para. 218; 321st Report, Case No. 2056, para. 137; 324th Report, Case No. 2072, para. 587; 326th Report, Case No. 2091, para. 154; 331st Report, Case No. 1937/2027, para. 105; and 333rd Report, Case No. 2164, para. 608.)

661. The dismissal of workers because of a strike constitutes serious discrimination in employment on grounds of legitimate trade union activities and is contrary to Convention No. 98.

(See the 1996 *Digest*, para. 591; 306th Report, Case No. 1904, para. 596; 326th Report, Case No. 2116, para. 356; 333rd Report, Case No. 2164, para. 608; 334th Report, Case No. 2267, para. 658, and Case No. 2211, para. 678; and 338th Report, Case No. 2046, para. 104.)

662. When trade unionists or union leaders are dismissed for having exercised the right to strike, the Committee can only conclude that they have been punished for their trade union activities and have been discriminated against.

(See the 1996 *Digest*, para. 592; 306th Report, Case No. 1904, para. 596; 318th Report, Case No. 1978, para. 218; 326th Report, Case No. 2116, para. 356; and 334th Report, Case No. 2267, para. 658.)

663. Respect for the principles of freedom of association requires that workers should not be dismissed or refused re-employment on account of their having participated in a strike or other industrial action. It is irrelevant for these purposes whether the dismissal occurs during or after the strike. Logically, it should also be irrelevant that the dismissal takes place in advance of a strike, if the purpose of the dismissal is to impede or to penalize the exercise of the right to strike.

(See the 1996 *Digest*, para. 593; 305th Report, Case No. 1870, para. 144; 308th Report, Case No. 1934, para. 132; and 327th Report, Case No. 2141, para. 324.)

664. The Committee could not view with equanimity a set of legal rules which: (a) appears to treat virtually all industrial action as a breach of contract on the part of those who participate therein; (b) makes any trade union or official thereof who instigates such breaches of contract liable in damages for any losses incurred by the employer in consequence of their actions; and (c) enables an employer faced with such action to obtain an injunction to prevent the commencement (or continuation) of the unlawful conduct. The cumulative effect of such provisions could be to deprive workers of the capacity lawfully to take strike action to promote and defend their economic and social interests.

(See the 1996 *Digest*, para. 594.)

665. The announcement by the government that workers would have to do overtime to compensate for the strike might in itself unduly influence the course of the strike.

(See the 1996 *Digest*, para. 596.)

666. The use of extremely serious measures, such as dismissal of workers for having participated in a strike and refusal to re-employ them, implies a serious risk of abuse and constitutes a violation of freedom of association.

(See the 1996 *Digest*, para. 597; 311th Report, Case No. 1954, para. 406; 329th Report, Case No. 2195, para. 738; and 333rd Report, Case No. 2281, para. 633.)

B. Cases of abuse while exercising the right to strike

667. The principles of freedom of association do not protect abuses consisting of criminal acts while exercising the right to strike.

(See the 1996 *Digest*, para. 598; 320th Report, Case No. 2007, para. 281; 332nd Report, Case No. 2187, para. 719; and 338th Report, Case No. 2363, para. 734.)

668. Penal sanctions should only be imposed as regards strikes where there are violations of strike prohibitions which are themselves in conformity with the principles of freedom of association. All penalties in respect of illegitimate actions linked to strikes should be proportionate to the offence or fault committed and the authorities should not have recourse to measures of imprisonment for the mere fact of organizing or participating in a peaceful strike.

(See the 1996 *Digest*, para. 599; and, for example, 303rd Report, Case No. 1810/1830, para. 62; 304th Report, Case No. 1851, para. 281; 310th Report, Case No. 1930, para. 354; 311th Report, Case No. 1950, para. 460; 320th Report, Case No. 2048, para. 718; 329th Report, Case No. 2195, para. 738; 331st Report, Case No. 1937/2027, para. 105; 332nd Report, Case No. 2252, para. 886; 336th Report, Case No. 2153, para. 174; and 338th Report, Case No. 2363, para. 734.)

669. The Committee considered that some of the temporary measures taken by the authorities as a result of a strike in an essential service (prohibition of the trade union's activities, cessation of the check-off of trade union dues, etc.) were contrary to the guarantees provided for in Article 3 of Convention No. 87. The Committee drew the Government's attention to the fact that the measures taken by the authorities to ensure the performance of essential services should not be out of proportion to the ends pursued or lead to excesses.

(See the 1996 *Digest*, para. 600.)

670. Fines which are equivalent to a maximum amount of 500 or 1,000 minimum wages per day of abusive strike may have an intimidating effect on trade unions and inhibit their legitimate trade union activities, particularly where the cancellation of a fine of this kind is subject to the provision that no further strike considered as abusive is carried out.

(See 306th Report, Case No. 1889, para. 175.)

C. In cases of peaceful strikes

(See also para. 77)

671. The authorities should not resort to arrests and imprisonment in connection with the organization of or participation in a peaceful strike; such measures entail serious risks of abuse and are a grave threat to freedom of association.

(See the 1996 *Digest*, para. 601; 299th Report, Case No. 1687, para. 457; 302nd Report, Case No. 1825, para. 493; 304th Report, Case No. 1712, para. 378; 320th Report, Case No. 2048, para. 716; and 327th Report, Case No. 1581, para. 111.)

672. No one should be deprived of their freedom or be subject to penal sanctions for the mere fact of organizing or participating in a peaceful strike.

(See the 1996 *Digest*, para. 602; 302nd Report, Case No. 1825, para. 493; 304th Report, Case No. 1712, para. 378; 306th Report, Case No. 1884, para. 686; 308th Report, Case No. 1773, para. 446; 320th Report, Case No. 2007, para. 283; and 332nd Report, Case No. 2234, para. 782, and Case No. 2252, para. 886.)

673. The peaceful exercise of trade union rights (strike and demonstration) by workers should not lead to arrests and deportations.

(See the 1996 *Digest*, para. 603.)

D. Large-scale sanctions

674. Arrests and dismissals of strikers on a large scale involve a serious risk of abuse and place freedom of association in grave jeopardy. The competent authorities should be given appropriate instructions so as to obviate the dangers to freedom of association that such arrests and dismissals involve.

(See the 1996 *Digest*, para. 604; 304th Report, Case No. 1719, para. 414; 326th Report, Case No. 2105, para. 445; and 338th Report, Case No. 2364, para. 977.)

Discrimination in favour of non-strikers

675. Concerning measures applied to compensate workers who do not participate in a strike by bonuses, the Committee considers that such discriminatory practices constitute a major obstacle to the right of trade unionists to organize their activities.

(See the 1996 *Digest*, para. 605; and 326th Report, Case No. 2105, para. 446.)

Closure of enterprises in the event of a strike

676. The closure of the enterprise in the event of a strike, as provided for in the law, is an infringement of the freedom of work of persons not participating in a strike and disregards the basic needs of the enterprise (maintenance of equipment, prevention of accidents and the right of employers and managerial staff to enter the installations of the enterprise and to exercise their activities).

(See 310th Report, Case No. 1931, para. 497.)

Dissolution and suspension of organizations 11

General principles

677. In a case involving the dissolution and suspension of the trade union organizations in a country, the Committee expressed its deep conviction that in no case does the solution to the economic and social problems besetting a country lie in isolating trade union organizations and suspending their activities. On the contrary, only through the development of free and independent trade union organizations and negotiations with these organizations can a government tackle such problems and solve them in the best interests of the workers and the nation.

(See the 1996 *Digest*, paras. 31 and 673; and 338th Report, Case No. 2006, para. 266.)

678. In view of the serious consequences which dissolution of a union involves for the occupational representation of workers, the Committee has considered that it would appear preferable, in the interest of labour relations, if such action were to be taken only as the last resort, and after exhausting other possibilities with less serious effects for the organization as a whole.

(See the 1996 *Digest*, para. 677.)

Voluntary dissolution

679. Where the decision to dissolve a trade union organization was freely taken by a congress convened in a regular manner by all the workers concerned, the Committee was of the opinion that this dissolution, or any consequence resulting from it, would not be regarded as an infringement of trade union rights.

(See the 1996 *Digest*, para. 660.)

Dissolution on account of insufficient membership

(See also para. 289)

680. A legal provision which requires the dissolution of a trade union if its membership falls below 20 or 40, depending on whether it is a works union or an occupational union, does not in itself constitute an infringement of the exercise of trade union rights, provided that such winding up is attended by all necessary legal guarantees to avoid any possibility of an abusive interpretation of the provision; in other words, the right of appeal to a court of law.

(See the 1996 *Digest*, para. 661.)

681. In one case where the legislation required that there be at least 20 persons in order to found a union, and where a court had ordered the dissolution of a union of homeopathy workers because of the insufficient number of persons legally qualified to practice this profession, the Committee considered that the dissolution did not appear to constitute a measure which could be considered an infringement of freedom of association.

(See the 1996 *Digest*, para. 662.)

682. In a case in which it concluded that the reduction in the number of union members to below the legal minimum of 25 was the consequence of anti-trade union dismissals or threats, the Committee requested the government, should it be concluded that these were anti-trade union dismissals and that the withdrawal from union membership of trade union leaders resulted from pressure or threats from the employer, to impose the penalties provided by the legislation, reinstate the dismissed workers in their jobs and permit the dissolved trade union to be reconstituted.

(See the 1996 *Digest*, para. 663.)

Dissolution and suspension by administrative authority

(See also para. 199)

683. Measures of suspension or dissolution by the administrative authority constitute serious infringements of the principles of freedom of association.

(See the 1996 *Digest*, para. 664; 302nd Report, Case No. 1849, para. 209; 304th Report, Case No. 1850, para. 214; 325th Report, Case No. 2090, para. 166; 327th Report, Case No. 1581, para. 110; 329th Report, Case No. 2181, para. 760; and 338th Report, Case No. 2364, para. 979.)

684. The administrative dissolution of trade union organizations constitutes a clear violation of Article 4 of Convention No. 87.

(See the 1996 *Digest*, para. 665; 304th Report, Case No. 1850, para. 214; 305th Report, Case No. 1893, para. 459; and 324th Report, Case No. 1880, para. 857.)

Cancellation of registration or trade union status

685. The Committee has emphasized that the cancellation of registration of an organization by the registrar of trade unions or their removal from the register is tantamount to the dissolution of that organization by administrative authority.

(See the 1996 *Digest*, para. 669; 318th Report, Case No. 2006, para. 348; 320th Report, Case No. 1953, para. 120; 323rd Report, Case No. 2075, para. 518; 327th Report, Case No. 2098, para. 759; 329th Report, Case No. 2181, para. 760; and 338th Report, Case No. 2364, para. 979.)

686. The cancellation of a trade union organization's registration by administrative authority because of an internal dispute – which in fact implies the suspension of its activities – is a serious infringement of the principles of freedom of association, and in particular of Article 4 of Convention No. 87 which provides that workers' and employers' organizations are not liable to be dissolved by administrative authority.

(See 300th Report, Case No. 1821, para. 153.)

687. Cancellation of a trade union's registration should only be possible through judicial channels.

(See the 1996 *Digest*, para. 670; 310th Report, Case No. 1888, para. 382; 318th Report, Case No. 2006, para. 348; and 324th Report, Case No. 1880, para. 857.)

688. De-registration measures, even when justified, should not exclude the possibility of a union application for registration to be entertained once a normal situation has been re-established.

(See the 1996 *Digest*, para. 671; and 329th Report, Case No. 2181, para. 760.)

689. Legislation which accords the minister the complete discretionary power to order the cancellation of the registration of a trade union, without any right of appeal to the courts, is contrary to the principles of freedom of association.

(See the 1996 *Digest*, para. 672; and 329th Report, Case No. 2181, para. 760.)

Dissolution by legislative measures

690. Dissolution by the executive branch of the government pursuant to a law conferring full powers, or acting in the exercise of legislative functions, like dissolution by virtue of administrative powers, does not ensure the right of defence which normal judicial procedure alone can guarantee and which the Committee considers essential.

(See the 1996 *Digest*, para. 675; and 302nd Report, Case No. 1849, para. 209.)

691. Noting that under a legal provision, the registration of existing trade unions was cancelled, the Committee considered that it is essential that any dissolution of workers' or employers' organizations should be carried out by the judicial authorities, which alone can guarantee the rights of defence. This principle, the Committee has pointed out, is equally applicable when such measures of dissolution are taken even during an emergency situation.

(See the 1996 *Digest*, para. 676.)

Reasons for dissolution

692. To deprive many thousands of workers of their trade union organizations because of a judgement that illegal activities have been carried out by some leaders or members constitutes a clear violation of the principles of freedom of association.

(See the 1996 *Digest*, para. 667; 310th Report, Case No. 1888, para. 382; 318th Report, Case No. 2006, para. 347; and 323rd Report, Case No. 2006, para. 427.)

693. If it was found that certain members of the trade union had committed excesses going beyond the limits of normal trade union activity, they could have been prosecuted under specific legal provisions and in accordance with ordinary judicial procedure, without involving the suspension and subsequent dissolution of an entire trade union movement.

(See 318th Report, Case No. 2006, para. 347; and 323rd Report, Case No. 2006, para. 427.)

694. In a case where trade union status was withdrawn from a trade union organization, mainly because of irregularities in the financial management of the organization, the Committee considered that, if the authorities found irregularities which might be detrimental to the union's social funds, they should have taken legal action based on these irregularities against the persons responsible rather than adopt measures depriving the union of all possibility of action.

(See the 1996 *Digest*, para. 668.)

695. Development needs should not justify maintaining the entire trade union movement of a country in an irregular legal situation, thereby preventing the workers from exercising their trade union rights, as well as preventing organizations from carrying out their normal activities. Balanced economic and social development requires the existence of strong and independent organizations which can participate in this process.

(See the 1996 *Digest*, paras. 25 and 674; 330th Report, Case No. 2189, para. 466; and 337th Report, Case No. 2189, para. 485.)

696. Given the extremely serious consequences that the dissolution of a union involves for the occupational representation of workers, the Committee has considered that the nomination of a representative of a federation as a candidate for the presidency of the country can in no way justify the dissolution of an entire federation.

(See 325th Report, Case No. 2090, para. 166.)

697. The dissolution of a trade union is an extreme measure and recourse to such action on the basis of a picket action resulting in the disruption of a public event, the temporary termination of an organization's activities or the disruption of transport, is clearly not in conformity with the principles of freedom of association.

(See 326th Report, Case No. 2090, para. 242.)

698. In view of the serious consequences which cancellation of trade union registration involves for the occupational representation of workers, the Committee considers that the use of the company's name in the title of the trade union should not result in the cancellation of trade union registration.

(See 337th Report, Case No. 2388, para. 1371.)

Intervention by the judicial authorities

(See also para. 464)

699. The Committee considers that the dissolution of trade union organizations is a measure which should only occur in extremely serious cases; such dissolutions should only happen following a judicial decision so that the rights of defence are fully guaranteed.

(See the 1996 Report, para. 666; 315th Report, Case No. 1935, para. 22; 327th Report, Case No. 1581, para. 110; and 329th Report, Case No. 2181, para. 760.)

700. The suspension of the legal personality of trade union organizations represents a serious restriction on trade union rights and in matters of this nature the rights of defence can only be fully guaranteed through due process of law.

(See the 1996 *Digest*, para. 678.)

701. Any measures of suspension or dissolution by administrative authority, when taken during an emergency situation, should be accompanied by normal judicial safeguards, including the right of appeal to the courts against such dissolution or suspension.

(See the 1996 *Digest*, para. 679; and 300th Report, Case No. 1799, para. 212.)

702. Even if they may be justified in certain circumstances, measures taken to withdraw the legal personality of a trade union and the blocking of trade union funds should be taken through judicial and not administrative action to avoid any risk of arbitrary decisions.

(See the 1996 *Digest*, para. 680.)

703. If the principle that an occupational organization may not be subject to suspension or dissolution by administrative decision is to be properly applied, it is not sufficient for the law to grant a right of appeal against such administrative decisions; such decisions should not take effect until the expiry of the statutory period for lodging an appeal, without an appeal having been entered, or until the confirmation of such decisions by a judicial authority.

(See the 1996 *Digest*, para. 681; and 306th Report, Case No. 1884, para. 690.)

704. Any possibility should be eliminated from the legislation of suspension or dissolution by administrative authority, or at the least it should provide that the administrative decision does not take effect until a reasonable time has been allowed for appeal and, in the case of appeal, until the judicial authority has ruled on the appeal made by the trade union organizations concerned.

(See the 1996 *Digest*, para. 682; 323rd Report, Case No. 2075, para. 518; and 327th Report, Case No. 1581, para. 110.)

705. Judges should be able to deal with the substance of a case to enable them to decide whether or not the provisions pursuant to which the administrative measures in question were taken constitute a violation of the rights accorded to occupational organizations by Convention No. 87. In effect, if the administrative authority has a discretionary right to register or cancel the registration of a trade union, the existence of a procedure of appeal to the courts does not appear to be a sufficient guarantee; the judges hearing such an appeal could only ensure that the legislation had been correctly applied. The same problem may arise in the event of the suspension or dissolution of an occupational organization.

(See the 1996 *Digest*, para. 683; and 310th Report, Case No. 1908, para. 22.)

Use made of the assets of organizations that are dissolved

A. General principles

706. The Committee has accepted the criterion that, when an organization is dissolved, its assets should be provisionally sequestered and eventually distributed among its former members or handed over to the organization that succeeds it, meaning the organization or organizations which pursue the aims for which the dissolved union was established, and which pursue them in the same spirit.

(See the 1996 *Digest*, para. 684; 308th Report, Case No. 1869, para. 497; 309th Report, Case No. 1938, para. 181; and 325th Report, Case No. 1888, para. 399.)

707. When a union ceases to exist, its assets could be handed over to the association that succeeds it or distributed in accordance with its own rules; but where there is no specific rule, the assets should be at the disposal of the workers concerned.

(See the 1996 *Digest*, para. 685.)

B. Transition to a situation of trade union pluralism

(See also para. 1088)

708. With regard to the issue of the distribution of trade union assets among various trade union organizations following a change from a situation of trade union monopoly to a situation of trade union pluralism, the Committee has emphasized the importance it attaches to the principle according to which the devolution of trade union assets (including real estate) or, in the event that trade union premises are made available by the State, the redistribution of this property must aim to ensure that all the trade unions are guaranteed on an equal footing the possibility of effectively exercising their activities in a fully independent manner. It would be desirable for the government and all the trade union organizations concerned to make efforts to conclude as soon as possible a definitive agreement regulating the distribution of the assets of the former trade union organization.

(See the 1996 *Digest*, para. 687.)

709. When examining a case concerning the devolution of the assets of the trade union organizations in a former communist country undergoing democratization, the Committee invited the government and all the trade union organizations concerned to establish, as soon as possible, a formula to settle the question of the assignment of the funds in question so that the government could recover the assets that corresponded to the accomplishment of the social functions which it now exercised and all the trade union organizations were guaranteed on an equal footing the possibility of effectively exercising their activities in a fully independent manner.

(See the 1996 *Digest*, para. 688.)

Right of employers' and workers' organizations to establish federations and confederations and to affiliate with international organizations of employers and workers

12

Establishment of federations and confederations

710. The principle laid down in Article 2 of Convention No. 87 that workers and employers shall have the right to establish and join organizations of their own choosing implies for the organizations themselves the right to establish and join federations and confederations of their own choosing.

(See the 1996 *Digest*, para 606; 327th Report, Case No. 2153, para. 155; 329th Report, Case No. 2140, para. 295; 330th Report, Case No. 2229, para. 942; 332nd Report, Case No. 2225, para. 378; 333rd Report, Case No. 2301, para. 592; and 336th Report, Case No. 2153, para. 170.)

711. The acquisition of legal personality by workers' organizations, federations and confederations shall not be made subject to conditions of such a nature as to restrict the exercise of the right referred to in the preceding paragraph.

(See the 1996 *Digest*, para. 607; 329th Report, Case No. 2140, para. 295; 332nd Report, Case No. 2225, para. 378; and 336th Report, Case No. 2153, para. 171.)

712. A provision whereby a minister may, at his or her discretion, approve or reject an application for the creation of a general confederation is not in conformity with the principles of freedom of association.

(See the 1996 *Digest*, para. 609; and 332nd Report, Case No. 2225, para. 380.)

713. The question as to whether a need to form federations and confederations is felt or not is a matter to be determined solely by the workers and their organizations themselves after their right to form them has been legally recognized.

(See the 1996 *Digest*, para 610; 330th Report, Case No. 2229, para. 942; and 333rd Report, Case No. 2301, para. 592.)

714. The requirement of an excessively high minimum number of trade unions to establish a higher-level organization conflicts with Article 5 of Convention No. 87 and with the principles of freedom of association.

(See the 1996 *Digest*, para. 611; and 330th Report, Case No. 2229, para. 945.)

715. Legislation which prevents the establishment of federations and confederations bringing together the trade unions or federations of different activities in a specific locality or area is incompatible with Article 5 of Convention No. 87.

(See the 1996 *Digest*, para 612.)

716. When only one confederation of workers may exist in a country, and the right to establish federations is limited to such federations as may be established by the unions mentioned in the law, as well as such new unions as might be registered with the consent of the minister, this is incompatible with Article 5 of Convention No. 87.

(See the 1996 *Digest*, para 613.)

717. Importance has been attached by the Committee to the right to form federations grouping unions of workers engaged in different occupations and industries. In this connection, the Committee of Experts on the Application of Conventions and Recommendations pointed out, in respect of a provision of national law prohibiting organizations of public officials from adhering to federations or confederations of industrial or agricultural organizations, that it seemed difficult to reconcile this provision with Article 5 of Convention No. 87. It indicated, in the same observation, that while the legislation permitted organizations of public officials to federate among themselves and that the resulting federation would be the only one recognized by the State, these provisions did not appear to be compatible with Article 6 of the Convention, which refers to Article 2 of the Convention with respect to the establishment of federations and confederations and adhesion to these higher organizations. According to these provisions of the Convention, trade union organizations should have the right to establish and to join federations or confederations "of their own choosing without previous authorization".

(See the 1996 *Digest*, para. 615; and 313th Report, Case No. 1967, para. 148.)

718. A provision prohibiting the establishment of federations by unions in different departments constitutes a restriction of the right of workers' organizations to establish federations and confederations, recognized by Article 5 of Convention No. 87.

(See the 1996 *Digest*, para. 616.)

719. Conditions laid down by law for the establishment of federations, and in particular a condition that founding unions based in different provinces must first ask permission (which may be refused) from the minister, are incompatible with the generally accepted principles of freedom of association, which include the right of trade unions to establish and join federations of their own choosing.

(See the 1996 *Digest*, para. 617.)

720. Any restriction, either direct or indirect, on the right of unions to establish and join associations of unions belonging to the same or different trades, on a regional basis, would not be in conformity with the principles of freedom of association.

(See the 1996 *Digest*, para. 618.)

721. The preferential rights granted to the most representative organizations should not give them the exclusive right to establish and join federations.

(See the 1996 *Digest*, para. 619; and 327th Report, Case No. 2153, para. 155.)

Affiliation with federations and confederations

722. A workers' organization should have the right to join the federation and confederation of its own choosing, subject to the rules of the organizations concerned, and without any previous authorization. It is for the federations and confederations themselves to decide whether or not to accept the affiliation of a trade union, in accordance with their own constitutions and rules.

(See the 1996 *Digest*, para. 608; and 308th Report, Case No. 1920, para. 521.)

723. In a case in which a confederation had been compelled to accept new members by the government, the Committee considered that actions of this kind may allow the authorities to influence the result of elections or the actions of a trade union by direct interference with the composition of its constituents.

(See 308th Report, Case No. 1920, para. 521.)

724. All workers should have the right to engage freely in the defence and promotion of their economic and social interests through the central organizations of their own choice.

(See the 1996 *Digest*, para. 614.)

725. Organizations of public servants should be able to affiliate, if they so choose, to federations or confederations of workers in the private sector if the rules of the latter so permit.

(See 313th Report, Case No. 1967, para. 147.)

726. It seems difficult to reconcile with Article 5 of Convention No. 87 any provision prohibiting organizations of public officials from adhering to federations or confederations of industrial organizations.

(See 336th Report, Case no. 2153, para. 170.)

727. A government's refusal to permit agricultural unions to affiliate with a national centre of workers' organizations comprising industrial unions is incompatible with Article 5 of the Convention.

(See the 1996 *Digest*, para. 620.)

728. The prohibition of the direct affiliation of certain persons to federations and confederations is contrary to the principles of freedom of association. It is for these organizations themselves to determine what the rules relating to their membership should be.

(See 300th Report, Case No. 1777, para. 70.)

729. It is for the statutes of the federations of a branch of activity to determine the number and type of organizations of which it is comprised.

(See 320th Report, Case No. 1953, para. 120.)

Rights of federations and confederations

(See also paras. 386, 387, 473, 483, 525, 561 and 562)

730. In order to defend the interests of their members more effectively, workers' and employers' organizations should have the right to form federations and confederations of their own choosing, which should themselves enjoy the various rights accorded to first-level organizations, in particular as regards their freedom of operation, activities and programmes.

(See the 1996 *Digest*, para. 621; 306th Report, Case No. 1884, para. 686; and 337th Report, Case No. 2327, para. 209.)

731. It is for union by-laws to determine the conditions of election of trade union officials.

(See 320th Report, Case No. 2007, para. 284.)

Affiliation with international organizations of workers and employers

A. General principles

732. International trade union solidarity constitutes one of the fundamental objectives of any trade union movement and underlies the principle laid down in Article 5 of Convention No. 87 that any organization, federation or confederation shall have the right to affiliate with international organizations of workers and employers.

(See the 1996 *Digest*, para. 622.)

733. Unions and confederations should be free to affiliate with international federations or confederations of their own choosing without intervention by the political authorities.

(See the 1996 *Digest*, para. 623.)

734. Article 5 of Convention No. 87 – as is clear from the preparatory work on the instrument – merely gives expression to the fact that workers or employers are united by a solidarity of interests, a solidarity which is not limited either to one specific undertaking or even to a particular industry, or even to the national economy, but extends to the whole international economy. Furthermore, the right to organize corresponds to the practice followed by the United Nations and the International Labour Organization, both of which have formally recognized international organizations of workers and employers by associating them directly with their own activities.

(See the 1996 *Digest*, para. 624.)

735. The Committee has emphasized the importance that it attaches to the fact that no obstacle should be placed in the way of the affiliation of workers' organizations, in full freedom, with any international organization of workers of their own choosing.

(See the 1996 *Digest*, para. 625.)

736. The Committee has considered that there might be justification for one complainant's contention that the principle of the right of workers' organizations to affiliate with international organizations of workers includes by implication the right to disaffiliate from an international organization.

(See the 1996 *Digest*, para. 626.)

B. Intervention by the public authorities

(See also para. 362)

737. Legislation which requires that government permission be obtained for the international affiliation of a trade union is incompatible with the principle of free and voluntary affiliation of trade unions with international organizations.

(See the 1996 *Digest*, para. 627; and 315th Report, Case No. 1935, para. 24.)

738. When a national organization seeks to affiliate with an international organization of workers, the conditions which the national organization attaches to its application and the question as to whether it agrees or disagrees with the international organization in its attitude to any political matter are matters which concern only the respective organizations themselves; while disagreement may influence the national organization in deciding whether to seek, maintain or withdraw from international affiliation, it should not form a basis for government intervention.

(See the 1996 *Digest*, para. 628.)

C. Consequences of international affiliation

(See also paras. 121, 152, 153, 171 and 766)

739. Any assistance or support that an international trade union organization might provide in setting up, defending or developing national trade union organizations is a legitimate trade union activity, even when the trade union tendency does not correspond to the tendency or tendencies within the country.

(See the 1996 *Digest*, para. 629; 300th Report, Case No. 1831, para. 397; and 328th Report, Case No. 2116, para. 368.)

740. Legislation which provides for the banning of any organization where there is evidence that it is under the influence or direction of any outside source, and also for the banning of any organization where there is evidence that it receives financial assistance or other benefits from any outside source, unless such financial assistance or other benefits be approved by and channelled through government, is incompatible with the principles set out in Article 5 of Convention No. 87.

(See the 1996 *Digest*, para. 630.)

741. The granting of advantages resulting from the international affiliation of a trade union organization must not conflict with the law, it being understood that the law should not be such as to render any such affiliation meaningless.

(See the 1996 *Digest*, para. 631; and 320th Report, Case No. 1963, para. 236.)

742. Legislation prohibiting the acceptance by a national trade union of financial assistance from an international organization of workers to which it is affiliated infringes the principles concerning the right to affiliate with international organizations of workers.

(See the 1996 *Digest*, para. 632; 305th Report, Case No. 1834, para. 380; and 325th Report, Case No. 2090, para. 168.)

743. Trade unions should not be required to obtain prior authorization to receive international financial assistance in their trade union activities.

(See the 1996 *Digest*, para. 633; 325th Report, Case No. 2090, para. 168; and 337th Report, Case No. 2327, para. 205.)

744. All national organizations of workers and employers should have the right to receive financial assistance from international organizations of workers and employers respectively, whether or not they are affiliated to the latter.

(See 305th Report, Case No. 1834, para. 380; and 321st Report, Case No. 2031, para. 172.)

745. The principle that national organizations of workers should have the right to affiliate with international organizations carries with it the right, for these organizations, to make contact with one another and, in particular, to exchange their trade union publications.

(See the 1996 *Digest*, para. 634; and 302nd Report, Case No. 1817, para. 324.)

746. The right to affiliate with international organizations of workers implies the right, for the representatives of national trade unions, to maintain contact with the international trade union organizations with which they are affiliated, to participate in the activities of these organizations and to benefit from the services and advantages which their membership offers.

(See the 1996 *Digest*, para. 635; 320th Report, Case No. 1963, para. 236; and 325th Report, Case No. 2108, para. 365.)

747. It is a fully legitimate trade union activity to seek advice and support from other well-established trade union movements in the region to assist in defending or developing the national trade union organizations, even when the trade union tendency does not correspond to the tendency or tendencies within the country, and visits made in this respect represent normal trade union activities.

(see 337th Report, Case No. 2365, para. 1667.)

748. The right of national trade unions to send representatives to international trade union congresses is a normal corollary of the right of those national organizations to join international workers' organizations.

(See the 1996 *Digest*, para. 636.)

749. Leaders of organizations of workers and employers should enjoy appropriate facilities for carrying out their functions, including the right to leave the country when their activities on behalf of the persons they represent so require; moreover, the free movement of these representatives should be ensured by the authorities.

(See the 1996 *Digest*, para. 637; and 320th Report, Case No. 1998, para. 253.)

750. Visits to affiliated national trade union organizations and participation in their congresses are normal activities for international workers' organizations, subject to the provisions of national legislation with regard to the admission of foreigners.

(See the 1996 *Digest*, para. 638; 307th Report, Case No. 1865, para. 234; 316th Report, Case No. 1773, para. 611; and 337th Report, Case No. 2365, para. 1667.)

751. The corollary of the above principle is that the formalities to which trade unionists and trade union leaders are subject in seeking entry to the territory of a State, or in attending to trade union business there, should be based on objective criteria and be free of anti-union discrimination.

(See the 1996 *Digest*, para. 639; 306th Report, Case No. 1885, para. 137; and 337th Report, Case No. 2365, para. 1667.)

752. The Committee has recognized that the refusal to grant a passport (or visa) to foreigners, or more generally the right to exclude persons from national territory, are matters which concern the sovereignty of a State.

(See the 1996 *Digest*, para. 640; and 307th Report, Case No. 1865, para. 234.)

753. Although it recognizes that the refusal to grant visas to foreigners is a matter which falls within the sovereignty of the State, the Committee has requested a government to ensure that the formalities required of international trade unionists to enter the country are based on objective criteria free of anti-trade unionism.

(See the 1996 *Digest*, para. 641.)

754. The formalities required before trade unionists can leave a country in order to take part in international meetings should be based on objective criteria that are free of anti-union discrimination, so as not to involve the risk of infringing the right of trade union organizations to send representatives to international trade union congresses.

(See the 1996 *Digest*, para. 642.)

755. In general, the authorities should not withhold official documents by reason of a person's membership in a workers' or employers' organization, as these documents are sometimes a prerequisite for important activities, for instance obtaining or maintaining employment. This is even more essential where persons hold a position in that organization, inasmuch as the refusal may prevent them from exercising their duties, such as travelling to an official meeting.

(See the 1996 *Digest*, para. 643.)

756. The imposition of sanctions, such as banishment or control of overseas travel for trade union reasons, constitutes a violation of freedom of association.

(See the 1996 *Digest*, para. 644.)

757. Participation in the work of international organizations must be based on the principle of the independence of the trade union movement. Within the framework of this principle, full freedom should be given to representatives of trade unions to take part in the work of the international workers' unions to which the organizations they represent are affiliated.

(See the 1996 *Digest*, para. 646.)

758. As regards a prohibition against foreign representatives of international organizations taking the floor at trade union meetings, the Committee has emphasized the importance which it attaches to safeguarding the right of trade union assembly and the right of national trade union organizations to maintain relations with international occupational organizations.

(See the 1996 *Digest*, para. 647.)

759. In all cases governments have the right to take the necessary measures to guarantee public order and national security. This includes ascertaining the purpose of visits to the country by persons against whom there are grounds for suspicion from this point of view. The authorities should verify each specific case as quickly as possible and should aim – on the basis of objective criteria – at ascertaining whether or not there exist facts which might have real repercussions on public order and security. It would be desirable, in situations of this kind, to seek an agreement through appropriate discussions in which the authorities, as well as the leaders and organizations concerned, may clarify their positions.

(See the 1996 *Digest*, para. 648.)

Participation in ILO meetings

760. The Committee strongly regretted that the arrest of a trade unionist as a result of an event arising directly from a strike should have had the effect of preventing a Worker member from attending a session of the Governing Body; it also considered that, once proceedings have been initiated, the independence of the judiciary cannot be invoked by the government as an excuse for the action which it itself has taken. The Committee therefore drew attention to the importance which the Governing Body attaches to the principle set forth in article 40 of the Constitution that members of the Governing Body shall enjoy such privileges and immunities as are necessary for the independent exercise of their functions.

(See the 1996 *Digest*, para. 649.)

761. It is important that no delegate to any organ or Conference of the ILO, and no member of the Governing Body, should in any way be hindered, prevented or deterred from carrying out their functions or from fulfilling their mandate.

(See the 1996 *Digest*, para. 650.)

762. It is the duty of a government to refrain from taking measures calculated to hinder delegates to an ILO Conference in the exercise of their functions, and to use its influence and take all reasonable steps to ensure that such delegates are in no way prejudiced by their acceptance of functions as delegates or by their conduct as delegates; measures on other grounds should not be envisaged against delegates in their absence, but should await their return so that they may be in a position to defend themselves.

(See the 1996 *Digest*, para. 651.)

763. A government decision which requires workers' representatives wishing to attend an international meeting outside the country to obtain permission from the authorities in order to leave the country is not, in the case of members of the Governing Body, compatible with the principles set forth in article 40 of the ILO Constitution.

(See the 1996 *Digest*, para. 652.)

764. In general, the refusal by a State to grant leave to one of its officials holding trade union office to attend an advisory meeting organized by the ILO does not constitute an infringement of the principles of freedom of association, unless this refusal is based on the trade union activities or functions of the person concerned.

(See the 1996 *Digest*, para. 653.)

765. Participation as a trade unionist in symposia organized by the ILO is a legitimate trade union activity, and a government should not refuse the necessary exit papers for this reason.

(See the 1996 *Digest*, para. 654.)

766. The Committee has reiterated the special importance it attaches to the right of workers' and employers' representatives to attend and to participate in meetings of international workers' and employers' organizations and of the ILO.

(See the 1996 *Digest*, para. 655.)

767. Apart from the specific protection granted in conformity with article 40 of the Constitution of the ILO to members of the Governing Body so as to enable them to carry out their functions vis-à-vis the Organization in full independence, participation as a trade unionist in meetings organized by the ILO is a fundamental trade union right. It is therefore incumbent on the government of any member State of the ILO to abstain from any measure which would prevent representatives of a workers' or employers' organization from exercising their mandate in full freedom and independence. In particular, a government must not withhold the documents necessary for this purpose.

(See the 1996 *Digest*, para. 657.)

768. The Committee considers that the prohibition on any individual, whether worker or employer, from participating more than once as a delegate or adviser to international labour conferences violates the principles of freedom of association, and particularly Articles 3 and 5 of Convention No. 87.

(See the 1996 *Digest*, para. 658.)

Protection against anti-union discrimination 13

General principles

769. Anti-union discrimination is one of the most serious violations of freedom of association, as it may jeopardize the very existence of trade unions.

(See 331st Report, Case No. 2169, para. 639.)

770. No person shall be prejudiced in employment by reason of trade union membership or legitimate trade union activities, whether past or present.

(See the 1996 *Digest*, para. 690; and, for example, 300th Report, Case No. 1823, para. 440; 304th Report, Case No. 1819, para. 155; 306th Report, Case No. 1867, para. 67; 310th Report, Case No. 1930, para. 364; 320th Report, Case No 1963, para. 226; 325th Report, Case No. 2068, para. 316; 327th Report, Case no. 2098, para. 757; 331st Report, Case No. 2187, para. 441; 336th Report, Case No. 2380, para. 794; and 388th Report, Case No. 2200, para. 325.)

771. No person should be dismissed or prejudiced in employment by reason of trade union membership or legitimate trade union activities, and it is important to forbid and penalize in practice all acts of anti-union discrimination in respect of employment.

(See the 1996 *Digest*, paras. 696 and 748; and, for example, 305th Report, Case No. 1874, para. 270; 309th Report, Case No. 1925, para. 116; 316th Report. Case No. 1972, para. 708; 320th Report, Case No. 1998, para. 254; 321st Report, Case No. 2055, para. 355; 327th Report, Case No. 2125, para. 778; 330th Report, Case No. 2203, para. 808; 331st Report, Case No. 2097, para. 277; 333rd Report, Case No. 2229, para. 108; and 334th Report, Case No. 2239, para. 394.)

772. No one should be subjected to discrimination or prejudice with regard to employment because of legitimate trade union activities or membership, and the persons responsible for such acts should be punished.

(See 299th Report, Case No. 1808, para. 377.)

773. Since inadequate safeguards against acts of anti-union discrimination, in particular against dismissals, may lead to the actual disappearance of trade unions composed only of workers in an undertaking, additional measures should be taken to ensure fuller protection for leaders of all organizations, and delegates and members of trade unions, against any discriminatory acts.

(See the 1996 *Digest*, para. 700; 304th Report, Case No. 1853, para. 299; 316th Report, Case No. 1970, para. 556; 336th Report, Case No. 2316, para. 55; and 337th Report, Case No. 2291, para. 136.)

774. The Committee considers that it is not its role to determine in federal States which are the internal standards regulating protection against anti-union discrimination and, in particular, whether the standards of general application or those of the province in question should be applicable. Nevertheless, irrespective of the procedural or substantive laws applying to public officials or employees in provinces of a federal State, the Committee is bound to examine whether the actual alleged anti-union discrimination measures are or are not in accordance with the provisions of ratified ILO Conventions and the principles of freedom of association.

(See 306th Report, Case No. 1867, paras. 63 and 64.)

Workers protected

775. Protection against anti-union discrimination applies equally to trade union members and former trade union officials as to current trade union leaders.

(See the 1996 *Digest*, para. 691; 327th Report, Case No. 2098, para. 757.)

776. No person should be prejudiced in his or her employment by reason of membership of a trade union, even if that trade union is not recognized by the employer as representing the majority of workers concerned.

(See the 1996 *Digest*, paras. 693 and 701; 316th Report, Case No. 1989, para. 194; 333rd Report, Case No. 2291, para. 917; 334th Report, Case No. 2316, para. 506; and 337th Report, Case No. 2241, para. 914.)

777. Noting in one case that conditions approaching civil war prevailed, the Committee considered that special restrictions for the purpose of eliminating sabotage in public utility undertakings should not in any case be such as to give rise to anti-union discrimination.

(See the 1996 *Digest*, para. 714.)

778. The Committee has pointed out that Article 8 of Convention No. 151 allows a certain flexibility in the choice of procedures for the settlement of disputes concerning public servants on condition that the confidence of the parties involved is ensured. The Committee itself has stated in relation to grievances concerning anti-union practices in both the public and private sectors that such complaints should normally be examined by national machinery which, in addition to being speedy, should not only be impartial but should also be seen to be such by the parties concerned.

(See the 1996 *Digest*, para. 918.)

Forms of discrimination

A. General principles

(See also paras. 338, 352, 353, 524 and 660)

779. The Committee is not called upon to pronounce upon the question of the breaking of a contract of employment by dismissal except in cases in which the provisions on dismissal imply anti-union discrimination.

(See the 1996 *Digest*, para. 692.)

780. Protection against anti-union discrimination should apply more particularly in respect of acts calculated to cause the dismissal of or otherwise prejudice a worker by reason of union membership or because of participation in union activities outside working hours or, with the employer's consent, during working hours.

(See the 1996 *Digest*, para. 694; 304th Report, Case No. 1787, para. 174; 329th Report, Case No. 2172, para. 351, and Case No. 2068, para. 436; and 330th Report, Case No. 2186, para. 379.)

781. Protection against acts of anti-union discrimination should cover not only hiring and dismissal, but also any discriminatory measures during employment, in particular transfers, downgrading and other acts that are prejudicial to the worker.

(See the 1996 *Digest*, para. 695; and, for example, 306th Report, Case No. 1867, para. 67; 307th Report, Case No. 1890, para. 372; 311th Report, Case No. 1942, para. 266; 320th Report, Case No. 1998, para. 254; 323rd Report, Case No. 1874, para. 60; 325th Report, Case No. 2087, para. 573; 326th Report, Case No. 2103, para. 295; 328th Report, Case No. 2068, para. 208; 330th Report, Case No. 2200, para. 1101; and 334th Report, Case No. 2222, para. 210.)

B. Discrimination in relation to hiring

782. Workers face many practical difficulties in proving the real nature of their dismissal or denial of employment, especially when seen in the context of blacklisting, which is a practice whose very strength lies in its secrecy. While it is true that it is important for employers to obtain information about prospective employees, it is equally true that employees with past trade union membership or activities should be informed about the information held on them and given a chance to challenge it, especially if it is erroneous and obtained from an unreliable source. Moreover, in these conditions, the employees concerned would be more inclined to institute legal proceedings since they would be in a better position to prove the real nature of their dismissal or denial of employment.

(See the 1996 *Digest*, paras. 173 and 710; 306th Report, Case No. 1862, para. 105; 330th Report, Case No. 2186, para. 372; and 335th Report, Case No. 2270, para. 1394.)

783. With regard to special committees set up under a law with a view to granting or refusing the "certificates of loyalty" required of certain workers in public utility undertakings if they were to be engaged or retained in service, the Committee recalled the desirability of ensuring that the special committees in question should not be used in such a manner as to give rise to anti-union discrimination.

(See the 1996 *Digest*, para. 713.)

784. Legislation should allow the possibility to appeal against discrimination in hiring, i.e. even before the workers can be qualified as "employees".

(See 338th Report, Case No. 2158, para. 186.)

C. Discrimination during employment

(See also paras. 675, 1054 and 1058)

785. The non-renewal of a contract for anti-union reasons constitutes a prejudicial act within the meaning of Article 1 of Convention No. 98.

(See 327th Report, Case No. 2147, para. 866.)

786. Acts of harassment and intimidation carried out against workers by reason of trade union membership or legitimate trade union activities, while not necessarily prejudicing workers in their employment, may discourage them from joining organizations of their own choosing, thereby violating their right to organize.

(See 302nd Report, Case No. 1826, para. 411.)

787. Granting bonuses to non-union member staff – even if it is not to all non-union workers – and excluding all workers who are union members from such bonuses during a period of collective conflict, constitutes an act of anti-union discrimination contrary to Convention No. 98.

(See 307th Report, Case No. 1886, para. 466.)

788. The government's obligations under Convention No. 98 and the principles on protection against anti-union discrimination cover not only acts of direct discrimination (such as demotion, dismissal, frequent transfer, and so on), but extend to the need to protect unionized employees from more subtle attacks which may be the outcome of omissions. In this respect, proprietorial changes should not remove the right to collective bargaining from employees, or directly or indirectly threaten unionized workers and their organizations.

(See the 1996 *Digest*, para. 715; and 313th Report, Case No. 1987, para. 115.)

D. Discriminatory dismissal

(See also paras. 268, 269, 408, 661 to 664, 666, 674 and 682)

789. The dismissal of workers on grounds of membership of an organization or trade union activities violates the principles of freedom of association.

(See the 1996 *Digest*, para. 702; and, for example, 300th Report, Case No. 1780, para. 142; 306th Report, Case No. 1884, para. 703; 310th Report, Case No. 1888, para. 389; 316th Report, Case No. 1970, para. 555; 321st Report, Case No. 1979, para. 391; 325th Report, Case No. 2068, para. 316; 328th Report, Case No. 2161, para. 674; 333rd Report, Case No. 2087, para. 1010; 336th Report, Case No. 2336, para. 535; and 337th Report, Case No. 2388, para. 1359.)

790. Subcontracting accompanied by dismissals of union leaders can constitute a violation of the principle that no one should be prejudiced in his or her employment on the grounds of union membership or activities.

(See the 1996 *Digest*, para. 705.)

791. It would not appear that sufficient protection against acts of anti-union discrimination, as set out in Convention No. 98, is granted by legislation in cases where employers can in practice, on condition that they pay the compensation prescribed by law for cases of unjustified dismissal, dismiss any worker, if the true reason is the worker's trade union membership or activities.

(See the 1996 *Digest*, para. 707; and, for example, 308th Report, Case No. 1934, para. 134; 310th Report, Case No. 1773, para. 459; 316th Report, Case No. 1934, para. 211; 318th Report, Case No. 2004, para. 400; 321st Report, Case No. 1978, para. 35; 332nd Report, Case No. 2262, para. 394; 333rd Report, Case No. 2186, para. 351; 335th Report, Case No. 2265, para. 1351; 336th Report, Case No. 2336, para. 535; and 337th Report, Case No. 2262, para. 262.)

792. Where public servants are employed under conditions of free appointment and removal from service, the exercise of the right to freely remove public employees from their posts should in no instance be motivated by the trade union functions or activities of the persons who could be affected by such measures.

(See the 1996 *Digest*, para. 708; and 332nd Report, Case No. 2187, para. 725.)

793. Not only dismissal, but also compulsory retirement, when imposed as a result of legitimate trade union activities, would be contrary to the principle that no person should be prejudiced in his or her employment by reason of trade union membership or activities.

(See the 1996 *Digest*, para. 716.)

794. In certain cases, the Committee has found it difficult to accept as a coincidence unrelated to trade union activity that heads of departments should have decided, immediately after a strike, to convene disciplinary boards which, on the basis of service records, ordered the dismissal not only of a number of strikers, but also of members of their union committee.

(See the 1996 *Digest*, para. 717; and 333rd Report, Case No. 2186, para. 353.)

795. Acts of anti-trade union discrimination should not be authorized under the pretext of dismissals based on economic necessity.

(See the 1996 *Digest*, para. 718; 304th Report, Case No. 1853, para. 299; 332nd Report, Case No. 2187, para. 725; and 335th Report, Case No. 2303, para. 1371.)

796. The application of staff reduction programmes musts not be used to carry out acts of anti-union discrimination.

(See 304th Report, Case No. 1796, para. 458; and 305th Report, Case No. 1855, para. 431.)

797. A corporate restructuring should not directly or indirectly threaten unionized workers and their organizations.

(See 320th Report, Case No. 1963, para. 226.)

798. Bipartite talks and the administrative procedure of permission to dismiss do not accord sufficient protection to workers against acts of anti-union discrimination when the legislation currently in force allows an employer merely to invoke lack of harmony in the working relationship to justify the dismissal of workers who only wish to exercise a fundamental right under the principles of freedom of association.

(See the 1996 *Digest*, para. 723.)

Trade union leaders and representatives

A. General principles

799. One of the fundamental principles of freedom of association is that workers should enjoy adequate protection against all acts of anti-union discrimination in respect of their employment, such as dismissal, demotion, transfer or other prejudicial measures. This protection is particularly desirable in the case of trade union officials because, in order to be able to perform their trade union duties in full independence, they should have a guarantee that they will not be prejudiced on account of the mandate which they hold from their trade unions. The Committee has considered that the guarantee of such protection in the case of trade union officials is also necessary in order to ensure that effect is given to the fundamental principle that workers' organizations shall have the right to elect their representatives in full freedom.

(See the 1996 *Digest*, para. 724; and, for example, 302nd Report, Case No. 1809, para. 381; 306th Report, Case No. 1796, para. 506; 311th Report, Case No. 1944, para. 543; 320th Report, Case No. 1995, para. 371; 332nd Report, Case No. 2262, para. 394; 334th Report, Case No. 2222, para. 210; 335th Report, Case No. 2226, para. 756; 336th Report, Case No. 2336, para. 538; 337th Report, Case No. 2262, para. 260; and 338th Report, Case No. 2402, para. 467.)

800. The Committee has drawn attention to the Workers' Representatives Convention (No. 135) and Recommendation (No. 143), 1971, in which it is expressly established that workers' representatives in the undertaking shall enjoy effective protection against any act prejudicial to them, including dismissal, based on their status or activities as workers' representatives or on union membership, or participation in union activities, in so far as they act in conformity with existing laws or collective agreements or other jointly agreed arrangements.

(See the 1996 *Digest*, para. 732; 324th Report, Case No. 2091, para. 893; 335th Report, Case No. 2276, para. 409; and 337th Report, Case No. 2395, para. 1191.)

801. The principle that a worker or trade union official should not suffer prejudice by reason of his or her trade union activities does not necessarily imply that the fact that a person holds a trade union office confers immunity against dismissal irrespective of the circumstances.

(See the 1996 *Digest*, para. 725; 316th Report, Case No. 1972, para. 706; and 335th Report, Case No. 2236, para. 963.)

802. A deliberate policy of frequent transfers of persons holding trade union office may seriously harm the efficiency of trade union activities.

(See the 1996 *Digest*, para. 733.)

B. Blacklists

803. All practices involving the blacklisting of trade union officials or members constitute a serious threat to the free exercise of trade union rights and, in general, governments should take stringent measures to combat such practices.

(See the 1996 *Digest*, paras. 709, 711 and 734; 304th Report, Case No. 1850, para. 217; 335th Report, Case No. 2274, para. 1125; and Case No. 2270, para. 1394.)

C. Dismissal of trade union leaders

(See also paras 830 and 865)

804. The Committee has pointed out that one way of ensuring the protection of trade union officials is to provide that these officials may not be dismissed, either during their period of office or for a certain time thereafter except, of course, for serious misconduct.

(See the 1996 *Digest*, para. 727; 311th Report, Case No. 1934, para. 129; 316th Report, Case No. 1972, para. 706; and 334th Report, Case No. 2046, para. 350.)

805. The dismissal of trade unionists for absence from work without the employer's permission, for example, to attend a workers' education course, does not appear in itself to constitute an infringement of freedom of association.

(See the 1996 *Digest*, para. 728; and 336th Report, Case No. 2328, para. 885.)

806. The Committee cannot accept that the failure to work on a non-workday should be considered a breach of labour discipline leading to the dismissal of trade union leaders.

(See 325th Report, Case No. 2090, para. 176.)

807. In a case in which trade union leaders could be dismissed without an indication of the motive, the Committee requested the government to take steps with a view to punishing acts of anti-union discrimination and to making appeal procedures available to the victims of such acts.

(See the 1996 *Digest*, para. 706; and 318th Report, Case No. 2004, para. 400.)

808. In no case should it be possible to dismiss a trade union officer merely for having presented a list of dispute grievances; this constitutes an extremely serious act of discrimination.

(See the 1996 *Digest*, para. 720; and 330th Report, Case No. 2158, para. 848.)

809. According to the findings of a court, one of the essential reasons for the dismissal of a trade union official was that he performed certain trade union activities in the employer's time, using the personnel of the employer for trade union purposes and using his business position to exercise improper pressure on another employee – all this without the consent of the employer. The Committee considered that, when trade union activities are carried on in this way, it is not possible for the person concerned to invoke the protection of Convention No. 98 or to contend that, in the event of dismissal, his legitimate trade union rights have been infringed.

(See the 1996 *Digest*, para. 729.)

810. In a case in which a trade union leader was dismissed and then reinstated a few days later, the Committee pointed out that the dismissal of trade union leaders by reason of union membership or activities is contrary to Article 1 of Convention No. 98, and could amount to intimidation aimed at preventing the free exercise of their trade union functions.

(See the 1996 *Digest*, para. 730; and 330th Report, Case No. 2186, para. 371.)

811. With regard to the reasons for dismissal, the activities of trade union officials should be considered in the context of particular situations which may be especially strained and difficult in cases of labour disputes and strike action.

(See the 1996 *Digest*, para. 731; 320th Report, Case No. 2014, para. 815; and 324th Report, Case No. 2091, para. 892.)

812. In a case involving a large number of dismissals of trade union leaders and other trade unionists, the Committee considered that it would be particularly desirable for the government to carry out an inquiry in order to establish the true reasons for the measures taken.

(See the 1996 *Digest*, para. 735.)

Need for rapid and effective protection

813. Legislation should lay down explicitly remedies and penalties against acts of anti-union discrimination in order to ensure the effective application of Article 1 of Convention No. 98.

(See the 1996 *Digest*, para. 697; 300th Report, Case No. 1799, para. 209; 329th Report, Case No. 2172, para. 351, and Case No. 2068, para. 436; 334th Report, Case No. 2222, para. 210; and 335th Report, Case No. 2265, para. 1347.)

814. Where a government has undertaken to ensure that the right to associate shall be guaranteed by appropriate measures, that guarantee, in order to be effective, should, when necessary, be accompanied by measures which include the protection of workers against anti-union discrimination in their employment.

(See the 1996 *Digest*, para. 698; and 329th Report, Case No. 2154, para. 813.)

815. In accordance with Convention No. 98, a government should take measures, whenever necessary, to ensure that protection of workers is effective, which implies that the authorities should refrain from any act likely to provoke, or have as its object, anti-union discrimination against workers in respect of their employment.

(See the 1996 *Digest*, para. 699.)

816. As long as protection against anti-union discrimination is in fact ensured, the methods adopted to safeguard workers against such practices may vary from one State to another; but if there is discrimination, the government concerned should take all necessary steps to eliminate it, irrespective of the methods normally used.

(See the 1996 *Digest*, para. 737; 307th Report, Case No. 1877, para. 403; and 330th Report, Case No. 2229, para. 950.)

817. The government is responsible for preventing all acts of anti-union discrimination and it must ensure that complaints of anti-union discrimination are examined in the framework of national procedures which should be prompt, impartial and considered as such by the parties concerned.

(See the 1996 *Digest*, para. 738; and, for example, 307th Report, Case No. 1877, para. 403; 310th Report, Case No. 1880, para. 539; 321st Report, Case No. 1972, para. 77; 327th Report, Case No. 1995, para. 211; 330th Report, Case No. 2126, para. 152; 334th Report, Case No. 2126, para. 73; 335th Report, Case No. 2228, para. 897; 336th Report, Case No. 2336, para. 536; 337th Report, Case No. 2395, para. 1200; and 338th Report, Case No. 2402, para. 467.)

818. The basic regulations that exist in the national legislation prohibiting acts of anti-union discrimination are inadequate when they are not accompanied by procedures to ensure that effective protection against such acts is guaranteed.

(See the 1996 *Digest*, paras. 739, 740 and 742; and, for example, 320th Report, Case No. 2034, para. 745; 324th Report, Case No. 2035, para. 574; 330th Report, Case No. 2186, para. 372; 331st Report, Case No. 2215, para. 178; 332nd Report, Case No. 2227, para. 608; 333rd Report, Case No. 2186, para. 350; 334th Report, Case No. 2222, para. 210, and Case No. 2215, para. 236; 335th Report, Case No. 2236, para. 967; 337th Report, Case No. 2395, para. 1200; and 338th Report, Case No. 2186, para. 53.)

819. It may often be difficult, if not impossible, for workers to furnish proof of an act of anti-union discrimination of which they have been the victim. This shows the full importance of Article 3 of Convention No. 98, which provides that machinery appropriate to national conditions shall be established, where necessary, to ensure respect for the right to organize.

(See the 1996 *Digest*, para. 740; 310th Report, Case No. 1867, para. 88; 311th Report, Case No. 1934, para. 127; 316th Report, Case No. 1970, para. 556; 330th Report, Case No. 2186, para. 372; 333rd Report, Case No. 2186, para. 354; and 335th Report, Case No. 2265, para. 1348.)

820. Respect for the principles of freedom of association clearly requires that workers who consider that they have been prejudiced because of their trade union activities should have access to means of redress which are expeditious, inexpensive and fully impartial.

(See the 1996 *Digest*, para. 741; and, for example, 310th Report, Case No. 1880, para. 539; 327th Report, Case No. 2098, para. 757; 328th Report, Case No. 2158, para. 319; 329th Report, Case No. 2172, para. 351, and Case No. 2176, para. 565; 330th Report, Case No. 2186, para. 372; 333rd Report, Case No. 2281, para. 633; 335th Report, Case No. 2236, para. 967; and 338th Report, Case No. 2378, para. 1145.)

821. The longer it takes for such a procedure to be completed, the more difficult it becomes for the competent body to issue a fair and proper relief, since the situation complained of has often been changed irreversibly, people may have been transferred, etc, to a point where it becomes impossible to order adequate redress or to come back to the status quo ante.

(See 329th Report, Case No. 2176, para. 565.)

822. Legislation must make express provision for appeals and establish sufficiently dissuasive sanctions against acts of anti-union discrimination to ensure the practical application of Articles 1 and 2 of Convention No. 98.

(See the 1996 *Digest*, paras. 743 and 745; 299th Report, Case No. 1687, para. 455; 307th Report, Case No. 1877, para. 401; 316th Report, Case No. 1934, para. 211; 330th Report, Case No. 2203, para. 808; 335th Report, Case No. 2236, para. 967, and Case No. 2265, para. 1315.)

823. Where a government has undertaken to ensure that the free exercise of trade union rights shall be guaranteed by appropriate measures, that guarantee, in order to be effective, should when necessary be accompanied by measures which include the protection of workers against anti-union discrimination in their employment.

(See the 1996 *Digest*, para. 744.)

824. The Committee has recalled the need to ensure by specific provisions accompanied by civil remedies and penal sanctions the protection of workers against acts of anti-union discrimination at the hands of employers.

(See the 1996 *Digest*, para. 746; 329th Report, Case No. 2154, para. 815; and 330th Report, Case No. 2186, para. 374.)

825. A system of protection against anti-union practices which includes severe fines in the case of anti-union dismissals, administrative orders to reinstate workers so dismissed and the possibility of closing down the enterprise does not infringe Convention No. 98.

(See the 1996 *Digest*, para. 747.)

826. Cases concerning anti-union discrimination contrary to Convention No. 98 should be examined rapidly, so that the necessary remedies can be really effective. An excessive delay in processing cases of anti-union discrimination, and in particular a lengthy delay in concluding the proceedings concerning the reinstatement of the trade union leaders dismissed by the enterprise, constitute a denial of justice and therefore a denial of the trade union rights of the persons concerned.

(See the 1996 *Digest*, para. 749; and, for example, 304th Report, Case No. 1719, para. 415; 309th Report, Case No. 1945, para. 66; 320th Report, Case No. 1937, para. 95; 329th Report, Case No. 1948/1955, para. 396; 331st Report, Case No. 1955, para. 18; 333rd Report, Case No. 2291, para. 915; 335th Report, Case No. 2228, para. 897; 336th Report, Case No. 2203, para. 428; 337th Report, Case No. 2395, para. 1194; and 338th Report, Case No. 1890, para. 179.)

827. In a case in which proceedings concerning dismissals had already taken 14 months, the Committee requested the judicial authorities, in order to avoid a denial of justice, to pronounce on the dismissals without delay and emphasized that any further undue delay in the proceedings could in itself justify the reinstatement of these persons in their posts.

(See 323rd Report, Case No. 2059, para. 476.)

828. Complaints against acts of anti-union discrimination should normally be examined by national machinery which, in addition to being speedy, should not only be impartial but also be seen to be such by the parties concerned, who should participate in the procedure in an appropriate and constructive manner.

(See the 1996 *Digest*, para. 750; 330th Report, Case No. 2158, para. 853; 331st Report, Case No. 2187, para. 443; 332nd Report, Case No. 2262, para. 397; and 334th Report, Case No. 2126, para. 73.)

829. The Committee has recalled that the Fact-Finding and Conciliation Commission on Freedom of Association had stressed the importance of providing expeditious, inexpensive and wholly impartial means of redressing grievances caused by acts of anti-union discrimination; it has drawn attention to the desirability of settling grievances wherever possible by discussion without treating the process of determining grievances as a form of litigation, but the Commission has concluded, in cases where honest differences of opinion or viewpoint exist, that resort should be had to impartial tribunals or individuals as the final step in the grievance procedure.

(See the 1996 *Digest*, para. 751.)

830. The Committee has drawn attention to the Workers' Representatives Recommendation, 1971 (No. 143), which recommends, as one of the measures that should be taken to ensure the effective protection of workers' representatives, the adoption of provision for laying upon the employer, in the case of any alleged discriminatory dismissal or unfavourable change in the conditions of employment of a workers' representative, the burden of proving that such action was in fact justified.

(See the 1996 *Digest*, para. 736.)

831. Besides preventive machinery to forestall anti-union discrimination (such as, for example, a request for the prior authorization of the labour inspectorate before dismissing a trade union leader), a further means of ensuring effective protection could be to make it compulsory for each employer to prove that the motive for the decision to dismiss a worker has no connection with the worker's union activities.

(See the 1996 *Digest*, para. 752; and 335th Report, Case No. 2265, para. 1348.)

832. In cases of staff reductions, the Committee has drawn attention to the principle contained in the Workers' Representatives Recommendation, 1971 (No. 143), which mentions amongst the measures to be taken to ensure effective protection to these workers, that recognition of a priority should be given to workers' representatives with regard to their retention in employment in case of reduction of the workforce.

(See the 1996 *Digest*, para. 960; 302nd Report, Case No. 1838, para. 121; 311th Report, Case No. 1865, para. 334; 313th Report, Case No. 1987, para. 115; 328th Report, Case No. 2165, para. 246; 330th Report, Case No. 2142, para. 58, and Case No. 2151, para. 536; 337th Report, Case No. 2356, para. 700; and 338th Report, Case No. 2226, para. 132.)

833. The Committee has emphasized the advisability of giving priority to workers' representatives with regard to their retention in employment in case of reduction of the workforce, to ensure their effective protection.

(See the 1996 *Digest*, para. 961; 305th Report, Case No. 1875, para. 180; 313th Report, Case No. 1987, para. 115; 322nd Report, Case No. 1962, para. 66; 325th Report, Case No. 2068, para. 334; 328th Report, Case No. 2068, para. 207; 331st Report, Case No. 2226, para. 302; and 337th Report, Case No. 2356, para. 700.)

834. The Committee has considered that governments should take the necessary measures to enable labour inspectors to enter freely and without previous notice any workplace liable to inspection, and to carry out any examination, test or inquiry which they may consider necessary in order to satisfy themselves that the legal provisions – including those relating to anti-union discrimination – are being strictly observed.

(See the 1996 Digest, para. 753; and 336th Report, Case No. 2316. para. 55.)

835. Where cases of alleged anti-union discrimination are involved, the competent authorities dealing with labour issues should begin an inquiry immediately and take suitable measures to remedy any effects of anti-union discrimination brought to their attention.

(See the 1996 *Digest*, para. 754; and, for example, 308th Report, Case No. 1897, para. 476; 309th Report, Case No. 1852, para. 335; 310th Report, Case No. 1880, para. 539; 318th Report, Case No. 1987, para. 56; 320th Report, Case No. 1989, para. 327; 328th Report, Case No. 2116, para. 364; 331st Report, Case No. 2068, para. 265; 334th Report, Case No. 2200, para. 757; 337th Report, Case No. 2371, para. 238; and 338th Report, Case No. 2407, para. 492.)

836. In a case in which the remedies available to undocumented workers dismissed for attempting to exercise their trade union rights included: (1) a cease and desist order in respect of violations of the law; and (2) the conspicuous posting of a notice to employees setting forth their rights under the law and detailing the prior unfair practices, the Committee considered that such remedies in no way sanctioned the act of anti-union discrimination already committed, but only acted as possible deterrents for future acts. Such an approach is likely to afford little protection to undocumented workers who can be indiscriminately dismissed for exercising freedom of association. The remedial measures in question are therefore inadequate to ensure effective protection against acts of anti-union discrimination.

(See 332nd Report, Case No. 2227, paras. 609 and 610.)

Reinstatement of trade unionists in their jobs

(See also para. 682)

837. No one should be subjected to anti-union discrimination because of legitimate trade union activities and the remedy of reinstatement should be available to those who are victims of anti-union discrimination.

(See the 1996 *Digest*, para. 755; 306th Report, Case No. 1867, para. 67; 316th Report, Case No. 1970, para. 555; 327th Report, Case No. 2046, para. 433; and 330th Report, Case No. 2186, para. 374.)

838. In the case of a country in which there was no legislation providing for the reinstatement of workers who had been dismissed without justification, the Committee requested the government to take measures to amend the legislation so that workers dismissed for the exercise of their trade union rights can be reinstated in their posts.

(See 332nd Report, Case No. 2201, para. 548.)

839. In cases of the dismissal of trade unionists on the grounds of their trade union membership or activities, the Committee has requested the government to take the necessary measures to enable trade union leaders and members who had been dismissed due to their legitimate trade union activities to secure reinstatement in their jobs and to ensure the application against the enterprises concerned of the corresponding legal sanctions.

(See the 1996 *Digest*, para. 756; 320th Report, Case No. 1995, para. 372; and 323rd Report, Case No. 2034, para. 403.)

840. In many cases, the Committee has requested the government to ensure that the persons in question are reinstated in their jobs without loss of pay.

(See, for example, 318th Report, Case No. 1974, para. 306, and Case No. 2004, para. 401; 319th Report, Case No. 1962, para. 152; 320th Report, Case No. 1989, para. 325; 323rd Report, Case No. 2034, para. 406; 324th Report, Case No. 2090, para. 212; 326th Report, Case No. 2103, para. 296; 327th Report, Case No. 2125, para. 778; and 328th Report, Case No. 2068, para. 206.)

841. If, given the considerable time that has elapsed since the dismissals, in violation of the principles of freedom of association, it is not practicable to reinstate the workers concerned, the Committee has requested the government to take steps to ensure that the workers receive full compensation without delay.

(See 319th Report, Case No. 1962, paras. 152 and 153.)

842. In certain cases of dismissals in which judicial proceedings were ongoing, if the decision concludes that there have been acts of anti-union discrimination, the Committee has requested the reinstatement of the workers concerned.

(See 324th Report, Case No. 1880, para. 853; 328th Report, Case No. 2158; para. 320; 329th Report, Case No. 2188, para. 214; 330th Report, Case No. 2186, para. 374, Case No. 2208, para. 600, and Case No. 2192, para. 1072; 332nd Report, Case No. 2187, para. 724; 333rd Report, Case No. 2286, para. 874; and 335th Report, Case No. 2283, para. 225.)

843. If the judicial authority determines that reinstatement of workers dismissed in violation of freedom of association is not possible, measures should be taken so that they are fully compensated.

(See 335th Report, Case No. 2274, para. 1118.)

844. The compensation should be adequate, taking into account both the damage incurred and the need to prevent the repetition of such situations in the future.

(See 336th Report, Case No. 2336, para. 537; 338th Report, Case No. 2404, para. 1053, and Case No. 2248, para. 1200.)

845. If reinstatement is not possible, the government should ensure that the workers concerned are paid adequate compensation which would represent a sufficient dissuasive sanction for anti-trade union dismissals.

(See 336th Report, Case No. 2380, para. 795; 337th Report, Case No. 2371, para. 239, Case No. 2262, para. 260, and Case No. 2268, paras. 1104, 1107 and 1109; 338th Report, Case No. 2228, para. 195, and Case No. 2399, para. 1172.)

846. In certain cases, the Committee has requested the government to carry out independent investigations of dismissals and, if it finds that they constitute anti-trade union acts, to take measures to ensure the reinstatement of the workers concerned.

(See, for example, 327th Report, Case No. 2098, para. 757, and Case No. 2126, para. 845; 329th Report, Case No. 2098, para. 125; 330th Report, Case No. 2103, para. 766; 331st Report, Case No. 2169, para. 639; 332nd Report, Case No. 2187, para. 725; 333rd Report, Case No. 2286, para. 876; 334th Report, Case No. 2239, para. 394; 337th Report, Case No. 2371, para. 239; 338th Report, Case No. 2096, para. 274, and Case No. 2303, para. 334.)

847. If the post occupied by the worker has been eliminated, she or he should be reinstated in a comparable post if the dismissal constituted an act of anti-union discrimination.

(See 329th Report, Case No. 2150, para. 314.)

848. Where the enterprise no longer exists, measures should be taken to ensure that workers dismissed for trade union activities are fully compensated.

(See 329th Report, Case No. 2097, para. 470.)

849. Declarations of loyalty or other similar commitment should not be imposed as a condition for reinstatement.

(See 309th Report, Case No. 1851/1922, para. 237.)

850. In a case of a strike by air traffic controllers in which public safety was endangered, the Committee considered that it could not ask the Government to allow the request for a return to work of those who were dismissed, as claimed by the complainant.

(See 309th Report, Case No. 1913, para. 305.)

851. In a case in which a trade union official had been dismissed for alleged robbery, and where the case against the official had not been upheld by the courts, the Committee considered that the person concerned should be reinstated without loss of pay and be authorized to exercise trade union activities.

(See 333rd Report, Case No. 2299, para. 560.)

852. The necessary measures should be taken so that trade unionists who have been dismissed for activities related to the establishment of a union are reinstated in their functions, if they so wish.

(See the 1996 *Digest*, paras. 302, 703 and 757; 304th Report, Case No. 1787, para. 174; 328th Report, Case No. 2160, para. 658; 335th Report, Case No 2283, para. 225, and Case No. 2265, para. 1351; 336th Report, Case No. 2336, para. 535, and Case No. 2380, para. 794; and 337th Report, Case No. 2262, para. 260.)

853. It is inconsistent with the right to strike for an employer to be permitted to refuse to reinstate some or all of the employees at the conclusion of the strike, lock-out or other industrial action without those employees having the right to challenge the fairness of that dismissal before an independent court or tribunal.

(See the 1996 *Digest*, para. 722; and 333rd Report, Case No. 2281, para. 633.)

Discrimination against employers

854. In relation to allegations concerning discrimination against employers' leaders on the grounds of agrarian reform, the Committee considered that the provisions concerning compensation for land expropriation should be reviewed to make sure that there is real and fair compensation for the losses thus sustained by owners, and that the Government should reopen the compensation files if so requested by persons who consider they have been despoiled in the agrarian reform process.

(See the 1996 *Digest*, para. 758.)

Protection against acts of interference

14

(See also para. 1119)

General principles

855. Article 2 of Convention No. 98 establishes the total independence of workers' organizations from employers in exercising their activities.

(See the 1996 *Digest*, para. 759; 325th Report, Case No. 2068, para. 321; 329th Report, Case No. 2198, para. 683; 330th Report, Case No 2186, para. 379; 331st Report, Case No. 2185, para. 676; 334th Report, Case No. 2316, para. 506; 337th Report, Case No. 2388, para. 1355; and 338th Report, Case No. 2374, para. 509.)

856. The closure of trade union offices, as a consequence of a legitimate strike, constitutes a violation of the principles of freedom of association and, if carried out by management, interference by the employer in the functioning of a workers' organization, which is prohibited under Article 2 of Convention No. 98.

(See 302nd Report, Case No. 1849, para. 215.)

857. The intervention by an employer to promote the constitution of the executive board of a trade union, and interference with its correspondence, are acts which constitute a grave violation of the principles of freedom of association

(See 311th Report, Case No. 1966, para. 360.)

858. As regards allegations of anti-union tactics in the form of bribes offered to union members to encourage their withdrawal from the union and the presentation of statements of resignation to the workers, as well as the alleged efforts made to create puppet unions, the Committee considers such acts to be contrary to Article 2 of Convention No. 98, which provides that workers' and employers' organizations shall enjoy adequate protection against any acts of interference by each other or each other's agents in their establishment, functioning or administration.

(See the 1996 *Digest*, para. 760; 324th Report, Case No. 2090, para. 209; 330th Report, Case No. 2090, para. 232, and Case No. 2203, para. 810; and 337th Report, Case No. 2388, para. 1354.)

859. Respect for the principles of freedom of association requires that the public authorities exercise great restraint in relation to intervention in the internal affairs of trade unions. It is even more important that employers exercise restraint in this regard. They should not, for example, do anything which might seem to favour one group within a union at the expense of another.

(See the 1996 *Digest*, para. 761; 327th Report, Case No. 2118, para. 641; 328th Report, Case No. 2124, para. 460; 329th Report, Case No. 2198, para. 685, and Case No. 2184, para. 828; 330th Report, Case No. 2118, para. 116; and 331st Report, Case No. 2132, para. 589.)

860. Where legislation does not contain specific provisions for the protection of workers' organizations from acts of interference by employers and their organizations (and provides that any case not provided for by the legislation should be decided, inter alia, in accordance with the provisions laid down in the Conventions and Recommendations adopted by the International Labour Organization, in so far as they are not contrary to laws of the country, and in accordance with Convention No. 98, by virtue of its ratification), it would be appropriate for the government to examine the possibility of adopting clear and precise provisions ensuring the adequate protection of workers' organizations against these acts of interference.

(See the 1996 *Digest*, para. 762; and 333rd Report, Case No. 2186, para. 358.)

861. The existence of legislative provisions prohibiting acts of interference on the part of the authorities, or by organizations of workers and employers in each other's affairs, is insufficient if they are not accompanied by efficient procedures to ensure their implementation in practice.

(See the 1996 *Digest*, para. 763; and 333rd Report, Case No. 2168, para. 358.)

862. Legislation must make express provision for appeals and establish sufficiently dissuasive sanctions against acts of interference by employers against workers and workers' organizations to ensure the practical application of Articles 1 and 2 of Convention No. 98.

(See the 1996 *Digest*, para. 764; 330th Report, Case No. 2203, para. 810; and 333rd Report, Case No. 2186, para. 358.)

863. Attempts by employers to persuade employees to withdraw authorizations given to a trade union could unduly influence the choice of workers and undermine the position of the trade union, thus making it more difficult to bargain collectively, which is contrary to the principle that collective bargaining should be promoted.

(See the 1996 *Digest*, para. 766; 304th Report, Case No. 1852, para. 494; and 337th Report, Case No. 2395, para. 1188.)

864. Legal provisions which allow employers to undermine workers' organizations through artificial promotions of workers constitute a violation of the principles of freedom of association.

(See the 1996 *Digest*, para. 767.)

865. In endorsing an observation made by the Committee of Experts on the Application of Conventions and Recommendations concerning a law, the Committee pointed out that it would be extremely difficult for a worker who was dismissed by an employer invoking, for example, "neglect of duty", to prove that the real motive for dismissal was to be found in his or her trade union activities. Further, since lodging an appeal in this case did not suspend the decision taken, the dismissed trade union leader had, by virtue of the law, to resign his or her trade union post when dismissed. The Committee considered that the law therefore made it possible for managements of undertakings to hinder the activities of a trade union, which is contrary to Article 2 of Convention No. 98, according to which workers' and employers' organizations shall enjoy adequate protection against any acts of interference by each other or each other's agents or members in their establishment, functioning or administration.

(See the 1996 *Digest*, para. 768; and 333rd Report, Case No. 2186, para. 357.)

866. The issue of circulars by a company requesting its employees to state to which trade union they belong, even though this is not intended to interfere with the exercise of trade union rights, may not unnaturally be regarded as such an interference.

(See the 1996 *Digest*, para. 769.)

867. The fact that one of the members of a government is at the same time a leader of a trade union which represents several categories of workers employed by the State creates a possibility of interference in violation of Article 2 of Convention No. 98.

(See the 1996 *Digest*, para. 770.)

868. Recalling the importance of the independence of the parties in collective bargaining, negotiations should not be conducted on behalf of employees or their organizations by bargaining representatives appointed by or under the domination of employers or their organizations.

(See the 1996 *Digest*, paras. 771 and 789; 329th Report, Case No. 2198, para. 683; 331st Report, Case No. 2217, para. 205, and Case No. 2185, para. 676; and 337th Report, Case No. 2388, para. 1354.)

Solidarist or other associations

A. Definition

869. An Act on solidarist associations provides that such associations may be formed by 12 or more workers, and defines them as follows: "Solidarist associations are bodies of indeterminate duration which have their own legal personality and which, to achieve their purposes (the promotion of justice and social peace, harmony between employers and workers and the general advancement of their members), may acquire goods of all kinds, conclude any type of contract and undertake legal operations of any sort aimed at improving their members' social and economic conditions so as to raise their standard of living and enhance their dignity. To this effect they may undertake savings, credit and investment operations and any other financially viable operations. They may also organize programmes in the areas of housing, science, sport, art, education and recreation, cultural and spiritual matters and social and economic affairs and any other programme designed legally to promote cooperation between workers and between workers and their employers." The income of solidarist associations comes from members' minimum monthly savings, the percentage of which shall be determined by the general meeting, and the employers' monthly contribution on behalf of the workers, which shall be determined by common agreement between the two sides.

(See the 1996 *Digest*, para. 772.)

870. Solidarist associations are associations of workers which are set up dependent on a financial contribution from the relevant employer and which are financed in accordance with the principles of mutual benefit societies by both workers and employers for economic and social purposes of material welfare (savings, credit, investment, housing and educational programmes, etc.) and of unity and cooperation between workers and employers; their deliberative bodies must be made up of workers, though an employers' representative may be included who may speak but not vote. In the Committee's opinion, although from the point of view of the principles contained in Conventions Nos. 87 and 98, nothing prevents workers and employers from seeking forms of cooperation, including those of a mutualist nature, to pursue social objectives, it is up to the Committee, in so far as such forms of cooperation crystallize into permanent structures and organizations, to ensure that the legislation on and the functioning of solidarist associations do not interfere with the activities and the role of trade unions.

(See the 1996 *Digest*, para. 773.)

B. Safeguards to prevent associations from carrying out trade union activities

871. The provisions governing “solidarist” associations should respect the activities of trade unions guaranteed by Convention No. 98.

(See the 1996 *Digest*, para. 774.)

872. The necessary legislative and other measures should be taken to guarantee that solidarist associations do not get involved in trade union activities, as well as measures to guarantee effective protection against any form of anti-union discrimination and to abolish any inequalities of treatment in favour of solidarist associations.

(See the 1996 *Digest*, para. 775; and 320th Report, Case No. 1984, para. 542.)

873. As regards allegations relating to “solidarism”, the Committee has recalled the importance it attaches, in conformity with Article 2 of Convention No. 98, to protection being ensured against any acts of interference by employers designed to promote the establishment of workers’ organizations under the domination of an employer.

(See the 1996 *Digest*, para. 776.)

874. As regards allegations concerning the activities of solidarist associations aimed at thwarting trade union activities, the Committee drew the Government’s attention to Article 2 of Convention No. 98, which provides that workers’ and employers’ organizations shall enjoy adequate protection against any acts of interference by each other and that measures designed to promote the establishment of workers’ organizations under the domination of employers or employers’ organizations, or to support workers’ organizations by financial and other means, with the object of placing such organizations under the control of employers or employers’ organizations, are specifically assimilated to such acts of interference.

(See the 1996 *Digest*, para. 777.)

875. The interference of solidarist associations in trade union activities, including collective bargaining, through direct settlements signed between an employer and a group of non-unionized workers, even when a union exists in the undertaking, does not promote collective bargaining as set out in Article 4 of Convention No. 98, which refers to the development of negotiations between employers or their organizations and workers’ organizations.

(See the 1996 *Digest*, paras. 778 and 790.)

876. Since solidarist associations are financed partly by employers, are comprised of workers but also of senior staff or personnel having the employers' confidence and are often started up by employers, they cannot play the role of independent organizations in the collective bargaining process, a process which should be carried out between an employer (or an employer's organization) and one or more workers' organizations totally independent of each other. This situation therefore gives rise to problems in the application of Article 2 of Convention No. 98, which sets out the principle of the full independence of workers' organizations in carrying out their activities.

(See the 1996 *Digest*, paras. 779 and 790.)

877. In relation to solidarist associations, the Committee emphasized the fundamental importance of the principle of tripartism advocated by the ILO, which presupposes organizations of workers and of employers which are independent of each other and of the public authorities. The Committee requested the Government to take measures, in consultation with the trade union confederations, to create the necessary conditions for strengthening the independent trade union movement and for developing its activities in the social field.

(See the 1996 *Digest*, para. 780.)

878. Workers' welfare associations cannot be substitutes for free and independent trade unions for as long as they fail to present guarantees of independence in their composition and functioning.

(See 333rd Report, Case No. 2268, para. 742.)

879. The Committee has recalled that legislative or other measures have to be taken in order to ensure that organizations that are separate from trade unions do not assume responsibility for trade union activities and to ensure effective protection against all forms of anti-union discrimination.

(See 334th Report, Case No. 2295, para. 596.)

Collective bargaining 15

The right to bargain collectively – General principles

880. Measures should be taken to encourage and promote the full development and utilization of machinery for voluntary negotiation between employers or employers' organizations and workers' organizations, with a view to the regulation of terms and conditions of employment by means of collective agreements.

(See the 1996 *Digest*, para. 781; and, for example, 308th Report, Case No. 1934, para. 127; 322nd Report, Case No. 2015, para. 102; 330th Report, Case No. 2186, para. 382; 331st Report, Case No. 2228, para. 469; 332nd Report, Case No. 2255, para. 945; 333rd Report, Case No. 2172, para. 318; 334th Report, Case No. 2222, para. 211; 336th Report, Case No. 2336, para. 528; 337th Report, Case No. 2349, para. 404; and 338th Report, Case No. 2253, para. 82.)

881. The right to bargain freely with employers with respect to conditions of work constitutes an essential element in freedom of association, and trade unions should have the right, through collective bargaining or other lawful means, to seek to improve the living and working conditions of those whom the trade unions represent. The public authorities should refrain from any interference which would restrict this right or impede the lawful exercise thereof. Any such interference would appear to infringe the principle that workers' and employers' organizations should have the right to organize their activities and to formulate their programmes.

(See the 1996 *Digest*, para. 782; 310th Report, Case No. 1928, para. 175; 311th Report, Case No. 1951, para. 220, and Case No. 1942, para. 269; 321st Report, Case No. 2019, para. 412; 327th Report, Case No. 2119, para. 253; and 338th Report, Case No. 2326, para. 450.)

882. The preliminary work for the adoption of Convention No. 87 clearly indicates that "one of the main objects of the guarantee of freedom of association is to enable employers and workers to combine to form organisations independent of the public authorities and capable of determining wages and other conditions of employment by means of freely concluded collective agreements". (Freedom of Association and Industrial Relations, Report VII, International Labour Conference, 30th Session, Geneva, 1947, p. 52.)

(See the 1996 *Digest*, para. 799; 308th Report, Case No. 1900, para. 186; 311th Report, Case No. 1951, para. 225; and 325th Report, Case No. 1951, para. 211.)

883. Federations and confederations should be able to conclude collective agreements.

(See the 1996 *Digest*, para. 783; 302nd Report, Case No. 1817, para. 320; and 332nd Report, Case No. 2216, para. 910.)

884. The Committee has pointed out the importance which it attaches to the right of representative organizations to negotiate, whether these organizations are registered or not.

(See the 1996 *Digest*, para. 784; 318th Report, Case No. 2012, para. 423; 329th Report, Case No. 2140, para. 296, and Case No. 2133, para. 546; and 333rd Report, Case No. 2133, para. 60.)

Workers covered by collective bargaining

(See also para. 577)

885. Convention No. 98, and in particular Article 4 thereof concerning the encouragement and promotion of collective bargaining, applies both to the private sector and to nationalized undertakings and public bodies.

(See the 1996 *Digest*, para. 792; and 334th Report, Case No. 2222, para. 211.)

886. All public service workers other than those engaged in the administration of the State should enjoy collective bargaining rights, and priority should be given to collective bargaining as the means to settle disputes arising in connection with the determination of terms and conditions of employment in the public service.

(See the 1996 *Digest*, paras. 793 and 893; and, for example, 308th Report, Case No. 1902, para. 702; 321st Report, Case No. 2019, para. 412; 325th Report, Case No. 2110, para. 265; 327th Report, Case No. 2138, para. 541; 328th Report, Case No. 2114, para. 414; 329th Report, Case No. 2114, para. 72; 330th Report, Case No. 2200, para. 1097; 334th Report, Case No. 2269, para. 792; and 338th Report, Case No. 2253, para. 84.)

887. A distinction must be drawn between, on the one hand, public servants who by their functions are directly engaged in the administration of the State (that is, civil servants employed in government ministries and other comparable bodies), as well as officials acting as supporting elements in these activities and, on the other hand, persons employed by the government, by public undertakings or by autonomous public institutions. Only the former category can be excluded from the scope of Convention No. 98.

(See the 1996 *Digest*, para. 794; 306th Report, Case No. 1882, para. 433; 329th Report, Case No. 2114, para. 72, and Case No. 2177/2183, para. 644; 334th Report, Case No. 2222, para. 209; and 338th Report, Case No. 2253, para. 84.)

888. The Committee has considered it useful to recall that, under the terms of the Labour Relations (Public Service) Convention, 1978 (No. 151) (Article 7): "Measures appropriate to national conditions shall be taken, where necessary, to encourage and promote the full development and utilisation of machinery for negotiation of terms and conditions of employment between the public authorities concerned and public employees' organisations, or of such other methods as will allow representatives of public employees to participate in the determination of these matters".

(See the 1996 *Digest*, para. 916.)

889. While recalling the terms of Article 7 of Convention No. 151, the Committee has emphasized that when national legislation opts for negotiation machinery, the State must ensure that such machinery is applied properly.

(See 308th Report, Case No. 1919, para. 322.)

890. Referring to Article 8 of Convention No. 151 concerning the settlement of disputes, the Committee has recalled that, in view of the preparatory work which preceded the adoption of the Convention, this Article has been interpreted as giving a choice between negotiation or other procedures (such as mediation, conciliation and arbitration) in settling disputes. The Committee has stressed the importance of the principle contained in Article 8 of Convention No. 151.

(See the 1996 *Digest*, para. 917.)

891. The Committee acknowledges that Article 7 of Convention No. 151 allows a degree of flexibility in the choice of procedures to be used in the determination of the terms and conditions of employment.

(See the 1996 *Digest*, para. 923.)

892. The mere fact that public servants are white-collar employees is not in itself conclusive of their qualification as employees engaged in the administration of the State; if this were not the case, Convention No. 98 would be deprived of much of its scope. To sum up, all public service workers, with the sole possible exception of the armed forces and the police and public servants directly engaged in the administration of the State, should enjoy collective bargaining rights.

(See 329th Report, Case No. 2177/2183, para. 644.)

893. It is imperative that the legislation contain specific provisions clearly and explicitly recognizing the right of organizations of public employees and officials who are not acting in the capacity of agents of the state administration to conclude collective agreements. From the point of view of the principles laid down by the supervisory bodies of the ILO in connection with Convention No. 98, this right could only be denied to officials working in ministries and other comparable government bodies, but not, for example, to persons working in public undertakings or autonomous public institutions.

(See the 1996 *Digest*, para. 795; 327th Report, Case No. 2104, para. 520; and 334th Report, Case No. 2253, para. 312.)

894. The workers of state-owned commercial or industrial enterprises should have the right to negotiate collective agreements.

(See the 1996 *Digest*, para. 796.)

895. Convention No. 98 applies to employees of the postal and telecommunications services.

(See the 1996 *Digest*, para. 797.)

896. In a case in which an attempt was being made to give the workers in the National Bank private sector status, the Committee considered that it was not within its purview to express an opinion as to whether the workers should be given public law or private law status. Considering that Conventions Nos. 87 and 98 apply to all workers in the banking sector, however, the Committee expressed the hope that the right of bank employees would be recognized to conclude collective agreements and join the federations of their choosing.

(See the 1996 *Digest*, para. 798.)

897. The staff of a national radio and television institute, a public undertaking, may not be excluded, by reason of their duties, from the principle concerning the promotion of collective bargaining.

(See the 1996 *Digest*, para. 800.)

898. No provision in Convention No. 98 authorizes the exclusion of staff having the status of contract employee from its scope.

(See the 1996 *Digest*, para. 802; 324th Report, Case No. 2083, para. 254; 327th Report, Case No. 2138, para. 544; and 335th Report, Case No. 2303, para. 1372.)

899. When examining legislation which made it possible to exclude seafarers not resident in the country from collective agreements, the Committee called on the Government to take measures to amend the Act so as to ensure that full and voluntary collective bargaining open to all seafarers employed on ships sailing under the national flag was once again a reality.

(See the 1996 *Digest*, para. 803.)

900. The Committee has drawn attention to the importance of promoting collective bargaining, as set out in Article 4 of Convention No. 98, in the education sector.

(See the 1996 *Digest*, para. 804; 302nd Report, Case No. 1820, para. 109; 310th Report, Case No. 1928, para. 175; 327th Report, Case No. 2119, para. 253; 328th Report, Case No. 2114, para. 414; 329th Report, Case No. 2177/2183, para. 645; and 334th Report, Case No. 2222, para. 212.).

901. In the Committee's opinion, teachers do not carry out tasks specific to officials in the state administration; indeed, this type of activity is also carried out in the private sector. In these circumstances, it is important that teachers with civil servant status should enjoy the guarantees provided for under Convention No. 98.

(See 302nd Report, Case No. 1820, para. 109.)

902. Air flight control personnel should have the right to engage in collective bargaining on their conditions of employment.

(See 304th Report, Case No. 1827, para. 529.)

903. Persons employed in public hospitals should enjoy the right to collective bargaining.

(See 306th Report, Case No. 1882, para. 433.)

904. Civil aviation technicians working under the jurisdiction of the armed forces cannot be considered, in view of the nature of their functions, as belonging to the armed forces and as such liable to be excluded from the guarantees laid down in Convention No. 98; the standards contained in Article 4 of the Convention concerning collective bargaining should be applied to them.

(See the 1996 *Digest*, para. 805.)

905. Convention No. 98 is applicable to locally recruited personnel in embassies.

(See 334th Report, Case No. 2197, para. 130.)

906. Temporary workers should be able to negotiate collectively.

(See 305th Report, Case No. 1829, para. 130.)

907. With regard to temporary job offers in the public sector to combat unemployment, in which the wages were not determined under the terms of the collective agreements governing remuneration of regular employees, the Committee expressed the hope that the Government would ensure that, in practice, the job offers remained of a limited duration and did not become an opportunity to fill permanent posts with unemployed persons, restricted in their right to bargain collectively as regards their remuneration.

(See the 1996 *Digest*, para. 912.)

908. People involved in community participation activities intended to combat unemployment, of a limited duration of six months, are not true employees of the organization which benefits from their labour and can therefore legitimately be excluded from the scope of collective agreements in force, at least in respect of wages.

(See 316th Report, Case No. 1975, para. 269; and 324th Report, Case No. 2022, para. 764.)

909. With reference to the above principle, the Committee however considered that the persons concerned perform work and provide a service of benefit to the organizations concerned. For this reason, they must enjoy a certain protection in respect of their working and employment conditions.

(See 316th Report, Case No. 1975, para. 270; and 324th Report, Case No. 2022, para. 764.)

910. In the context of measures to combat unemployment and the introduction of job offer schemes which imposed a ceiling on hourly wage rates, the Committee emphasized that the Government should ensure, in practice, that job pools are not resorted to on a successive basis in order to fill regular jobs with unemployed persons restricted in their right to bargain collectively in respect of wages. The Committee urged the Government to set up tripartite procedures in order to prevent any abuse.

(See 312th Report, Case No. 1958, para. 75.)

911. In a case in which some collective agreements applied only to the parties to the agreement and their members and not to all workers, the Committee considered that this is a legitimate option – just as the contrary would be – which does not appear to violate the principles of freedom of association, and one which is practised in many countries.

(See 305th Report, Case No. 1765, para. 100.)

Subjects covered by collective bargaining

(See also paras. 480 and 481)

912. Measures taken unilaterally by the authorities to restrict the scope of negotiable issues are often incompatible with Convention No. 98; tripartite discussions for the preparation, on a voluntary basis, of guidelines for collective bargaining are a particularly appropriate method of resolving these difficulties.

(See 308th Report, Case No. 1897, para. 473.)

913. Matters which might be subject to collective bargaining include the type of agreement to be offered to employees or the type of industrial instrument to be negotiated in the future, as well as wages, benefits and allowances, working time, annual leave, selection criteria in case of redundancy, the coverage of the collective agreement, the granting of trade union facilities, including access to the workplace beyond what is provided for in legislation etc.; these matters should not be excluded from the scope of collective bargaining by law, or as in this case, by financial disincentives and considerable penalties applicable in case of non-implementation of the Code and Guidelines.

(See 338th Report, Case No. 2326, para. 450.)

914. Legislation excluding working time from the scope of collective bargaining, unless there is government authorization, would seem to infringe the right of workers' organizations to negotiate freely their working conditions with employers, as guaranteed under Article 4 of Convention No. 98.

(See the 1996 *Digest*, para. 806.)

915. As regards the legislative ban on including secondary boycott clauses in collective agreements, the Committee has considered that restrictions on such clauses should not be included in the legislation.

(See the 1996 *Digest*, para. 807.)

916. It should be possible for collective agreements to provide for a system for the collection of union dues, without interference by the authorities.

(See the 1996 *Digest*, paras. 327 and 808; and 332nd Report, Case No. 2187, para. 722.)

917. Where job distribution is subject to legal restrictions, the Committee has drawn attention to the fact that such provisions may tend to prevent the negotiation by collective agreement of better terms and conditions, mainly concerning access to particular employment, and thereby to infringe the rights of the workers concerned to bargain collectively and to improve their working conditions.

(See the 1996 *Digest*, para. 809.)

918. Legislation amending collective agreements which have already been in force for some time, and which prohibits collective agreements concerning the manning of ships from being concluded in the future, is not in conformity with Article 4 of Convention No. 98.

(See the 1996 *Digest*, para. 810.)

919. Legislation establishing that the ministry of labour has powers to regulate wages, working hours, rest periods, leave and conditions of work, that these regulations must be observed in collective agreements, and that such important aspects of conditions of work are thus excluded from the field of collective bargaining, is not in harmony with Article 4 of Convention No. 98.

(See the 1996 *Digest*, para. 811.)

920. With regard to allegations concerning the refusal to bargain collectively on certain matters in the public sector, the Committee has recalled the view of the Fact-Finding and Conciliation Commission on Freedom of Association that "there are certain matters which clearly appertain primarily or essentially to the management and operation of government business; these can reasonably be regarded as outside the scope of negotiation". It is equally clear that certain other matters are primarily or essentially questions relating to conditions of employment and that such matters should not be regarded as falling outside the scope of collective bargaining conducted in an atmosphere of mutual good faith and trust.

(See the 1996 *Digest*, para. 812; 306th Report, Case No. 1859, para. 242; 310th Report, Case No. 1928, para. 175; 311th Report, Case No. 1951, para. 220; 327th Report, Case No. 2119, para. 253; and 329th Report, Case No. 2177/2183, para. 646.)

921. While staffing levels or the departments to be affected as a result of financial difficulties may be considered to be matters which appertain primarily or essentially to the management and operation of government business and therefore reasonably regarded as outside the scope of negotiation, the larger spectrum of job security in general includes questions which relate primarily or essentially to conditions of employment, such as pre-dismissal rights, indemnities, etc., which should not be excluded from the scope of collective bargaining.

(See 306th Report, Case No. 1859, para. 242; and 311th Report, Case No. 1951, para. 220.)

922. The determination of the broad lines of educational policy is not a matter for collective bargaining between the competent authorities and teachers' organizations, although it may be normal to consult these organizations on such matters.

(See the 1996 *Digest*, para. 813; 310th Report, Case No. 1928, para. 175; 311th Report, Case No. 1951, para. 220; and 330th Report, Case No. 2173, para. 300.)

923. Free collective bargaining should be allowed on the consequences for conditions of employment of decisions on educational policy.

(See 325th Report, Case No. 1951, para. 206; and 327th Report, Case No. 2119, para. 253.)

924. The bargaining partners are best equipped to weigh the justification and determine the modalities (and, as far as employers are concerned, the financial practicability) of negotiated compulsory retirement clauses before the legal retirement age, be it by reason of the difficult nature of the job, or for health and safety reasons.

(See 330th Report, Case No. 2171, para. 1048.)

The principle of free and voluntary negotiation

925. The voluntary negotiation of collective agreements, and therefore the autonomy of the bargaining partners, is a fundamental aspect of the principles of freedom of association.

(See the 1996 *Digest*, para. 844; 321st Report, Case No. 1975, para. 117; 327th Report, Case No. 2146, para. 896; 330th Report, Case No. 2196, para. 304, and Case No. 2171, para. 1048; 331st Report, Case No. 2132, para. 590; 332nd Report, Case No. 2233, para. 639; and 337th Report, Case No. 2349, para. 404.)

926. Collective bargaining, if it is to be effective, must assume a voluntary character and not entail recourse to measures of compulsion which would alter the voluntary nature of such bargaining.

(See the 1996 *Digest*, para. 845; and 337th Report, Case No. 2349, para. 404.)

927. Nothing in Article 4 of Convention No. 98 places a duty on the government to enforce collective bargaining by compulsory means with a given organization; such an intervention would clearly alter the nature of bargaining.

(See the 1996 *Digest*, para. 846; 311th Report, Case No. 1942, para. 269; 313th Report, Case No. 1959, para. 217; 316th Report, Case No. 1996, para. 667; 328th Report, Case No. 2149, para. 579; and 332nd Report, Case No. 2252, para. 880.)

928. Article 4 of Convention No. 98 in no way places a duty on the government to enforce collective bargaining, nor would it be contrary to this provision to oblige social partners, within the framework of the encouragement and promotion of the full development and utilization of collective bargaining machinery, to enter into negotiations on terms and conditions of employment. The public authorities should however refrain from any undue interference in the negotiation process.

(See 328th Report, Case No. 2149, para. 581.)

929. Although nothing in Article 4 of Convention No. 98 places a duty on the government to enforce collective bargaining by compulsory means with a given organization, as such an intervention would clearly alter the voluntary nature of collective bargaining, this does not mean that governments should abstain from any measure whatsoever aiming to establish a collective bargaining mechanism.

(See 338th Report, Case No. 2253, para. 82.)

930. Legislation which lays down mandatory conciliation and prevents the employer from withdrawing, irrespective of circumstances, at the risk of being penalized by payment of wages in respect of strike days, in addition to being disproportionate, runs counter to the principle of voluntary negotiation enshrined in Convention No. 98.

(See 318th Report, Case No. 1931, para. 369.)

931. The opportunity which employers have, according to the legislation, of presenting proposals for the purposes of collective bargaining – provided these proposals are merely to serve as a basis for the voluntary negotiation to which Convention No. 98 refers – cannot be considered as a violation of the principles applicable in this matter.

(See the 1996 *Digest*, para. 849; and 337th Report, Case No. 2331, para. 592.)

Mechanisms to facilitate collective bargaining

932. The bodies appointed for the settlement of disputes between the parties to collective bargaining should be independent, and recourse to these bodies should be on a voluntary basis.

(See the 1996 *Digest*, para. 858; 320th Report, Case No. 2025, para. 408; 327th Report, Case No. 2145, para. 305; and 335th Report, Case No. 2305, para. 506.)

933. Certain rules and practices can facilitate negotiations and help to promote collective bargaining and various arrangements may facilitate the parties' access to certain information concerning, for example, the economic position of their bargaining unit, wages and working conditions in closely related units, or the general economic situation; however, all legislation establishing machinery and procedures for arbitration and conciliation designed to facilitate bargaining between both sides of industry must guarantee the autonomy of parties to collective bargaining. Consequently, instead of entrusting the public authorities with powers to assist actively, even to intervene, in order to put forward their point of view, it would be better to convince the parties to collective bargaining to have regard voluntarily in their negotiations to the major reasons put forward by the government for its economic and social policies of general interest.

(See the 1996 *Digest*, para. 859; and 318th Report, Case No. 2012, para. 424.)

The principle of bargaining in good faith

(See also para. 657)

934. The Committee recalls the importance which it attaches to the obligation to negotiate in good faith for the maintenance of the harmonious development of labour relations.

(See the 1996 *Digest*, para. 814; and, for example, 307th Report, Case No. 1873, para. 98; 311th Report, Case No. 1944, para. 546; 318th Report, Case No. 2005, para. 184; 325th Report, Case No. 2106, para. 485; 330th Report, Case No. 2186, para. 380; 332nd Report, Case No. 2263, para. 298; 333rd Report, Case No. 2288, para. 826; 335th Report, Case No. 2274, para. 1121; 337th Report, Case No. 2244, para. 1258; and 338th Report, Case No. 2404, para. 1047.)

935. It is important that both employers and trade unions bargain in good faith and make every effort to reach an agreement; moreover genuine and constructive negotiations are a necessary component to establish and maintain a relationship of confidence between the parties.

(See the 1996 *Digest*, para. 815; and, for example, 300th Report, Case No. 1806, para. 125; 316th Report, Case No. 1970, para. 566; 318th Report, Case No. 2020, para. 319; 324th Report, Case No. 2092/2101, para. 732; 325th Report, Case No. 2110, para. 265; 326th Report, Case No. 2122, para. 316; 329th Report, Case No. 2198, para. 679; 332nd Report, Case No. 2263, para. 298; 333rd Report, Case No. 2288, para. 826; and 338th Report, Case No. 2404, para. 1047.)

936. Both employers and trade unions should bargain in good faith and make every effort to come to an agreement, and satisfactory labour relations depend primarily on the attitudes of the parties towards each other and on their mutual confidence.

(See 299th Report, Case No. 1768, para. 107.)

937. The principle that both employers and trade unions should negotiate in good faith and make efforts to reach an agreement means that any unjustified delay in the holding of negotiations should be avoided.

(See the 1996 *Digest*, para. 816; 300th Report, Case No. 1804, para. 322; 316th Report, Case No. 1970, para. 566; 318th Report, Case No. 2009, para. 295, and Case No. 1994, para. 455; 330th Report, Case No. 2186, para. 380; 332nd Report, Case No. 2252, para. 880; 335th Report, Case No. 2311, para. 1148; and 338th Report, Case No. 2404, para. 1047.)

938. While the question as to whether or not one party adopts an amenable or uncompromising attitude towards the other party is a matter for negotiation between the parties, both employers and trade unions should bargain in good faith making every effort to reach an agreement.

(See the 1996 *Digest*, para. 817; 307th Report, Case No. 1873, para. 99; 320th Report, Case No. 2048, para. 720; 324th Report, Case No. 2093, para. 436, and Case No. 2091, para. 890; 325th Report, Case No. 2068, para. 326; 327th Report, Case No. 2127, para. 195; 328th Report, Case No. 2149, para. 580; and 337th Report, Case No. 2337, para. 443.)

939. Agreements should be binding on the parties.

(See the 1996 *Digest*, para. 818; and, for example, 311th Report, Case No. 1944, para. 546; 320th Report, Case No. 2048, para. 720; 323rd Report, Case No. 1960, para. 244; 324th Report, Case No. 1965, para. 801; 325th Report, Case No. 2106, para. 481; 327th Report, Case No. 2138, para. 540; 330th Report, Case No. 2212, para. 745; 331st Report, Case No. 2187, para. 437; 333rd Report, Case No. 2288, para. 826; and 337th Report, Case No. 2362, para. 760.)

940. Mutual respect for the commitment undertaken in collective agreements is an important element of the right to bargain collectively and should be upheld in order to establish labour relations on stable and firm ground.

(See 308th Report, Case No. 1919, para. 325; 323rd Report, Case No. 1960, para. 244; 325th Report, Case No. 2068, para. 329; 328th Report, Case No. 2165, para. 248; and 337th Report, Case No. 2362, para. 760.)

941. Collective bargaining implies both a give-and-take process and a reasonable certainty that negotiated commitments will be honoured, at the very least for the duration of the agreement, such agreement being the result of compromises made by both parties on certain issues, and of certain bargaining demands dropped in order to secure other rights which were given more priority by trade unions and their members. If these rights, for which concessions on other points have been made, can be cancelled unilaterally, there could be neither reasonable expectation of industrial relations stability, nor sufficient reliance on negotiated agreements.

(See 330th Report, Case No. 2171, para. 1048.)

942. A legal provision which allows the employer to modify unilaterally the content of signed collective agreements, or to require that they be renegotiated, is contrary to the principles of collective bargaining.

(See the 1996 *Digest*, para. 848; 330th Report, Case No. 2171, para. 1047; 332nd Report, Case No. 2242, para. 824; and 336th Report, Case No. 2324, para. 278.)

943. Failure to implement a collective agreement, even on a temporary basis, violates the right to bargain collectively, as well as the principle of bargaining in good faith.

(See 327th Report, Case No. 2118, para. 639.)

Collective bargaining with representatives of non-unionized workers

(See also paras. 868, 875 and 876)

944. The Collective Agreements Recommendation, 1951 (No. 91), emphasizes the role of workers' organizations as one of the parties in collective bargaining; it refers to representatives of unorganized workers only when no organization exists.

(See the 1996 *Digest*, para. 785; 299th Report, Case No. 1512, para. 424; 302nd Report, Case No. 1781, para. 253; 308th Report, Case No. 1926, para. 628; 321st Report, Case No. 1926, para. 65; 327th Report, Case No. 2138, para. 545; 331st Report, Case No. 2243, para. 618; 332nd Report, Case No. 2216, para. 909; and 333rd Report, Case No. 2251, para. 977.)

945. The Collective Agreements Recommendation, 1951 (No. 91), provides that: "For the purpose of this Recommendation, the term 'collective agreements' means all agreements in writing regarding working conditions and terms of employment concluded between an employer, a group of employers or one or more employers' organisations, on the one hand, and one or more representative workers' organisations, or, in the absence of such organisations, the representatives of the workers duly elected and authorised by them in accordance with national laws and regulations, on the other." In this respect, the Committee has emphasized that the said Recommendation stresses the role of workers' organizations as one of the parties in collective bargaining. Direct negotiation between the undertaking and its employees, by-passing representative organizations where these exist, might in certain cases be detrimental to the principle that negotiation between employers and organizations of workers should be encouraged and promoted.

(See the 1996 *Digest*, para. 786; 318th Report, Case No. 2018, para. 512; 322nd Report, Case No. 2046, para. 138; 325th Report, Case No. 2107, para. 234; 334th Report, Case No. 2046, para. 345; 337th Report, Case No. 2362, para. 762; and 338th Report, Case No. 2386, para. 1249.)

946. The Workers' Representatives Convention, 1971 (No. 135), and the Collective Bargaining Convention, 1981 (No. 154), also contain explicit provisions guaranteeing that, where there exist in the same undertaking both trade union representatives and elected representatives, appropriate measures are to be taken to ensure that the existence of elected representatives is not used to undermine the position of the trade unions concerned.

(See the 1996 *Digest*, para. 787; 308th Report, Case No. 1934, para. 127; 310th Report, Case No. 1887, para. 104; 325th Report, Case No. 2090, para. 162; and 332nd Report, Case No. 2255, para. 944.)

947. The possibility for staff delegates who represent 10 per cent of the workers to conclude collective agreements with an employer, even where one or more organizations of workers already exist, is not conducive to the development of collective bargaining in the sense of Article 4 of Convention No. 98; in addition, in view of the small percentage required, this possibility could undermine the position of the workers' organizations, contrary to Article 3, paragraph 2, of Convention No. 154.

(See the 1996 *Digest*, para. 788.)

948. Where an offer made directly by the company to its workers is merely a repetition of the proposals previously made to the trade union, which has rejected them, and where negotiations between the company and the trade union are subsequently resumed, the Committee considers that the complainants have not demonstrated in such a situation that there has been a violation of trade union rights.

(See the 1996 *Digest*, para. 791.)

Recognition of the most representative organizations

(See also paras. 356 and 358)

949. The Collective Bargaining Recommendation, 1981 (No. 163), enumerates various means of promoting collective bargaining, including the recognition of representative employers' and workers' organizations (Paragraph 3(a)).

(See the 1996 *Digest*, para. 819.)

950. Systems of collective bargaining with exclusive rights for the most representative trade union and those where it is possible for a number of collective agreements to be concluded by a number of trade unions within a company are both compatible with the principles of freedom of association.

(See 328th Report, Case No. 2136, para. 526; and 329th Report, Case No. 2136, para. 99.)

951. In a case where the right to represent all the employees in the sector in question appeared to have been granted to organizations which were representative only to a limited extent at the national level, the Committee considered that, if national legislation establishes machinery for the representation of the occupational interests of a whole category of workers, this representation should normally lie with the organizations which have the largest membership in the category concerned, and the public authorities should refrain from any intervention that might undermine this principle.

(See the 1996 *Digest*, para. 820.)

952. Employers, including governmental authorities in the capacity of employers, should recognize for collective bargaining purposes the organizations representative of the workers employed by them.

(See the 1996 *Digest*, para. 821; 305th Report, Case No. 1861, para. 251; 311th Report, Case No. 1942, para. 269; 316th Report, Case No. 1996, para. 667; 318th Report, Case No. 1978, para. 217; 333rd Report, Case No. 2301, para. 595, and Case No. 2291, para. 916; and 336th Report, Case No. 1996, para. 93.)

953. Recognition by an employer of the main unions represented in the undertaking, or the most representative of these unions, is the very basis for any procedure for collective bargaining on conditions of employment in the undertaking.

(See the 1996 *Digest*, para. 822; 307th Report, Case No. 1890, para. 373; 333rd Report, Case No. 2301, para. 595, Case No. 2281, para. 635, and Case No. 2291, para. 916; and 338th Report, Case No. 2378, para. 1141.)

954. Employers should recognize for the purposes of collective bargaining organizations that are representative of workers in a particular industry.

(See the 1996 *Digest*, para. 823; 333rd Report, Case No. 1996, para. 98; and 336th Report, Case No. 1996, para. 93.)

955. Where difficulties with regard to the interpretation of rules concerning the election of trade union officers create situations where the employers refuse to negotiate with the union concerned and, more in general, to recognize such a union, problems of compatibility with Convention No. 87 arise.

(See 338th Report, Case No. 2096, para. 273.)

Determination of the trade union(s) entitled to negotiate

956. The requirement of the majority of not only the number of workers, but also of enterprises, in order to be able to conclude a collective agreement on the branch or occupational level could raise problems with regard to the application of Convention No. 98.

(See the 1996 *Digest*, para. 854; 302nd Report, Case No. 1845, para. 514; and 306th Report, Case No. 1906, para. 553.)

957. For a trade union at the branch level to be able to negotiate a collective agreement at the enterprise level, it should be sufficient for the trade union to establish that it is sufficiently representative at the enterprise level.

(See 302nd Report, Case No. 1845, para. 516.)

958. In relation to a provision under which a majority union in an enterprise cannot engage in collective bargaining if it is not affiliated to a representative federation, the Committee recalled the importance to be attached to the right to bargain collectively of the majority union in an enterprise.

(See 305th Report, Case No. 1765, para. 99.)

959. The competent authorities should, in all cases, have the power to proceed to an objective verification of any claim by a union that it represents the majority of the workers in an undertaking, provided that such a claim appears to be plausible. If the union concerned is found to be the majority union, the authorities should take appropriate conciliatory measures to obtain the employer's recognition of that union for collective bargaining purposes.

(See the 1996 *Digest*, paras. 824 and 835; 305th Report, Case No. 1861, para. 251; 309th Report, Case No. 1852, para. 337; 311th Report, Case No. 1873, para. 108; 316th Report, Case No. 1996, para. 667; 332nd Report, Case No. 2250, para. 281, and Case No. 2187, para. 726; 333rd Report, Case No. 2281, para. 635; 334th Report, Case No. 2316, para. 504; and 338th Report, Case No. 2378, para. 1141.)

960. If a union other than that which concluded an agreement has in the meantime become the majority union and requests the cancellation of this agreement, the authorities, notwithstanding the agreement, should make appropriate representations to the employer regarding the recognition of this union.

(See the 1996 *Digest*, para. 825; and 330th Report, Case No. 2229, para. 955.)

961. If the authorities have the power to hold polls for determining the majority union which is to represent the workers for the purposes of collective bargaining, such polls should always be held in cases where there are doubts as to which union the workers wish to represent them.

(See the 1996 *Digest*, paras. 826 and 837; 323rd Report, Case No. 2006, para. 428; and 329th Report, Case No. 2175, para. 697.)

962. Where, under the system in force, the most representative union enjoys preferential or exclusive bargaining rights, decisions concerning the most representative organization should be made by virtue of objective and pre-established criteria so as to avoid any opportunities for partiality or abuse.

(See the 1996 *Digest*, para. 827; 307th Report, Case No. 1890, para. 373; and 328th Report, Case No. 2136, para. 525.)

963. While the public authorities have the right to decide whether they will negotiate at the regional or national level, the workers, whether negotiating at the regional or national level, should be entitled to choose the organization which shall represent them in the negotiations.

(See the 1996 *Digest*, para. 828.)

964. In a case in which, in order to claim to be representative and have the capacity to be the sole signatory to collective agreements, the organizations in question needed to demonstrate national and multi-sectoral representativeness, the Committee considered that the combination of these requirements raises problems with regard to the principles of freedom of association in terms of representativeness. Their application could have the consequence of preventing a representative union in a given sector from being the sole signatory to the collective agreements resulting from the collective negotiations in which it has participated.

(See 324th Report, Case No. 1980, para. 669.)

965. The association of an organization with the negotiation process, in order to be fully effective and real, implies that the organization should be able to sign, and where necessary to be the sole signatory to, resulting agreements when it wishes, provided that its representativeness in the sector has been objectively demonstrated.

(See 324th Report, Case No. 1980, para. 679.)

966. Participation in collective bargaining and in signing the resulting agreements necessarily implies independence of the signatories from the employer or employers' organizations, as well as from the authorities. It is only when their independence is established that trade union organizations may have access to bargaining.

(See 324th Report, Case No. 1980, para. 671.)

967. In order to determine whether an organization has the capacity to be the sole signatory to collective agreements, two criteria should be applied: representativeness and independence. The determination of which organizations meet these criteria should be carried out by a body offering every guarantee of independence and objectivity.

(See 324th Report, Case No. 1980, para. 672.)

968. A minimum membership requirement of 1,000 set out in the law for the granting of exclusive bargaining rights might be liable to deprive workers in small bargaining units or who are dispersed over wide geographical areas of the right to form organizations capable of fully exercising trade union activities, contrary to the principles of freedom of association.

(See the 1996 *Digest*, para. 832; 310th Report, Case No. 1996, para. 662; and 338th Report, Case No. 2378, para. 1149.)

969. It is not necessarily incompatible with Convention No. 87 to provide for the certification of the most representative union in a given unit as the exclusive bargaining agent for that unit. This is the case, however, only if a number of safeguards are provided. The Committee has pointed out that in several countries in which the procedure of certifying unions as exclusive bargaining agents has been established, it has been regarded as essential that such safeguards should include the following: (a) certification to be made by an independent body; (b) the representative organizations to be chosen by a majority vote of the employees in the unit concerned; (c) the right of an organization which fails to secure a sufficiently large number of votes to ask for a new election after a stipulated period; (d) the right of an organization other than the certificated organizations to demand a new election after a fixed period, often 12 months, has elapsed since the previous election.

(See the 1996 *Digest*, para. 834; 300th Report, Case No. 1741, para. 55; 302nd Report, Case No 1826, para. 407; 328th Report, Case No. 2136, para. 525; and 332nd Report, Case No. 2252, para. 879.)

970. If there is a change in the relative strength of unions competing for a preferential right or the power to represent workers exclusively for collective bargaining purposes, then it is desirable that it should be possible to review the factual bases on which that right or power is granted. In the absence of such a possibility, a majority of the workers concerned might be represented by a union which, for an unduly long period, could be prevented – either in fact or in law – from organizing its administration and activities with a view to fully furthering and defending the interests of its members.

(See the 1996 *Digest*, para. 836; 329th Report, Case No. 2175, para. 696; and 330th Report, Case No. 2229, para. 955.)

971. In order to encourage the harmonious development of collective bargaining and to avoid disputes, it should always be the practice to follow, where they exist, the procedures laid down for the designation of the most representative unions for collective bargaining purposes when it is not clear by which unions the workers wish to be represented. In the absence of such procedures, the authorities, where appropriate, should examine the possibility of laying down objective rules in this respect.

(See the 1996 *Digest*, para. 838; and 311th Report, Case No. 1942, para. 269.)

972. In one case a Bill concerning negotiating committees for the public service provided for a count to be taken of the paid-up membership of the trade unions in order to determine their representative character, and for a verification of such representative character to be carried out by a board presided over by a magistrate (every six years or at any time at the request of a union). The Committee considered that although, in general, a vote might be a desirable means of ascertaining how representative trade unions are, the inquiries provided for in the Bill seemed to offer strong guarantees of secrecy and impartiality which are indispensable in such an operation.

(See the 1996 *Digest*, para. 839.)

973. In one case where the government, in the light of national conditions, had restricted the right to engage in collective bargaining to the two most representative national unions of workers in general, the Committee considered that this should not prevent a union representing the majority of workers of a certain category from furthering the interests of its members. The Committee recommended that the Government be requested to examine the measures that it might take under national conditions to afford this union the possibility of being associated with the collective bargaining process so as to permit it adequately to represent and defend the collective interests of its members.

(See the 1996 *Digest*, para. 843.)

Rights of minority unions

(See also paras. 326, 358 and 359)

974. The Committee has recalled the position of the Committee of Experts on the Application of Conventions and Recommendations that, where the law of a country draws a distinction between the most representative trade union and other trade unions, such a system should not have the effect of preventing minority unions from functioning and at least having the right to make representations on behalf of their members and to represent them in cases of individual grievances.

(See the 1996 *Digest*, para. 829.)

975. The granting of exclusive rights to the most representative organization should not mean that the existence of other unions to which certain involved workers might wish to belong is prohibited. Minority organizations should be permitted to carry out their activities and at least to have the right to speak on behalf of their members and to represent them.

(See 300th Report, Case No. 1741, para. 55.)

976. Where, under a system for nominating an exclusive bargaining agent, there is no union representing the required percentage to be so designated, collective bargaining rights should be granted to all the unions in this unit, at least on behalf of their own members.

(See the 1996 *Digest*, para. 830.)

977. If there is no union covering more than 50 per cent of the workers in a unit, collective bargaining rights should nevertheless be granted to the unions in this unit, at least on behalf of their own members.

(See the 1996 *Digest*, para. 833; 302nd Report, Case No. 1817, para. 321; 316th Report, Case No. 1996, para. 663; 333rd Report, Case No. 2301, para. 595; 337th Report, Case No. 2118, para. 85; and 338th Report, Case No. 2303, para. 337.)

978. With regard to a provision that stipulates that a collective agreement may be negotiated only by a trade union representing an absolute majority of the workers in an enterprise, the Committee considered that the provision does not promote collective bargaining in the sense of Article 4 of Convention No. 98 and it invited the government to take steps, in consultation with the organizations concerned, to amend the provision in question so as to ensure that when no trade union represents the absolute majority of the workers, the organizations may jointly negotiate a collective agreement applicable to the enterprise or the bargaining unit, or at least conclude a collective agreement on behalf of their members.

(See the 1996 *Digest*, para. 831; 316th Report, Case No. 1996, para. 663; 335th Report, Case No. 2303, para. 1373; and 338th Report, Case No. 2386, para. 1248.)

979. The requirement established by law that a union has to establish its authority for all the workers it claims to represent in negotiations for a collective employment contract is excessive and in contradiction with freedom of association principles as it may be applied so as to constitute an impediment to the right of a workers' organization to represent its members.

(See 1996 *Digest*, para. 840.)

980. In so far as the persons who conclude collective agreements are trade union representatives, the requirement that they be approved by an absolute majority of the workers involved may constitute an obstacle to collective bargaining which is incompatible with the provisions of Article 4 of Convention No. 98.

(See the 1996 *Digest*, para. 841.)

Determination of employers' organizations entitled to negotiate

981. Employers should be able to choose the organization which they wish to represent their interests in the collective bargaining process.

(See 327th Report, Case No. 2146, para. 897.)

982. The principle of representation for collective bargaining purposes cannot be applied in an equitable fashion in respect of employers' associations if membership in the Chamber of Commerce is compulsory and the Chamber of Commerce is empowered to bargain collectively with trade unions.

(See 327th Report, Case No. 2146, para. 896; and 332nd Report, Case No. 2233, para. 641.)

983. Granting collective bargaining rights to the Chamber of Commerce which is created by law and to which affiliation is compulsory impairs the employers' freedom of choice in respect of the organization to represent their interests in collective bargaining.

(See 327th Report, Case No. 2146, para. 897.)

Representation of organizations in the collective bargaining process

984. Workers' organizations must themselves be able to choose which delegates will represent them in collective bargaining without the interference of the public authorities.

(See 307th Report, Case No. 1910, para. 174.)

985. Excessively strict prescriptions on such matters as the composition of the representatives of the parties in the process of collective bargaining may limit its effectiveness and this is a matter which should be determined by the parties themselves.

(See 310th Report, Case No. 1931, para. 504.)

986. Organizations of employers and workers should have the right to choose, without any hindrance, the persons from whom they wish to seek assistance during collective bargaining and dispute settlement procedures.

(See 306th Report, Case No. 1865, para. 331.)

987. With regard to the ban on third party intervention in the settlement of disputes, the Committee is of the opinion that such an exclusion constitutes a serious restriction on the free functioning of trade unions, since it deprives them of assistance from advisers.

(See the 1996 *Digest*, para. 850.)

Level of bargaining

(See also paras. 336 and 963)

988. According to the principle of free and voluntary collective bargaining embodied in Article 4 of Convention No. 98, the determination of the bargaining level is essentially a matter to be left to the discretion of the parties and, consequently, the level of negotiation should not be imposed by law, by decision of the administrative authority or by the case-law of the administrative labour authority.

(See the 1996 *Digest*, para. 851; 302nd Report, Case No. 1845, para. 514; 306th Report, Case No. 1906, para. 553; 308th Report, Case No. 1926, para. 629; 321st Report, Case No. 1975, para. 117; 325th Report, Case No. 2099, para. 193; 338th Report, Case No. 2326, para. 448, Case No. 2403, para. 600, and Case No. 2375, para. 1226.)

989. The determination of the bargaining level is essentially a matter to be left to the discretion of the parties. Thus, the Committee does not consider the refusal by employers to bargain at a particular level as an infringement of freedom of association.

(See the 1996 *Digest*, para. 852; and 321st Report, Case No. 1975, para. 117.)

990. Legislation should not constitute an obstacle to collective bargaining at the industry level.

(See the 1996 *Digest*, para. 853.)

991. The best procedure for safeguarding the independence of the parties involved in collective bargaining is to allow them to decide by mutual agreement the level at which bargaining should take place. Nevertheless, it appears that, in many countries, this question is determined by a body that is independent of the parties themselves. The Committee considers that in such cases the body concerned should be truly independent.

(See the 1996 *Digest*, para. 855; and 338th Report, Case No. 2375, para. 1226.)

Restrictions on the principle of free and voluntary bargaining

A. Compulsory arbitration

(See also paras. 566 and 567)

992. The imposition of a compulsory arbitration procedure if the parties do not reach agreement on a draft collective agreement raises problems in relation to the application of Convention No. 98.

(See the 1996 *Digest*, para. 861; 332nd Report, Case No. 2261, para. 665; and 333rd Report, Case No. 2281, para. 631.)

993. Provisions which establish that, failing agreement between the parties, the points at issue in collective bargaining must be settled by the arbitration of the authority are not in conformity with the principle of voluntary negotiation contained in Article 4 of Convention No. 98.

(See the 1996 *Digest*, paras. 518 and 862; and 338th Report, Case No. 2329, para. 1276.)

994. Recourse to compulsory arbitration in cases where the parties do not reach agreement through collective bargaining is permissible only in the context of essential services in the strict sense of the term (i.e. services the interruption of which would endanger the life, personal safety or health of the whole or part of the population).

(See the 1996 *Digest*, para. 860; 320th Report, Case No. 2025, para. 408; 327th Report, Case No. 2145, para. 305; 332nd Report, Case No. 2261, para. 665; and 335th Report, Case No. 2305, para. 506.)

995. In order to gain and retain the parties' confidence, any arbitration system should be truly independent and the outcomes of arbitration should not be predetermined by legislative criteria.

(See 299th Report, Case No. 1768, para. 110.)

996. In certain cases, the Committee has regretted that the government has not given priority to collective bargaining as a means of regulating employment conditions in a non-essential service, but rather that it felt compelled to have recourse to compulsory arbitration in the dispute in question.

(See the 1996 *Digest*, para. 864.)

997. The use of collective bargaining to settle problems of rationalization in undertakings and improve their efficiency may yield valuable results for both the workers and the undertakings. Nevertheless, if this type of collective bargaining has to follow a special pattern which imposes bargaining on the trade union organizations on those aspects determined by the labour authority and stipulates that the period of negotiation shall not exceed a specified time; and failing agreement between the parties, the points at issue shall be submitted to arbitration by the said authority, such a statutory system does not conform to the principle of voluntary negotiation which is the guiding principle of Article 4 of Convention No. 98.

(See the 1996 *Digest*, paras. 847 and 865.)

B. Intervention by the authorities in collective bargaining

(See also paras. 919, 1086 and 1087)

(a) General principles

998. In cases of government intervention to restrict collective bargaining, the Committee has considered that it is not its role to express a view on the soundness of the economic arguments used by the Government to justify its position or on the measures it has adopted. However, it is for the Committee to express its views on whether, in taking such action, the Government has gone beyond what the Committee has considered to be acceptable restrictions that might be placed temporarily on free collective bargaining

(See 299th Report, Case No. 1800, para. 180, Case No. 1733, para. 241, and Case No. 1802, para. 275; and 300th Report, Case No. 1806, para. 120.)

999. In any case, any limitation on collective bargaining on the part of the authorities should be preceded by consultations with the workers' and employers' organizations in an effort to obtain their agreement.

(See the 1996 *Digest*, para. 884; 330th Report, Case No. 2194, para. 791; and 335th Report, Case No. 2293, para. 1237.)

1000. In a case in which the government had, on many occasions over the past decade, resorted to statutory limitations on collective bargaining, the Committee pointed out that repeated recourse to statutory restrictions on collective bargaining could, in the long term, only prove harmful and destabilize labour relations, as it deprived workers of a fundamental right and means of furthering and defending their economic and social interests.

(See the 1996 *Digest*, para. 885.)

(b) The drafting of collective agreements

1001. State bodies should refrain from intervening to alter the content of freely concluded collective agreements.

(See 299th Report, Case No. 1733, para. 243.)

1002. The intervention by a representative of the public authorities in the drafting of collective agreements, unless it consists exclusively of technical aid, is inconsistent with the spirit of Article 4 of Convention No. 98.

(See the 1996 *Digest*, para. 866.)

1003. The Committee recognizes that there comes a time in bargaining where, after protracted and fruitless negotiations, the authorities might be justified in stepping in when it is obvious that the deadlock in bargaining will not be broken without some initiative on their part.

(See 299th Report, Case No. 1768, para. 109; and 330th Report, Case No. 2170, para. 888.)

1004. With reference to the above principle, the Committee has however expressed the view that the mere existence of a deadlock in a collective bargaining process is not in itself a sufficient ground to justify an intervention from the public authorities to impose arbitration on the parties to the labour dispute. Any intervention by the public authorities in collective disputes must be consistent with the principle of free and voluntary negotiations; this implies that the bodies appointed for the settlement of disputes between the parties to collective bargaining should be independent and recourse to these bodies should be on a voluntary basis, except where there is an acute national crisis.

(See 330th Report, Case No. 2170, para. 888.)

1005. Where intervention by the public authorities is essentially for the purpose of ensuring that the negotiating parties subordinate their interests to the national economic policy pursued by the government, irrespective of whether they agree with that policy or not, this is not compatible with the generally accepted principles that workers' and employers' organizations should enjoy the right freely to organize their activities and to formulate their programmes, that the public authorities should refrain from any interference which would restrict this right or impede the lawful exercise thereof, and that the law of the land should not be such as to impair or be so applied as to impair the enjoyment of such right.

(See the 1996 *Digest*, para. 867.)

1006. Legislation which permits the refusal to approve a collective agreement on grounds of errors of pure form is not in conflict with the principle of voluntary negotiation. If this legislation, however, implies that the filing of a collective agreement may be refused on grounds such as incompatibility with the general policy of the government, it would amount to a requirement that prior approval be obtained before a collective agreement can come into force.

(See the 1996 *Digest*, para. 868.)

1007. In a case in which, in the context of a stabilization policy, the provisions of collective agreements relating to remuneration were suspended (in the public and private sectors), the Committee emphasized that collective agreements which were in force should be applied fully (unless otherwise agreed by the parties).

(See the 1996 *Digest*, para. 883; and 318th Report, Case No. 1976, para. 613.)

1008. The suspension or derogation by decree – without the agreement of the parties – of collective agreements freely entered into by the parties violates the principle of free and voluntary collective bargaining established in Article 4 of Convention No. 98. If a government wishes the clauses of a collective agreement to be brought into line with the economic policy of the country, it should attempt to persuade the parties to take account voluntarily of such considerations, without imposing on them the renegotiation of the collective agreements in force.

(See the 1996 *Digest*, para. 876; 307th Report, Case No. 1899, para. 84; and 323rd Report, Case No. 2089, para. 491.)

1009. While the Committee appreciates that the introduction of wage restraint measures must be timed in order to obtain the maximum impact on the economic situation, it nevertheless considers that the interruption of already negotiated contracts is not in conformity with the principles of free collective bargaining because such contracts should be respected.

(See the 1996 *Digest*, para. 877; 299th Report, Case No. 1802, para. 279, and Case No. 1807, para. 356.)

1010. The harmonious development of labour relations would be facilitated if the public authorities, when dealing with the problems concerning the workers' loss of purchasing power, adopted solutions which did not involve modifications of agreements without the consent of both parties.

(See the 1996 *Digest*, para. 880; and 332nd Report, Case No. 2187, para. 720.)

1011. The public authorities should promote free collective bargaining and not prevent the application of freely concluded collective agreements, particularly when these authorities are acting as employers or have assumed responsibility for the application of agreements by countersigning them.

(See 299th Report, Case No. 1807, para. 356.)

(c) Administrative approval of freely concluded collective agreements and the national economic policy

1012. Making the validity of collective agreements signed by the parties subject to the approval of these agreements by the authorities is contrary to the principles of collective bargaining and of Convention No. 98.

(See 320th Report, Case No. 2030, para. 596.)

1013. Legal provisions which make collective agreements subject to the approval of the ministry of labour for reasons of economic policy, so that employers' and workers' organizations are not able to fix wages freely, are not in conformity with Article 4 of Convention No. 98 respecting the promotion and full development of machinery for voluntary collective negotiations.

(See the 1996 *Digest*, para. 869.)

1014. The requirement of Cabinet approval for negotiated agreements and of conformity with the policy and guidelines unilaterally set for the public sector are not in full conformity with the principles of freedom of association, which apply to all workers covered by Convention No. 98.

(See the 1996 *Digest*, para. 870.)

1015. The requirement of previous approval by a government authority to make an agreement valid might discourage the use of voluntary collective bargaining between employers and workers for the settlement of conditions of employment. Even though a refusal by the authorities to give their approval may sometimes be the subject of an appeal to the courts, the system of previous administrative authorization in itself is contrary to the whole system of voluntary negotiation.

(See the 1996 *Digest*, para. 871; and 310th Report, Case No. 1930, para. 346.)

1016. Objections by the Committee to the requirement that prior approval of collective agreements be obtained from the government do not signify that ways could not be found of persuading the parties to collective bargaining to have regard voluntarily in their negotiations to considerations relating to the economic or social policy of the government and the safeguarding of the general interest. But to achieve this, it is necessary first of all that the objectives to be recognized as being in the general interest should have been widely discussed by all parties on a national scale through a consultative body in accordance with the principle laid down in the Consultation (Industrial and National Levels) Recommendation, 1960 (No. 113). It might also be possible to envisage a procedure whereby the attention of the parties could be drawn, in certain cases, to the considerations of general interest which might call for further examination of the terms of agreement on their part. However, in this connection, persuasion is always to be preferred to constraint. First, instead of making the validity of collective agreements subject to governmental approval, it might be provided that every collective agreement filed with the ministry of labour would normally come into force a reasonable length of time after being filed; if the public authority considered that the terms of the proposed agreement were manifestly in conflict with the economic policy objectives recognized as being desirable in the general interest, the case could be submitted for advice and recommendation to an appropriate consultative body, it being understood, however, that the final decision in the matter rested with the parties to the agreement.

(See the 1996 *Digest*, para. 872.)

1017. The requirement of ministerial approval before a collective agreement can come into effect is not in full conformity with the principles of voluntary negotiation laid down in Convention No. 98. In cases where certain collective agreements contain terms which appear to conflict with considerations of general interest, it might be possible to envisage a procedure whereby the attention of the parties could be drawn to these considerations to enable them to examine the matter further, it being understood that the final decision thereon should rest with the parties. The setting up of a system of this kind would be in conformity with the principle that trade unions should enjoy the right to endeavour to improve, by means of collective bargaining, the conditions of living and of work of their members and that the authorities should refrain from any interference which might limit this right.

(See the 1996 *Digest*, para. 873.)

1018. A provision which establishes as a ground for refusing approval the existence in a collective agreement of a clause which interferes with “the right reserved to the State to coordinate and have the overall control of the economic life of the nation” involves the risk of seriously restricting the voluntary negotiation of collective agreements.

(See the 1996 *Digest*, para. 874.)

(d) Administrative interventions which require the renegotiation of existing collective agreements

1019. Repeated recourse to legislative restrictions on collective bargaining can only, in the long term, prejudice and destabilize the labour relations climate, if the legislator frequently intervenes to suspend or terminate the exercise of rights recognized for unions and their members. Moreover, this may have a detrimental effect on workers’ interests in unionization, since members and potential members could consider useless joining an organization the main objective of which is to represent its members in collective bargaining, if the results of such bargaining are constantly cancelled by law.

(See the 1996 *Digest*, para. 875; 330th Report, Case No. 2196, para. 304; and 336th Report, Case No. 2324, para. 283.)

1020. Legislation which obliges the parties to renegotiate acquired trade union rights is contrary to the principles of collective bargaining.

(See the 1996 *Digest*, para. 878.)

1021. In examining allegations of the annulment and forced renegotiation of collective agreements for reasons of economic crisis, the Committee was of the view that legislation which required the renegotiation of agreements in force was contrary to the principles of free and voluntary collective bargaining enshrined in Convention No. 98 and insisted that the government should have endeavoured to ensure that the renegotiation of collective agreements in force resulted from an agreement reached between the parties concerned.

(See the 1996 *Digest*, para. 879; and 307th Report, Case No. 1887, para. 67.)

1022. It would not be objectionable if, once it became clear that the implementation of an agreement concerning pension funds dependent on the State budget would be practically impossible, and after having exhausted all good faith efforts to achieve the implementation of the agreement, the Government undertook concrete efforts to renegotiate the agreement in order to find a solution that would be commonly acceptable to the parties.

(See 330th Report, Case No. 2212, para. 746.)

(e) Compulsory extension of the period for which collective agreements are in force

1023. Referring to an Act on the extension of collective agreements which followed other government interventions in collective bargaining, the Committee pointed out that such action, involving as it did statutory intervention in the collective bargaining process, should only be taken in cases of emergency and for brief periods of time. The Committee hoped that in future no similar measures would be taken to interfere with free collective bargaining or to restrict the right of workers to defend their economic and social interests through industrial action.

(See the 1996 *Digest*, para. 881.)

(f) Restrictions imposed by the authorities on future collective bargaining

(See also para. 918)

1024. If, as part of its stabilization policy, a government considers that wage rates cannot be settled freely through collective bargaining, such a restriction should be imposed as an exceptional measure and only to the extent that is necessary, without exceeding a reasonable period, and it should be accompanied by adequate safeguards to protect workers' living standards.

(See the 1996 *Digest*, para. 882; 299th Report, Case No. 1733, para. 242; 300th Report, Case No. 1806, para. 121; 306th Report, Case No. 1882, para. 432; 324th Report, Case No. 2060, para. 524; 330th Report, Case No. 2194, para. 789; 332nd Report, Case No. 2132, para. 104; and 335th Report, Case No. 2293, para. 1235.)

1025. A three-year period of limited collective bargaining on remuneration within the context of a policy of economic stabilization constitutes a substantial restriction, and the legislation in question should cease producing effects at the latest at the dates mentioned in the Act, or indeed earlier if the fiscal and economic situation improves.

(See the 1996 *Digest*, para. 886.)

1026. Restraints on collective bargaining for three years are too long.

(See the 1996 *Digest*, para. 1996; and 330th Report, Case No. 2166, para. 293.)

1027. Where wage restraint measures are taken by a government to impose financial controls, care should be taken to ensure that collective bargaining on non-monetary matters can be pursued and that unions and their members can fully exercise their normal trade union activity.

(See the 1996 *Digest*, para. 888.)

1028. The Committee is not mandated to decide on acceptable amounts of financial restraint, but where possible these measures should only extend to the sectors actually facing an emergency situation.

(See the 1996 *Digest*, para. 889; and 325th Report, Case No. 2106, para. 479.)

1029. As regards the obligation for future collective agreements to respect productivity criteria, the Committee recalled that if, within the context of a stabilization policy, a government may consider for compelling reasons that wage rates cannot be fixed freely by collective bargaining (in the present case the fixing of wage scales excludes index-linking mechanisms and must be adjusted to increases in productivity), such a restriction should be imposed as an exceptional measure and only to the extent necessary, without exceeding a reasonable period and it should be accompanied by adequate safeguards to protect workers' living standards. This principle is all the more important because successive restrictions may lead to a prolonged suspension of wage negotiations, which goes against the principle of encouraging voluntary collective negotiation.

(See the 1996 *Digest*, para. 890; and 332nd Report, Case No. 2250, para. 949.)

(g) Restrictions on clauses to index wages to the cost of living

1030. Legislative provisions prohibiting the negotiation of wage increases beyond the level of the increase in the cost of living are contrary to the principle of voluntary collective bargaining embodied in Convention No. 98; such a limitation would be admissible only if it remained within the context of an economic stabilization policy, and even then only as an exceptional measure and only to the extent necessary, without exceeding a reasonable period of time.

(See the 1996 *Digest*, para. 891.)

1031. In a case where government measures had fixed the base reference for the indexation of wages, whereas the parties had fixed another indexation system, the Committee recalled that the intervention of a government in areas which traditionally have always been negotiated freely by the parties could call into question the principle of free collective bargaining recognized by Article 4 of Convention No. 98, if it is not accompanied by certain guarantees and in particular if its period of application is not limited in time.

(See the 1996 *Digest*, para. 892.)

1032. The determination of criteria to be applied by the parties in fixing wages (cost-of-living increases, productivity, etc.) is a matter for negotiation between the parties and it is not for the Committee to express an opinion on the criteria that should be applied in fixing pay adjustments.

(See 310th Report, Case No. 1946, para. 268.)

(h) Budgetary powers and collective bargaining

1033. The reservation of budgetary powers to the legislative authority should not have the effect of preventing compliance with collective agreements entered into by, or on behalf of, that authority.

(See the 1996 *Digest*, para. 894; and 330th Report, Case No. 2212, para. 745.)

1034. The Committee has considered that the exercise of financial powers by the public authorities in a manner that prevents or limits compliance with collective agreements already entered into by public bodies is not consistent with the principle of free collective bargaining.

(See the 1996 *Digest*, para. 895; and 325th Report, Case No. 2106, para. 481.)

1035. A fair and reasonable compromise should be sought between the need to preserve as far as possible the autonomy of the bargaining parties, on the one hand, and measures which must be taken by governments to overcome their budgetary difficulties, on the other.

(See 297th Report, Case No. 1758, para. 229; and 299th Report, Case No. 1800, para. 184.)

1036. In so far as the income of public enterprises and bodies depends on state budgets, it would not be objectionable – after wide discussion and consultation between the concerned employers' and employees' organizations in a system having the confidence of the parties – for wage ceilings to be fixed in state budgetary laws, and neither would it be a matter for criticism that the Ministry of Finance prepare a report prior to the commencement of collective bargaining with a view to ensuring respect of such ceilings.

(See the 1996 *Digest*, paras. 896 and 898; 318th Report, Case No. 1993, para. 590; 325th Report, Case No. 2068, para. 325, and Case No. 2106, para. 486; 327th Report, Case No. 1865, para. 501; and 330th Report, Case No. 2166/2173/2180/2196, para. 290.)

1037. With regard to the requirement that draft collective agreements in the public sector must be accompanied by a preliminary opinion on their financial implications issued by the financial authorities, and not by the public body or enterprise concerned, the Committee noted that it was aware that collective bargaining in the public sector called for verification of the available resources in the various public bodies or undertakings, that such resources were dependent on state budgets and that the period of duration of collective agreements in the public sector did not always coincide with the duration of the State Budgetary Law – a situation which could give rise to difficulties. The body issuing the above opinion could also formulate recommendations in line with government economic policy or seek to ensure that the collective bargaining process did not give rise to any discrimination in the working conditions of the employees in different public institutions or undertakings. Provision should therefore be made for a mechanism which ensured that, in the collective bargaining process in the public sector, both trade union organizations and the employers and their associations were consulted and could express their points of view to the authority responsible for assessing the financial consequences of draft collective agreements. Nevertheless, notwithstanding any opinion submitted by the financial authorities, the parties to collective bargaining should be able to conclude an agreement freely.

(See the 1996 *Digest*, paras. 897 and 898; 306th Report, Case No. 1878, para. 537; 318th Report, Case No. 1993, para. 590; 325th Report, Case No. 2106, para. 482; 327th Report, Case No. 1865, para. 501; and 330th Report, Case No. 2166/2173/2180/2196, para. 290.)

1038. The Committee has endorsed the point of view expressed by the Committee of Experts in its 1994 General Survey:

> While the principle of autonomy of the parties to collective bargaining is valid as regards public servants covered by Convention No. 151, the special characteristics of the public service described above require some flexibility in its application. Thus, in the view of the Committee, legislative provisions which allow Parliament or the competent budgetary authority to set upper and lower limits for wage negotiations or to establish an overall "budgetary package" within which the parties may negotiate monetary or standard-setting clauses (for example: reduction of working hours or other arrangements, varying wage increases according to levels of remuneration, fixing a timetable for readjustment provisions) or those which give the financial authorities the right to participate in collective bargaining alongside the direct employer, are compatible with the Convention, provided they leave a *significant* role to collective bargaining. It is essential, however, that workers and their organizations be able to participate fully and meaningfully in designing this overall bargaining framework, which implies in particular that they must have access to all the financial, budgetary and other data enabling them to assess the situation on the basis of the facts.
>
> This is not the case of legislative provisions which, on the grounds of the economic situation of a country, impose unilaterally, for example, a specific percentage increase and rule out any possibility of bargaining, in particular by prohibiting the exercise of means of pressure subject to the application of severe sanctions. The Committee is aware that collective bargaining in the public sector "calls for verification of the available resources in the various public bodies or undertakings, that such resources are dependent on state budgets and that the period of duration of collective agreements in the public sector does not always coincide with the duration of budgetary laws – a situation which can give rise to difficulties". The Committee therefore takes full account of the serious financial and budgetary difficulties facing governments, particularly during periods of prolonged and widespread economic stagnation. However, it considers that the authorities should give preference as far as possible to collective bargaining in determining the conditions of employment of public servants; where the circumstances rule this out, measures of this kind should be limited in time and protect the standard of living of the workers who are the most affected. In other words, a fair and reasonable compromise should be sought between the need to preserve as far as possible the autonomy of the parties to bargaining, on the one hand, and measures which must be taken by governments to overcome their budgetary difficulties, on the other.

(See the 1996 *Digest*, para. 899; and, for example, 299th Report, Case No. 1561, para. 38; 300th Report, Case No. 1806, para. 122; 306th Report, Case No. 1859, para. 238; 307th Report, Case No. 1873, para. 98; 308th Report, Case No. 1921, para. 571; 318th Report, Case No. 1999, para. 168; 329th Report, Case No. 2123, para. 531; 330th Report, Case No. 2166/2173/2180/2196, para. 290; 333rd Report, Case No. 2288, para. 826; and 337th Report, Case No. 2356, para. 704.)

1039. It is acceptable that in the bargaining process the employer side representing the public administration seek the opinion of the Ministry of Finances or an economic and financial body that verifies the financial impact of draft collective agreements.

(See 306th Report, Case No. 1878, para. 537; and 318th Report, Case No. 1993, para. 590.)

1040. In context of economic stabilization, priority should be given to collective bargaining as a means of determining the employment conditions of public servants, rather than adopting legislation to restrain wages in the public sector.

(See the 1996 *Digest*, para. 900; 331st Report, Case No. 2187, para. 438; and 337th Report, Case No. 2349, para. 406.)

1041. The Committee deplored that, despite its previous calls to the government to refrain from intervening in the collective bargaining process, it once again failed to give priority to collective bargaining as a means of negotiating a change in the employment conditions of public servants, and that the legislative authority felt compelled to adopt the Public Sector Reduced Work-week and Compensation Management Act, particularly in view of the fact that this Act followed immediately the previous legislative intervention which had frozen public sector wages for one year.

(See the 1996 *Digest*, para. 901.)

1042. Even though the principle of the autonomy of the parties in the collective bargaining process remains valid with regard to public servants and public employees covered by Convention No. 151, this may be applied with a certain degree of flexibility given the particular characteristics of the public administration, while at the same time, the authorities should, to the greatest possible extent, promote the collective bargaining process as a mechanism for determining the conditions of employment of public servants.

(See 337th Report, Case No. 2331, para. 594; and Case No. 2356, para. 704.)

1043. A system in which public employees may only present "appropriate written representations" which are non-negotiable, in particular with regard to conditions of employment, which may only be determined by the authorities who have exclusive competence in this matter, is not in conformity with Conventions Nos. 98, 151 and 154.

(See 337th Report, Case No. 2331, para. 594.)

(i) Other forms of intervention by the authorities

1044. In one case it was alleged that Article 4 of Convention No. 98 had been infringed because, when lengthy negotiations had reached a deadlock, the Government gave effect to the claims of the union by an enactment. The Committee pointed out that such an argument would, if carried to its logical conclusion, mean that, in nearly every country where the workers were not sufficiently strongly organized to obtain a minimum wage, and that this standard was prescribed by law, Article 4 of Convention No. 98 would be infringed. Such an argument would clearly be untenable. If a government, however, adopted a systematic policy of granting by law what the unions could not obtain by negotiation, the situation might call for reappraisal.

(See the 1996 *Digest*, para. 902.)

1045. In a case in which general wage increases in the private sector were established by law, which were added to the increases agreed upon in collective agreements, the Committee drew to the Government's attention the fact that the harmonious development of industrial relations would be promoted if the public authorities, in tackling problems relating to the loss of the workers' purchasing power, were to adopt solutions which did not entail modifications of what had been agreed upon between workers' and employers' organizations without the consent of both parties.

(See the 1996 *Digest*, para. 903.)

Time-limits for bargaining

1046. In one case where the legislation contained a provision whereby a time-limit of up to 105 days was fixed, within which employers had to reply to proposals by the workers, and a time-limit of six months fixed within which collective agreements had to be concluded (which could be prolonged once for a further six months), the Committee expressed the view that it would be desirable to reduce these periods in order to encourage and promote the development of voluntary negotiation, particularly in view of the fact that the workers in the country in question were unable to take strike action.

(See the 1996 *Digest*, para. 904.)

Duration of collective agreements

1047. The duration of collective agreements is primarily a matter for the parties involved, but if government action is being considered any legislation should reflect tripartite agreement.

(See 320th Report, Case No. 2047, para. 361.)

1048. The Committee has considered that amendments removing the upper limit on the term of collective agreements, and their effect on the time periods for assessing representativity, collective bargaining, change of union allegiance and affiliation, do not constitute a violation of the principles of freedom of association. However, the Committee is aware that, at least potentially, the possibility of concluding collective agreements for a very long term entails a risk that a union with borderline representativity may be tempted to consolidate its position by accepting an agreement for a longer term to the detriment of the workers' genuine interests.

(See the 1996 *Digest*, para. 905; and 320th Report, Case No. 2047, para. 361.)

1049. A statutory provision providing that a collective agreement should be in force for two years when no other period has been agreed by the parties does not constitute a violation of the right to collective bargaining.

(See 330th Report, Case No. 2229, para. 956.)

Extension of collective agreements

1050. In a case where the public authorities decreed the extension of collective agreements when current collective agreements had been concluded by minority organizations in the face of opposition by an organization which allegedly represented the large majority of workers in the sector, the Committee considered that the Government could have carried out an objective appraisal of representativity of the occupational associations in question since, in the absence of such appraisal, the extension of an agreement could be imposed on an entire sector of activity contrary to the views of the majority organization representing the workers in the category covered by the extended agreement, and thereby limiting the right of free collective bargaining of that majority organization.

(See the 1996 *Digest*, para. 906.)

1051. Any extension of collective agreements should take place subject to tripartite analysis of the consequences it would have on the sector to which it is applied.

(See the 1996 *Digest*, para. 907.)

1052. When the extension of the agreement applies to non-member workers of enterprises covered by the collective agreement, this situation in principle does not contradict the principles of freedom of association, in so far as under the law it is the most representative organization that negotiates on behalf of all workers, and the enterprises are not composed of several establishments (a situation in which the decision respecting extension should be left to the parties).

(See the 1996 *Digest*, para. 908.)

1053. The extension of an agreement to an entire sector of activity contrary to the views of the organization representing most of the workers in a category covered by the extended agreement is liable to limit the right of free collective bargaining of that majority organization. This system makes it possible to extend agreements containing provisions which might result in a worsening of the conditions of employment of the category of workers concerned.

(See the 1996 *Digest*, para. 909; and 307th Report, Case No. 1725, para. 29.)

Relationship between individual employment contracts and collective agreements

1054. When in the course of collective bargaining with the trade union, the enterprise offers better working conditions to non-unionized workers under individual agreements, there is a serious risk that this might undermine the negotiating capacity of the trade union and give rise to discriminatory situations in favour of the non-unionized staff; furthermore, it might encourage unionized workers to withdraw from the union.

(See 306th Report, Case No. 1845, para. 517.)

1055. As individual agreements on specific subjects will prevail over collective agreements, the system does not encourage and promote the full development and utilization of machinery for voluntary negotiation between employers or employers' organizations and workers' organizations with a view to the regulation of terms and conditions of employment by means of collective agreements.

(See 330th Report, Case No. 2178, para. 582.)

1056. The relationship between individual employment contracts and collective agreements, and in particular the possibility that the former may override certain clauses in the latter under specific conditions, is dealt with differently in the various countries and under the various types of collective bargaining systems concerned. The basic task of the Committee is to decide whether the facts of the case are compatible with the Conventions and principles concerning freedom of association. In a case in which the relationship between individual contracts and the collective agreement seems to have been agreed between the employer and the trade union organizations, the Committee considered that the case did not call for further examination.

(See the 1996 *Digest*, para. 910.)

1057. In one case, the Committee found it difficult to reconcile the equal status given in the law to individual and collective contracts with the ILO principles on collective bargaining, according to which the full development and utilization of machinery for voluntary negotiation between employers or employers' organizations and workers' organizations should be encouraged and promoted, with a view to the regulation of terms and conditions of employment by means of collective agreements. In effect, it seemed that the Act allowed collective bargaining by means of collective agreements, along with other alternatives, rather than promoting and encouraging it.

(See the 1996 Digest, para. 911; and 329th Report, Case No. 2172, para. 354.)

Incentives to workers to give up the right to collective bargaining

1058. When examining various cases in which workers who refused to give up the right to collective negotiation were denied a wage rise, the Committee considered that it raised significant problems of compatibility with the principles of freedom of association, in particular as regards Article 1, paragraph 2(b), of Convention No. 98. In addition, such a provision can hardly be said to constitute a measure to "encourage and promote the full development and utilization of machinery for voluntary negotiation ... with a view to the regulation of terms and conditions of employment by means of collective agreements", as provided in Article 4 of Convention No. 98.

(See the 1996 *Digest*, para. 913; 321st Report, Case No. 2020, para. 50; 330th Report, Case No. 2186, para. 382; and 333rd Report, Case No. 2281, para. 637.)

Closure of the enterprise and application of the collective agreement

1059. The closing of an enterprise should not in itself result in the extinction of the obligations resulting from the collective agreement, in particular as regards compensation in the case of dismissal.

(See the 1996 *Digest*, para. 914.)

1060. In a case related to insolvency and bankruptcy proceedings, the Committee considered that insisting on full compliance with the provisions of the collective agreement might threaten the continued operation of the enterprise and the maintenance of the workers' jobs.

(See 307th Report, Case No. 1887, para. 67.)

Relationship between ILO Conventions

1061. Convention No. 151, which was intended to complement the Right to Organize and Collective Bargaining Convention, 1949 (No. 98), by laying down certain provisions concerning, in particular, protection against anti-union discrimination and the determination of terms and conditions of employment for the public service as a whole, does not in any way contradict or dilute the basic right of association guaranteed to all workers by virtue of Convention No. 87.

(See the 1996 *Digest*, para. 915.)

1062. The Committee acknowledges that the special nature of the functions of public servants engaged in the administration of the State and, in particular, the fact that their terms and conditions of employment may be determined otherwise than by a free collective bargaining process, was recognized by Convention No. 98, and that Convention No. 151, which was intended to make more specific provision for that category of public servants who were excluded from the scope of Convention No. 98, recognized that certain categories of public servants (including those in highly confidential positions) may be excluded from the more general provisions guaranteeing to public servants protection against acts of anti-union discrimination or ensuring the existence of methods of participation in the determination of their conditions of employment. In the opinion of the Committee, however, the exclusion of certain categories of workers in Conventions Nos. 98 and 151 cannot be interpreted as affecting or minimizing in any way the basic right to organize of all workers guaranteed by Convention No. 87. Nothing in either Convention No. 98 or Convention No. 151 indicates an intention to limit the scope of Convention No. 87. On the contrary, both the terms of these Conventions and the preparatory work leading to the adoption of Convention No. 98 show a contrary intention.

(See the 1996 *Digest*, para. 920.)

1063. The Committee has drawn attention to the terms of Article 6 of Convention No. 98, which provide that: “This Convention does not deal with the position of public servants engaged in the administration of the State, nor shall it be construed as prejudicing their rights or status in any way”. Unlike Article 5 of the Convention (dealing with the armed forces and the police), Article 6, in providing that the Convention shall not be construed as in any way prejudicing the rights or the status of public servants, at the same time removed the possible conflict between the Convention and Convention No. 87 and expressly preserved the rights of public servants, including those guaranteed in Convention No. 87. The argument that the effect of the provisions of Convention No. 87 is limited if reference is made to Article 6 of Convention No. 98 conflicts with the express terms of that Article. Likewise, Article 1, paragraph 1, of Convention No. 151 provides that the Convention applies to all persons employed by the public authorities “to the extent that more favourable provisions in other international labour Conventions are not applicable to them”. If, therefore, Convention No. 98 left intact the rights granted to public servants by Convention No. 87, it follows that Convention No. 151 has not impaired them either.

(See the 1996 *Digest*, para. 921.)

1064. Article 4 of Convention No. 98 offers more favourable provisions than Article 7 of Convention No. 151 in a branch of activity such as that of public education, where both Conventions are applicable, since it includes the concept of voluntary negotiation and the independence of the negotiating parties. In such cases, taking into account Article 1 of Convention No. 151, Article 4 of Convention No. 98 should be applicable in preference to Article 7 of Convention No. 151, which calls upon the public authorities to promote collective bargaining either by means of procedures that make such bargaining possible, or by such other methods as will allow public servants to participate in the determination of their terms and conditions of employment.

(See the 1996 *Digest*, para. 922.)

Consultation with the organizations of workers and employers 16

General principles

(See also para. 1090)

1065. The Committee has expressed the importance, for the preservation of a country's social harmony, of regular consultations with employers' and workers' representatives; such consultations should involve the whole trade union movement, irrespective of the philosophical or political beliefs of its leaders.

(See the 1996 *Digest*, paras. 26 and 924; and 331st Report, Case No. 2090, para. 165.)

1066. The Committee has emphasized that the principle of consultation and cooperation between public authorities and employers' and workers' organizations at the industrial and national levels is one to which importance should be attached.

(See the 1996 *Digest*, para. 925; 306th Report, Case No. 1882, para. 437; and 329th Report, Case No. 2090, para. 266.)

1067. The Committee has emphasized the importance it attaches to the promotion of dialogue and consultations on matters of mutual interest between the public authorities and the most representative occupational organizations of the sector involved.

(See the 1996 *Digest*, para. 926; 299th Report, Case No. 1808, para. 380; 320th Report, Case No. 2032, para. 697; 330th Report, Case No. 2229, para. 953; 332nd Report, Case No. 2221, para. 224; and 336th Report, Case No. 2324, para. 283.)

1068. The Committee has considered it useful to refer to the Consultation (Industrial and National Levels) Recommendation, 1960 (No. 113), Paragraph 1 of which provides that measures should be taken to promote effective consultation and cooperation between public authorities and employers' and workers' organizations without discrimination of any kind against these organizations. In accordance with Paragraph 5 of the Recommendation, such consultation should aim at ensuring that the public authorities seek the views, advice and assistance of these organizations, particularly in the preparation and implementation of laws and regulations affecting their interests.

(See the 1996 *Digest*, para. 928; 316th Report, Case No. 1972, para. 703; 325th Report, Case No. 2110, para. 263; and 337th Report, Case No. 2244, para. 1254.)

1069. As reaffirmed by the Declaration of Philadelphia, the war against want requires to be carried on with unrelenting vigour within each nation, and by continuous and concerted international effort in which the representatives of workers and employers, enjoying equal status with those of governments, join with them in free discussion and democratic decision with a view to the promotion of the common welfare.

(See 334th Report, Case No. 2254, para. 1066.)

1070. Tripartite consultation should take place before the Government submits a draft to the Legislative Assembly or establishes a labour, social or economic policy.

(See 334th Report, Case No. 2254, para. 1066.)

1071. It is important that consultations take place in good faith, confidence and mutual respect, and that the parties have sufficient time to express their views and discuss them in full with a view to reaching a suitable compromise. The Government must also ensure that it attaches the necessary importance to agreements reached between workers' and employers' organizations.

(See 328th Report, Case No. 2167, para. 296.)

Consultation during the preparation and application of legislation

1072. The Committee has emphasized the value of consulting organizations of employers and workers during the preparation and application of legislation which affects their interests.

(See the 1996 *Digest*, para. 929; 316th Report, Case No. 1972, para. 703; 327th Report, Case No. 2145, para. 308; 329th Report, Case No. 2123, para. 526; and 335th Report, Case No. 2305, para. 508.)

1073. The Committee has drawn the attention of governments to the importance of prior consultation of employers' and workers' organizations before the adoption of any legislation in the field of labour law.

(See the 1996 *Digest*, para. 930; 304th Report, Case No. 1851, para. 279; 306th Report, Case No. 1884, para. 685; 309th Report, Case No. 1851/1922, para. 248; 311th Report, Case No. 1969, para. 149; 329th Report, Case No. 2177/2183, para. 651; 335th Report, Case No. 2276, para. 410; and 336th Report, Case No. 2381, para. 574.)

1074. The Committee has emphasized the importance that should be attached to full and frank consultation taking place on any questions or proposed legislation affecting trade union rights.

(See the 1996 *Digest*, para. 927; and, for example, 327th Report, Case No. 2145, para. 308, and Case No. 2132, para. 660; 330th Report, Case No. 2144, para. 717, and Case No. 2229, para. 938; 331st Report, Case No. 2187, para. 440; 332nd Report, Case No. 2187, para. 721; 335th Report, Case No. 2305, para. 508; 336th Report, Case No. 2324, para. 283; 337th Report, Case No. 2244, para. 1254; and 338th Report, Case No. 2281, para. 249.)

1075. It is essential that the introduction of draft legislation affecting collective bargaining or conditions of employment should be preceded by full and detailed consultations with the appropriate organizations of workers and employers.

(See the 1996 *Digest*, para. 931; 302nd Report, Case No. 1817, para. 318; 311th Report, Case No. 1969, para. 149; 320th Report, Case No. 2025, para. 410; 326th Report, Case No. 2095, para. 193; 327th Report, Case No. 2118, para. 637; 329th Report, Case No. 2177/2183, para. 651; 330th Report, Case No. 2180, para. 302; 334th Report, Case No. 2269, para. 792; and 338th Report, Case No. 2326, para. 436.)

1076. The process of consultation on legislation and minimum wages helps to give laws, programmes and measures adopted or applied by public authorities a firmer justification and helps to ensure that they are well respected and successfully applied. The Government should seek general consensus as much as possible, given that employers' and workers' organizations should be able to share in the responsibility of securing the well-being and prosperity of the community as a whole. This is particularly important given the growing complexity of the problems faced by societies. No public authority can claim to have all the answers, nor assume that its proposals will naturally achieve all of their objectives.

(See 328th Report, Case No. 2167, para. 295; 330th Report, Case No. 2067, para. 175; 334th Report, Case No. 2254, para. 1065; and 337th Report, Case No. 2254, para. 1592.)

1077. While the refusal to permit or encourage the participation of trade union organizations in the preparation of new legislation or regulations affecting their interests does not necessarily constitute an infringement of trade union rights, the principle of consultation and cooperation between public authorities and employers' and workers' organizations at the industrial and national levels is one to which importance should be attached. In this connection, the Committee has drawn attention to the provisions of the Consultation (Industrial and National Levels) Recommendation, 1960 (No. 113).

(See the 1996 *Digest*, para. 933; and 328th Report, Case No. 2167, para. 296.)

Consultation and employment flexibility

1078. A contraction of the public sector and/or greater employment flexibility (for example, the generalization of short-term contracts) do not in themselves constitute violations of freedom of association. However, there is no doubt that these changes have significant consequences in the social and trade union spheres, particularly in view of the increased job insecurity to which they can give rise. Employers' and workers' organizations should therefore be consulted as to the scope and form of the measures adopted by the authorities.

(See the 1996 *Digest*, para. 934; and 336th Report, Case No. 2324, para. 278.)

Consultation and processes of restructuring, rationalization and staff reduction

1079. The Committee can examine allegations concerning economic rationalization programmes and restructuring processes, whether or not they imply redundancies or the transfer of enterprises or services from the public to the private sector, only in so far as they might have given rise to acts of discrimination or interference against trade unions. In any case, the Committee can only regret that in the rationalization and staff-reduction process, the government did not consult or try to reach an agreement with the trade union organizations.

(See the 1996 *Digest*, para. 935; and, for example, 299th Report, Case No. 1808, para. 374; 305th Report, Case No. 1875, para. 180; 314th Report, Case No. 1962, para. 91; 316th Report, Case No. 1996, para. 665; 321st Report, Case No. 2052, para. 250; 330th Report, Case No. 2151, para. 535; 333rd Report, Case No. 2272, para. 539; 334th Report, Case No. 2297, para. 403; 336th Report, Case No. 2324, para. 280; and 338th Report, Case No. 2384, para. 753.)

1080. Rationalization and staff reduction processes should involve consultations or attempts to reach agreement with the trade union organizations, instead of giving preference to proceeding by decree and ministerial decision.

(See the 1996 *Digest*, para. 936; 331st Report, Case No. 2169, para. 637; and 337th Report, Case No. 2356, para. 702.)

1081. The Committee has emphasized that it is important that governments consult with trade union organizations to discuss the consequences of restructuring programmes on the employment and working conditions of employees.

(See the 1996 *Digest*, para. 937; 306th Report, Case No. 1787, para. 289; 314th Report, Case No. 1962, para. 91; 321st Report, Case No. 2052, para. 250; 325th Report, Case No. 2068, para. 333, and Case No. 2052, para. 412; 329th Report, Case No. 2154, para. 813; 331st Report, Case No. 2068, para. 263; 332nd Report, Case No. 2187, para. 728; 333rd Report, Case No. 2288, para. 828; and 334th Report, Case No. 2310, para. 719.)

1082. The Committee requests that, in the cases where new staff reduction programmes are undertaken, negotiations take place between the enterprise concerned and the trade union organizations.

(See 291st Report, Case No. 1648/1650, para. 472; and 304th Report, Case No. 1796, para. 458.)

1083. When voluntary retirement programmes are carried out, the trade union organizations in the sector should be consulted.

(See 316th Report, Case No. 1970, para. 562.)

1084. With regard to the allegation concerning measures taken to induce workers in the public sector to give up their posts in the context of redundancy programmes in return for financial compensation, the Committee regretted that in the course of the staff reduction process there was no consultation and no attempt to come to an agreement with the trade union organizations.

(See the 1996 *Digest*, para. 939.)

1085. Although it is not within the Committee's competence to comment on economic measures which a government may take in difficult times or on the recommendations of the International Monetary Fund, the Committee nevertheless notes that decisions involving the dismissal of large numbers of workers should be discussed extensively with the trade union organizations concerned with a view to planning the occupational future of these workers in the light of the country's opportunities.

(See the 1996 *Digest*, para. 940.)

Consultation concerning the bargaining process

1086. The Committee has stated, in the same way as the Committee of Experts, that where a government seeks to alter bargaining structures in which it acts actually or indirectly as employer, it is particularly important to follow an adequate consultation process, whereby all objectives perceived as being in the overall national interest can be discussed by all parties concerned. Such consultations imply that they be undertaken in good faith and that both partners have all the information necessary to make an informed decision.

(See the 1996 *Digest*, paras. 856 and 941; and, for example, 299th Report, Case No. 1802, para. 281; 300th Report, Case No. 1806, para. 126; 310th Report, Case No. 1928, para. 183; 311th Report, Case No. 1951, para. 228; 318th Report, Case No. 1976, para. 613; 325th Report, Case No. 2110, para. 263; 329th Report, Case No. 2177/2183, para. 651; 330th Report, Case No. 2173, para. 299; 333rd Report, Case No. 2277, para. 272; and 338th Report, Case No. 2403, para. 598.)

1087. In view of the implications for the standard of living of the workers of the fixing of wages by the government, by-passing the collective bargaining process, and of the government's wage policy in general, the Committee has pointed out the importance it attaches to the effective promotion of consultation and cooperation between public authorities and workers' organizations in this respect, in accordance with the principles laid down in Recommendation No. 113, for the purpose of considering jointly matters of mutual concern with a view to arriving, to the fullest possible extent, at agreed solutions.

(See the 1996 *Digest*, para. 949.)

Consultations on the redistribution of the assets of trade unions which have been dissolved

1088. In a case relating to the redistribution of the assets of trade unions which had been dissolved, the Committee recalled that it is for the Government and the trade unions to cooperate to seek an arrangement consistent with the principles of freedom of association and acceptable to the parties concerned so that the trade unions are able to carry out their activities in full independence and on an equal footing.

(See 309th Report, Case No. 1938, para. 181.)

Participation of organizations of workers and employers in various bodies and procedures 17

(See also para. 516)

1089. The Committee considered that it was not called upon to express an opinion as to the right of a particular organization to be invited to take part in joint or consultative bodies unless its exclusion constituted a clear case of discrimination affecting the principle of freedom of association. This is a matter to be determined by the Committee in the light of the facts of each given case.

(See the 1996 *Digest*, para. 942; 299th Report, Case No. 1753, para. 69; 302nd Report, Case No. 1841, para. 77; and 305th Report, Case No. 1871, para. 79.)

1090. Any decisions concerning the participation of workers' organizations in a tripartite body should be taken in full consultation with all the trade unions whose representativity has been objectively proved.

(See the 1996 *Digest*, para. 943; 327th Report, Case No. 2132, para. 660; 328th Report, Case No. 2139, para. 444; 329th Report, Case No. 2090, para. 268; and 331st Report, Case No. 2132, para. 586.)

1091. The fact that a trade union organization is debarred from membership of joint committees does not necessarily imply infringement of the trade union rights of that organization. But for there to be no infringement, two conditions must be met: first, that the reason for which a union is debarred from participation in a joint committee must lie in its non-representative character, determined by objective criteria; second, that in spite of such non-participation, the other rights which it enjoys and the activities it can undertake in other fields must enable it effectively to further and defend the interests of its members within the meaning of Article 10 of Convention No. 87.

(See the 1996 *Digest*, paras. 842 and 946; 305th Report, Case No. 1857, para. 447; 328th Report, Case No. 2139, para. 443; and 335th Report, Case No. 2317, para. 1083.)

1092. If the circumstances are such that an organization considered to be the most representative of workers or of employers in a country were prevented from taking part in joint and tripartite inter-occupational bodies for the economic sectors or branches of which it is representative, the Committee would consider that the principles of freedom of association had been infringed.

(See 302nd Report, Case No. 1841, para. 77.)

1093. When setting up joint committees dealing with matters affecting the interests of workers, governments should make appropriate provision for the representation of different sections of the trade union movement having a substantial interest in the questions at issue.

(See the 1996 *Digest*, para. 944; 328th Report, Case No. 2139, para. 444; and 330th Report, Case No. 2090, para. 230.)

1094. The Committee has accepted that, under certain conditions, it is not contrary to the principles of freedom of association that a minority organization may not under the law be entitled to be represented on consultative bodies.

(See the 1996 *Digest*, para. 945.)

1095. In determining whether an organization is representative for the purpose of participation in the membership of arbitration tribunals, it is important that the State should not intervene other than to give formal recognition to situations of fact, and it is indispensable that any decision should be based on objective criteria laid down in advance by an independent body.

(See the 1996 *Digest*, para. 947.)

1096. The establishment of a tripartite group to examine the question of wages and the anti-inflationary measures that should be taken is in accordance with the provision in Recommendation No. 113 which provides that consultation and cooperation should be promoted between public authorities and employers' and workers' organizations with the general objective of achieving mutual understanding and good relations between them with a view to developing the economy as a whole or individual branches thereof, improving conditions of work and raising standards of living. In particular, the authorities should seek the views, advice and assistance of employers' and workers' organizations in an appropriate manner in respect of such matters as the preparation and implementation of laws and regulations affecting their interests.

(See the 1996 *Digest*, para. 948.)

1097. While the principles of freedom of association do not require that there be an absolute proportional representation (which might prove impossible, and indeed is not advisable due to the risks of excessive representational fragmentation), the authorities should at the very least make some allowance to recognize the plurality of trade unions, reflect the choice of workers and demonstrate in practice that fair and reasonable efforts are made to treat all representative workers' organizations on an equal footing.

(See 328th Report, Case No. 2139, para. 444.)

Facilities for workers' representatives 18

General principles

1098. Convention No. 135 calls on ratifying member States to supply such facilities in the undertaking as may be appropriate in order to enable workers' representatives to carry out their functions promptly and efficiently, and in such a manner as not to impair the efficient operation of the undertaking concerned.

(See the 1996 *Digest*, para. 950; 308th Report, Case No. 1897, para. 474; and 337th Report, Case No. 2395, para. 1197.)

1099. The Workers' Representatives Convention, 1971 (No. 135), and the Collective Bargaining Convention, 1981 (No. 154), contain explicit provisions guaranteeing that, where there exist in the same undertaking both trade union representatives and elected representatives, appropriate measures are to be taken to ensure that the existence of elected representatives in an enterprise is not used to undermine the position of the trade unions concerned.

(See the 1996 *Digest*, para. 951; and 331st Report, Case No. 2243, para. 618.)

Collection of dues

1100. The Committee has drawn attention to the Workers' Representatives Recommendation, 1971 (No. 143), concerning protection and facilities to be afforded to workers' representatives in the undertaking, which provides that, in the absence of other arrangements for the collection of trade union dues, workers' representatives authorized to do so by the trade union should be permitted to collect such dues regularly on the premises of the undertaking.

(See the 1996 *Digest*, paras. 436 and 953.)

Access to the management

1101. In a case of the refusal by the management of an enterprise to establish communications with the representatives of the trade union, the Committee pointed out that Paragraph 13 of the Workers' Representatives Recommendation (No. 143) provides that workers' representatives should be granted without undue delay access to the management of the undertaking and to management representatives empowered to take decisions, as may be necessary for the proper exercise of their functions.

(See 304th Report, Case No. 1852, para. 493.)

Access to the workplace

1102. The Committee has drawn the attention of governments to the principle that workers' representatives should enjoy such facilities as may be necessary for the proper exercise of their functions, including access to workplaces.

(See the 1996 *Digest*, para. 957; 304th Report, Case No. 1852, para. 493; 333rd Report, Case No. 2255, para. 131; and 334th Report, Case No. 2316, para. 505.)

1103. Governments should guarantee the access of trade union representatives to workplaces, with due respect for the rights of property and management, so that trade unions can communicate with workers in order to apprise them of the potential advantages of unionization.

(See the 1996 *Digest*, para. 954; 309th Report, Case No. 1852, para. 338; 327th Report, Case No. 1948/1955, para. 358; 330th Report, Case No. 2208, para. 604; 332nd Report, Case No. 2046, para. 446; 333rd Report, Case No. 2255, para. 131; 334th Report, Case No. 2316, para. 505; 335th Report, Case No. 2317, para. 1087; and 336th Report, Case No. 2316, para. 58, and Case No. 2255, para. 112.)

1104. Workers' representatives should be granted access to all workplaces in the undertaking where such access is necessary to enable them to carry out their representation function.

(See 318th Report, Case No. 2012, para. 426.)

1105. Trade union representatives who are not employed in the undertaking but whose trade union has members employed therein should be granted access to the undertaking. The granting of such facilities should not impair the efficient operation of the undertaking concerned.

(See 334th Report, Case No. 2316, para. 505.)

1106. For the right to organize to be meaningful, the relevant workers' organizations should be able to further and defend the interests of their members, by enjoying such facilities as may be necessary for the proper exercise of their functions as workers' representatives, including access to the workplace of trade union members.

(See 334th Report, Case No. 2222, para. 220.)

1107. The denial of access by trade union leaders to the premises of enterprises on the grounds that a list of dispute grievances had been presented constitutes a serious violation of the right of organizations to carry out their activities freely, which includes the presentation of grievances even by a trade union other than that which concluded the collective agreement in force.

(See the 1996 *Digest*, para. 955.)

1108. The necessary measures should be taken to ensure that access is granted freely to farmworkers, domestic workers and workers in the mining industry by trade unions and their officials for the purpose of carrying out normal union activities although on the premises of employers.

(See the 1996 *Digest*, para. 956.)

1109. Access to the workplace should not of course be exercised to the detriment of the efficient functioning of the administration or public institutions concerned. Therefore, the workers' organizations concerned and the employer should strive to reach agreements so that access to workplaces, during and outside working hours, should be granted to workers' organizations without impairing the efficient functioning of the administration or the public institution concerned.

(See 334th Report, Case No. 2222, para. 220.)

Free time accorded to workers' representatives

1110. When examining an allegation concerning the denial of time off to participate in trade union meetings, the Committee recalled that, while account should be taken of the characteristics of the industrial relations system of the country, and while the granting of such facilities should not impair the efficient operation of the undertaking concerned, Paragraph 10, subparagraph 1, of the Workers' Representatives Recommendation, 1971 (No. 143), provides that workers' representatives in the undertaking should be afforded the necessary time off from work, without loss of pay or social and fringe benefits, for carrying out their representation functions. Subparagraph 2 of Paragraph 10 also specifies that, while workers' representatives may be required to obtain permission from the management before taking time off, such permission should not be unreasonably withheld.

(See the 1996 *Digest*, para. 952; 311th Report, Case No. 1934, para. 130, and Case No. 1944, para. 542; 318th Report, Case No. 2009, para. 296; 325th Report, Case No. 2068, para. 312; 330th Report, Case No. 2192, para. 1075; and 336th Report, Case No. 2046, para. 322.)

1111. The affording of facilities to representatives of public employees, including the granting of time off, has as its corollary ensuring the "efficient operation of the administration or service concerned". This corollary means that there can be checks on requests for time off for absences during hours of work by the competent authorities solely responsible for the "efficient operation" of their services.

(See 335th Report, Case No. 2306, para. 353.)

Facilities on plantations

1112. The Committee has recognized that plantations are private property on which the workers not only work but also live. It is therefore only by having access to plantations that trade union officials can carry out normal trade union activities among the workers. For this reason, it is of special importance that the entry of trade union officials into plantations for the purpose of carrying out lawful trade union activities should be readily permitted, provided that there is no interference with the carrying on of the work during working hours and subject to any appropriate precautions being taken for the protection of the property. In this connection, the Committee has also drawn attention to the resolution adopted by the Plantations Committee at its First Session in 1950, which provides that employers should remove existing hindrances, if any, in the way of the organization of free, independent and democratically controlled trade unions by plantation workers and they should provide such unions with facilities for the conduct of their normal activities, including free office accommodation, freedom to hold meetings and freedom of entry.

(See the 1996 *Digest*, para. 958.)

Conflicts within the trade union movement 19

(See also para. 431)

1113. A matter involving no dispute between the government and the trade unions, but which involves a conflict within the trade union movement itself, is the sole responsibility of the parties themselves.

(See the 1996 *Digest*, para. 962.)

1114. The Committee is not competent to make recommendations on internal dissentions within a trade union organization, so long as the government does not intervene in a manner which might affect the exercise of trade union rights and the normal functioning of an organization.

(See the 1996 *Digest*, para. 963; 321st Report, Case No. 2070, para. 372; 325th Report, Case No. 1888, para. 397; and 338th Report, Case No. 2382, para. 527.)

1115. While the Committee has no competence to examine the merits of disputes within the various tendencies of a trade union movement, a complaint against another organization, if couched in sufficiently precise terms to be capable of examination on its merits, may bring the government of the country concerned into question – for example, if the acts of the organization complained against are wrongfully supported by the government or are of a nature which the government is under a duty to prevent by virtue of its having ratified an international labour Convention.

(See the 1996 *Digest*, para. 964; and 332nd Report, Case No. 2090, para. 346.)

1116. In cases of internal dissentions within a trade union organization, the Committee has pointed out that judicial intervention would permit a clarification of the situation from the legal point of view for the purpose of settling the question of the leadership and representation of the organization concerned.

(See the 1996 *Digest*, para. 965; 307th Report, Case No. 1918, para. 249; 308th Report, Case No. 1915, para. 271; 311th Report, Case No. 1969, para. 144; 328th Report, Case No. 2124, para. 458; 336th Report, Case No. 2153, para. 165; and 338th Report, Case No. 2382, para. 527.)

1117. In the case of internal dissention within one and the same trade union federation, by virtue of Article 3 of Convention No. 87, the only obligation of the government is to refrain from any interference which would restrict the right of the workers' and employers' organizations to draw up their constitutions and rules, to elect their representatives in full freedom, to organize their administration and activities and to formulate their programmes, and to refrain from any interference which would impede the lawful exercise of that right.

(See the 1996 *Digest*, para. 966; and 335th Report, Case No. 2345, para. 207.)

1118. Article 2 of Convention No. 98 is designed to protect workers' organizations against employers' organizations or their agents or members and not against other workers' organizations or the agents or members thereof. Inter-union rivalry is outside the scope of the Convention.

(See the 1996 *Digest*, para. 967.)

1119. With regard to the existence of two executive committees within the trade union, one of which is allegedly manipulated by the employer, the Committee recalled the need to lay down explicitly in legislation remedies and penalties for acts of anti-union discrimination and acts of interference by employers in workers' organizations in order to ensure the effective application of Article 2 of Convention No. 98.

(See the 1996 *Digest*, paras. 765 and 968.)

1120. In cases of internal dissention, the Committee has invited the government to persevere with its efforts, in consultation with the organizations concerned, to put in place as soon as possible impartial procedures to enable the workers concerned freely to choose their representatives.

(See the 1996 *Digest*, para. 969; and 311th Report, Case No. 1969, para. 145.)

1121. When two executive committees each proclaim themselves to be the legitimate one, the dispute should be settled by the judicial authority or an independent arbitrator, and not by the administrative authority.

(See the 1996 *Digest*, para. 970; and 335th Report, Case No. 2345, para. 207.)

1122. When internal disputes arise in a trade union organization they should be resolved by the persons concerned (for example, by a vote), by appointing an independent mediator with the agreement of the parties concerned, or by intervention of the judicial authorities.

(See the 1996 *Digest*, para. 971; 311th Report, Case No. 1969, para. 144; and 331st Report, Case No. 2217, para. 202.)

1123. Conflicts within a trade union lie outside the competence of the Committee and should be resolved by the parties themselves or by recourse to the judicial authority or an independent arbitrator.

(See the 1996 *Digest*, para. 972; and 333rd Report, Case No. 2068, para. 485.)

1124. In cases of internal conflict, the Committee has pointed out that judicial intervention would permit a clarification of the situation from the legal point of view for the purpose of settling questions concerning the management and representation of the trade union federation concerned. Another possible means of settlement would be to appoint an independent arbitrator to be agreed on by the parties concerned, to seek a joint solution to existing problems and, if necessary, to hold new elections. In either case, the government should recognize the leaders designated as the legitimate representatives of the organization.

(See the 1996 *Digest*, para. 973; and 300th Report, Case No. 1821, para. 153.)

1125. Violence resulting from inter-union rivalry might constitute an attempt to impede the free exercise of trade union rights. If this were the case and if the acts in question were sufficiently serious, it appears that the intervention of the authorities, in particular the police, would be called for in order to provide adequate protection of those rights. The question of infringement of trade union rights by the government would only arise to the extent that it may have acted improperly with regard to the alleged violence.

(See the 1996 *Digest*, para. 974.)

Special procedures for the examination in the International Labour Organization of complaints alleging violations of freedom of association

The outline given below of the current procedure for the examination of complaints alleging infringements of trade union rights is based on the provisions adopted by common consent by the Governing Body of the International Labour Office and the Economic and Social Council of the United Nations in January and February 1950, and also on the decisions taken by the Governing Body at its 117th Session (November 1951), 123rd Session (November 1953), 132nd Session (June 1956), 140th Session (November 1958), 144th Session (March 1960), 175th Session (May 1969), 184th Session (November 1971), 202nd Session (March 1977), 209th Session (May-June 1979) and 283rd Session (March 2002) with respect to the internal procedure for the preliminary examination of complaints, and lastly on certain decisions adopted by the Committee on Freedom of Association itself.[1]

Background

1. In January 1950 the Governing Body, following negotiations with the Economic and Social Council of the United Nations, set up a Fact-Finding and Conciliation Commission on Freedom of Association, composed of independent persons, and defined the terms of reference of the Commission and the general lines of its procedure. It also decided to communicate to the Economic and Social Council a certain number of suggestions with a view to formulating a procedure for making the services of the Commission available to the United Nations.

[1] Most of the procedural rules referred to in this Annex are contained under the heading "procedural questions" in the following documents: First Committee Report, paras. 6 to 32, in Sixth Report of the International Labour Organisation to the United Nations (Geneva, ILO, 1952), Appendix V; the 6th Report in Seventh Report of the International Labour Organisation to the United Nations (Geneva, ILO, 1953), Appenix V, paras. 14 to 21; the 9th Report in Eighth Report of the International Labour Organisation to the United Nations (Geneva, ILO, 1954), Appendix II, paras. 2 to 40; the 29th and 43rd Reports in the *Official Bulletin*, Vol. XLIII, 1960, No. 3; the 111th Report, *ibid.*, Vol. LII, 1969 No. 4, paras. 7 to 20; the 127th Report, *ibid.*, Vol. LV, 1972, Supplement, paras. 9 to 28; the 164th Report, *ibid.*, Vol. LX, 1977, No. 2, paras. 19 to 28; the 193rd Report, *ibid.*, Vol. LXII, 1979, No. 1; and the 327th Report, *ibid.*, Vol. LXXXV, 2002, paras. 17 to 26.

2. The Economic and Social Council, at its Tenth Session, on 17 February 1950, noted the decision of the Governing Body and adopted a resolution in which it formally approved this decision, considering that it corresponded to the intent of the Council's resolution of 2 August 1949 and that it was likely to prove a most effective way of safeguarding trade union rights. It decided to accept, on behalf of the United Nations, the services of the ILO and the Fact-Finding and Conciliation Commission and laid down a procedure, which was supplemented in 1953.

Complaints received by the United Nations

3. All allegations regarding infringements of trade union rights received by the United Nations from governments or trade union or employers' organizations against ILO member States will be forwarded by the Economic and Social Council to the Governing Body of the International Labour Office, which will consider the question of their referral to the Fact-Finding and Conciliation Commission.

4. Similar allegations received by the United Nations regarding any Member of the United Nations which is not a Member of the ILO will be transmitted to the Commission through the Governing Body of the ILO when the Secretary-General of the United Nations, acting on behalf of the Economic and Social Council, has received the consent of the government concerned, and if the Economic and Social Council considers these allegations suitable for transmission. If the government's consent is not forthcoming, the Economic and Social Council will give consideration to the position created by such refusal, with a view to taking any appropriate alternative action calculated to safeguard the rights relating to freedom of association involved in the case. If the Governing Body has before it allegations regarding infringements of trade union rights that are brought against a Member of the United Nations which is not a Member of the ILO, it will refer such allegations in the first instance to the Economic and Social Council.

Bodies competent to examine complaints

5. In accordance with a decision originally taken by the Governing Body, complaints against member States of the ILO were submitted in the first instance to the Officers of the Governing Body for preliminary examination. Following discussions at its 116th and 117th Sessions, the Governing Body decided to set up a Committee on Freedom of Association to carry out this preliminary examination.

6. At the present time, therefore, there are three bodies which are competent to hear complaints alleging infringements of trade union rights that are lodged with the ILO, viz. the Committee on Freedom of Association set up by the Governing Body, the Governing Body itself, and the Fact-Finding and Conciliation Commission on Freedom of Association.

Composition and functioning of the Committee on Freedom of Association

7. This body is a Governing Body organ reflecting the ILO's own tripartite character. Since its creation in 1951, it has been composed of nine regular members representing in equal proportion the Government, Employer and Worker groups of the Governing Body; each member participates in a personal capacity. Nine substitute members, also appointed by the Governing Body, were originally called upon to participate in the meetings only if, for one reason or another, regular members were not present, so as to maintain the initial composition.

8. The present practice adopted by the Committee in February 1958 and specified in March 2002 gives substitute members the right to participate in the work of the Committee, whether or not all the regular members are present. They have therefore acquired the status of deputy members and must respect the same rules as regular members.

9. At its most recent examination of the procedure in March 2002, the Committee expressed the hope that, in view of the rule that all the members are appointed in their individual capacity, the nominations of Government members would be made in a personal capacity so as to ensure a relative permanence of government representation.

10. No representative or national of the State against which a complaint has been made, or person occupying an official position in the national organization of employers or workers which has made the complaint, may participate in the Committee's deliberations or even be present during the hearing of the complaint in question. Similarly, the documents concerning the case are not supplied to them.

11. The Committee always endeavours to reach unanimous decisions.

Mandate and responsibility of the Committee

12. By virtue of its Constitution, the ILO was established in particular to improve working conditions and to promote freedom of association in the various countries. Consequently, the matters dealt with by the Organization in this connection no longer fall within the exclusive sphere of States and the action taken by the Organization for the purpose cannot be considered to be interference in internal affairs, since it falls within the terms of reference that the ILO has received from its Members with a view to attaining the aims assigned to it.[2]

13. The function of the International Labour Organization in regard to freedom of association and the protection of the individual is to contribute to the effectiveness of the general principles of freedom of association, as one of the primary safeguards of peace and social justice.[3] Its function is to secure and promote the right of association of workers and employers. It does not level charges at, or condemn, governments. In fulfilling its task the Committee takes the utmost care, through the procedures it has developed over many years, to avoid dealing with matters which do not fall within its specific competence.

[2] See *Freedom of Association: Digest of decisions and principles of the Freedom of Association Committee of the Governing Body of the ILO*, fifth (revised) edition, 2006, para. 2.

[3] See 2006 *Digest*, para. 1.

14. The mandate of the Committee consists in determining whether any given legislation or practice complies with the principles of freedom of association and collective bargaining laid down in the relevant Conventions.[4]

15. It is within the mandate of the Committee to examine whether, and to what extent, satisfactory evidence is presented to support allegations; this appreciation goes to the merits of the case and cannot support a finding of irreceivability.[5]

16. With a view to avoiding the possibility of misunderstanding or misinterpretation, the Committee considers it necessary to make it clear that its task is limited to examining the allegations submitted to it. Its function is not to formulate general conclusions concerning the trade union situation in particular countries on the basis of vague general statements, but simply to evaluate specific allegations.

17. The usual practice of the Committee has been not to make any distinction between allegations levelled against governments and those levelled against persons accused of infringing freedom of association, but to consider whether or not, in each particular case, a government has ensured within its territory the free exercise of trade union rights.

18. The Committee (after a preliminary examination, and taking account of any observations made by the governments concerned, if received within a reasonable period of time) reports to the Governing Body that a case does not call for further examination if it finds, for example, that the alleged facts, if proved, would not constitute an infringement of the exercise of trade union rights, or that the allegations made are so purely political in character that it is undesirable to pursue the matter further, or that the allegations made are too vague to permit a consideration of the case on its merits, or that the complainant has not offered sufficient evidence to justify reference of the matter to the Fact-Finding and Conciliation Commission.

19. The Committee may recommend that the Governing Body draw the attention of the governments concerned to the anomalies which it has observed and invite them to take appropriate measures to remedy the situation.

The Committee's competence to examine complaints

20. The Committee has considered that it is not within its competence to reach a decision on violations of ILO Conventions on working conditions since such allegations do not concern freedom of association.

21. The Committee has recalled that questions concerning social security legislation fall outside its competence.

22. The questions raised related to landownership and tenure governed by specific national legislation have nothing to do with the problems of the exercise of trade union rights.

23. It is not within the Committee's terms of reference to give an opinion on the type or characteristics – including the degree of legislative regulation – of the industrial relations system in any particular country.[6]

[4] See 2006 *Digest*, para. 6.

[5] See 2006 *Digest*, para. 9.

[6] See 287th Report, Case No. 1627, para. 32.

24. The Committee always takes account of national circumstances, such as the history of labour relations and the social and economic context, but the freedom of association principles apply uniformly and consistently among countries.[7]

25. Where the government concerned considers that the questions raised are purely political in character, the Committee has decided that, even though allegations may be political in origin or present certain political aspects, they should be examined in substance if they raise questions directly concerning the exercise of trade union rights.

26. The question of whether issues raised in a complaint concern penal law or the exercise of trade union rights cannot be decided unilaterally by the government against which a complaint is made. It is for the Committee to rule on the matter after examining all the available information.[8]

27. When it has had to deal with precise and detailed allegations regarding draft legislation, the Committee it has taken the view that the fact that such allegations relate to a text that does not have the force of law should not in itself prevent it from expressing its opinion on the merits of the allegations made. It has considered it desirable that, in such cases, the government and the complainant should be made aware of the Committee's point of view with regard to the proposed bill before it is enacted, since it is open to the government, on whose initiative such a matter depends, to make any amendments thereto.

28 Where national legislation provides for appeal procedures before the courts or independent tribunals, and these procedures have not been used for the matters on which the complaint is based, the Committee takes this into account when examining the complaint.

29. When a case is being examined by an independent national jurisdiction whose procedures offer appropriate guarantees, and the Committee considers that the decision to be taken could provide additional information, it will suspend its examination of the case for a reasonable time to await this decision, provided that the delay thus encountered does not risk prejudicing the party whose rights have allegedly been infringed.

30. Although the use of internal legal procedures, whatever the outcome, is undoubtedly a factor to be taken into consideration, the Committee has always considered that, in view of its responsibilities, its competence to examine allegations is not subject to the exhaustion of national procedures.

Receivability of complaints

31. Complaints lodged with the ILO, either directly or through the United Nations, must come either from organizations of workers or employers or from governments. Allegations are receivable only if they are submitted by a national organization directly interested in the matter, by international organizations of employers or workers having consultative status with the ILO, or other international organizations of employers or workers where the allegations relate to matters directly affecting their affiliated organizations. Such complaints may be presented whether or not the country concerned has ratified the freedom of association Conventions.

[7] See 2006 *Digest*, para. 10.

[8] See 268th Report, Case No. 1500, para. 693.

32. The Committee has full freedom to decide whether an organization may be deemed to be an employers' or workers' organization within the meaning of the ILO Constitution, and it does not consider itself bound by any national definition of the term.

33. The Committee has not regarded any complaint as being irreceivable simply because the government in question had dissolved, or proposed to dissolve, the organization on behalf of which the complaint was made, or because the person or persons making the complaint had taken refuge abroad.

34. The fact that a trade union has not deposited its by-laws, as may be required by national laws, is not sufficient to make its complaint irreceivable since the principles of freedom of association provide precisely that the workers shall be able, without previous authorization, to establish organizations of their own choosing.

35. The fact that an organization has not been officially recognized does not justify the rejection of allegations when it is clear from the complaints that this organization has at least a *de facto* existence.

36. In cases in which the Committee is called upon to examine complaints presented by an organization concerning which no precise information is available, the Director-General is authorized to request the organization to furnish information on the size of its membership, its statutes, its national or international affiliations and, in general, any other information calculated, in any examination of the receivability of the complaint, to lead to a better appreciation of the precise nature of the complainant organization.

37. The Committee will only take cognizance of complaints presented by persons who, through fear of reprisals, request that their names or the origin of the complaints should not be disclosed, if the Director-General, after examining the complaint in question, informs the Committee that it contains allegations of some degree of gravity which have not previously been examined by the Committee. The Committee can then decide what action, if any, should be taken with regard to such complaints.

Repetitive nature of complaints

38. In any case in which a complaint concerns exactly the same infringements as those on which the Committee has already given a decision, the Director-General may, in the first instance, refer the complaint to the Committee, which will decide whether it is appropriate to take action on it.

39. The Committee has taken the view that it could only reopen a case which it had already examined in substance and in which it had submitted final recommendations to the Governing Body if new evidence is adduced and brought to its notice. Similarly, the Committee does not re-examine allegations on which it has already given an opinion: for example, when a complaint refers to a law that it has already examined and, as such, does not contain new elements.[9]

[9] See 297th Report, para. 13.

Form of the complaint

40. Complaints must be presented in writing, duly signed by a representative of a body entitled to present them, and they must be as fully supported as possible by evidence of specific infringements of trade union rights.

41. When the Committee receives, either directly or through the United Nations, mere copies of communications sent by organizations to third parties, such communications do not constitute formal complaints and do not call for action on its part.

42. Complaints originating from assemblies or gatherings which are not bodies having a permanent existence or even bodies organized as definite entities and with which it is impossible to correspond, either because they have only a temporary existence or because the complaints do not contain any addresses of the complainants, are not receivable.

Rules concerning relations with complainants

43. Complaints which do not relate to specific infringements of trade union rights are referred by the Director-General to the Committee on Freedom of Association for opinion, and the Committee decides whether or not any action should be taken on them. In cases of this kind, the Director-General is not bound to wait until the Committee meets, but may contact the complainant organization directly to inform it that the Committee's mandate only permits it to deal with questions concerning freedom of association and to ask it to specify, in this connection, the particular points that it wishes to have examined by the Committee.

44. The Director-General, on receiving a new complaint concerning specific cases of infringement of freedom of association, either directly from the complainant organization or through the United Nations, informs the complainant that any information he may wish to furnish in substantiation of the complaint should be communicated to him within a period of one month. In the event that supporting information is sent to the ILO after the expiry of the one month period provided for in the procedures it will be for the Committee to determine whether this information constitutes new evidence which the complainant would not have been in a position to adduce within the appointed period; in the event that the Committee considers that this is not the case, the information in question is regarded as irreceivable. On the other hand, if the complainant does not furnish the necessary information in substantiation of a complaint (where it does not appear to be sufficiently substantiated) within a period of one month from the date of the Director-General's acknowledgement of receipt of the complaint, it is for the Committee to decide whether any further action in the matter is appropriate.

45. In cases in which a considerable number of copies of an identical complaint are received from separate organizations, the Director-General is not required to request each separate complainant to furnish further information; it is normally sufficient for the Director-General to address the request to the central organization in the country to which the bodies presenting the copies of the identical complaint belong or, where the circumstances make this impracticable, to the authors of the first copy received, it being understood that this does not preclude the Director-General from communicating with more than one of the said bodies if this appears to be warranted by any special circumstances of the particular case. The Director-General will transmit to the government

concerned the first copy received, but will also inform the government of the names of the other complainants presenting the copies of the identical complaints.

46. When a complaint has been communicated to the government concerned and the latter has presented its observations thereon, and when the statements contained in the complaint and the government's observations merely cancel one another out but do not contain any valid evidence, thereby making it impossible for the Committee to reach an informed opinion, the Committee is authorized to seek further information in writing from the complainant in regard to questions concerning the terms of the complaint requiring further elucidation. In such cases, it has been understood that, on the one hand, the government concerned, as defendant, would have an opportunity to reply in its turn to any additional comments the complainants may make, and, on the other hand, that this method would not be followed automatically in all cases but only in cases where it appears that such a request to the complainants would be helpful in establishing the facts.

47. Subject to the two conditions mentioned in the preceding paragraph, the Committee may, moreover, inform the complainants, in appropriate cases, of the substance of the government's observations and invite them to submit their comments thereon within a given period of time. In addition, the Director-General may ascertain whether, in the light of the observations sent by the government concerned, further information or comments from the complainants are necessary on matters relating to the complaint and, if so, may write directly to the complainants, in the name of the Committee and without waiting for its next session, requesting the desired information or the comments on the government's observations by a given date, the government's right to reply being respected as is pointed out in the preceding paragraph.

48. In order to keep the complainant regularly informed of the principal stages in the procedure, the complainant is notified, after each session of the Committee, that the complaint has been put before the Committee and, if the Committee has not reached a conclusion appearing in its report, that – as appropriate – examination of the case has been adjourned in the absence of a reply from the government or the Committee has asked the government for certain additional information.

Prescription

49. While no formal rules fixing any particular period of prescription are embodied in the procedure for the examination of complaints, it may be difficult – if not impossible – for a government to reply in detail to allegations regarding matters which occurred a long time ago.

Withdrawal of complaints

50. When the Committee has been confronted with a request submitted to it for the withdrawal of a complaint, it has always considered that the desire expressed by an organization which has submitted a complaint to withdraw this complaint constitutes an element of which full account should be taken, but it is not sufficient in itself for the Committee to automatically cease to proceed further with the case. In such cases, the

Committee has decided that it alone is competent to evaluate in full freedom the reasons put forward to explain the withdrawal of a complaint and to endeavour to establish whether these appear to be sufficiently plausible so that it may be concluded that the withdrawal is being made in full independence. In this connection, the Committee has noted that there might be cases in which the withdrawal of a complaint by the organization presenting it was the result not of the fact that the complaint had become without purpose, but of pressure exercised by the government against the complainants, the latter being threatened with an aggravation of the situation if they did not consent to this withdrawal.

Rules for relations with the governments concerned

51. By membership of the International Labour Organization, each member State is bound to respect a certain number of principles, including the principles of freedom of association which have become customary rules above the Conventions.[10]

52. If the original complaint or any further information received in response to the acknowledgement of the complaint is sufficiently substantiated, the complaint and any such further information are communicated by the Director-General to the government concerned as quickly as possible; at the same time the government is requested to forward to the Director-General, before a given date, fixed in advance with due regard to the date of the next meeting of the Committee, any observations which it may care to make. When communicating allegations to governments, the Director-General draws their attention to the importance which the Governing Body attaches to receiving the governments' replies within the specified period, in order that the Committee may be in a position to examine cases as soon as possible after the occurrence of the events to which the allegations relate. If the Director-General has any difficulty in deciding whether a particular complaint can be regarded as sufficiently substantiated to justify him in communicating it to the government concerned for its observations, it is open to him to consult the Committee before taking a decision on the matter.

53. In cases in which the allegations concern specific enterprises, or in appropriate cases, the letter by which the allegations are transmitted to the government requests it to obtain the views of all the organizations and institutions concerned so that it can provide a reply to the Committee that is as complete as possible. However, the application of this rule of procedure should not result in practice in delay in having recourse to urgent appeals made to governments, nor in the examination of cases.

54. A distinction is drawn between urgent cases, which are addressed on a priority basis, and less urgent cases. Matters involving human life or personal freedom, or new or changing conditions affecting the freedom of action of a trade union movement as a whole, cases arising out of a continuing state of emergency and cases involving the dissolution of an organization, are treated as cases of urgency. Priority of treatment is also given to cases on which a report has already been submitted to the Governing Body.

55. In all cases, if the first reply from the government in question is of too general a character, the Committee requests the Director-General to obtain all necessary additional information from the government, on as many occasions as it judges appropriate.

[10] Report of the Fact-Finding and Conciliation Commission on Freedom of Association concerning the situation in Chile, 1975, para. 466.

56. The Director-General is further empowered to ascertain without, however, making any appreciation of the substance of a case, whether the observations of governments on the subject matter of a complaint or governments' replies to requests for further information are sufficient to permit the Committee to examine the complaint and, if not, to write directly to the government concerned, in the name of the Committee, and without waiting for its next session, to inform it that it would be desirable if it were to furnish more precise information on the points raised by the Committee or the complainant.

57. The purpose of the whole procedure set up in the ILO for the examination of allegations of violations of freedom of association is to promote respect for trade union rights in law and in fact. If the procedure protects governments against unreasonable accusations, governments on their side should recognize the importance for their own reputation of formulating, so as to allow objective examination, detailed replies to the allegations brought against them. The Committee wishes to stress that, in all the cases presented to it since it was first set up, it has always considered that the replies from governments against whom complaints are made should not be limited to general observations.

58. In cases where governments delay in forwarding their observations on the complaints communicated to them, or the further information requested of them, the Committee mentions these governments in a special introductory paragraph to its reports after the lapse of a reasonable time, which varies according to the degree of urgency of the case and of the questions involved. This paragraph contains an urgent appeal to the governments concerned and, as soon as possible afterwards, special communications are sent to these governments by the Director-General on behalf of the Committee.

59. These governments are warned that at its following session the Committee may submit a report on the substance of the matter, even if the information awaited from the governments in question has still not been received.

60. Cases in respect of which governments continue to fail to cooperate with the Committee, or in which certain difficulties persist, are mentioned in a special paragraph of the introduction to the Committee's report. The governments concerned are then immediately informed that the chairman of the Committee will, on behalf of the Committee, make contact with their representatives attending the session of the Governing Body or the International Labour Conference. The chairman will draw their attention to the particular cases involved and, where appropriate, to the gravity of the difficulties in question, discuss with them the reasons for the delay in transmitting the observations requested by the Committee and examine with them various means of remedying the situation. The chairman then reports to the Committee on the results of such contacts.

61. In appropriate cases, where replies are not forthcoming, ILO external offices may approach governments in order to elicit the information requested of them, either during the examination of the case or in connection with the action to be taken on the Committee's recommendations, approved by the Governing Body. With this end in view the ILO external offices are sent detailed information with regard to complaints concerning their particular area and are requested to approach governments which delay in transmitting their replies, in order to draw their attention to the importance of supplying the observations or information requested of them.

62. In cases where the governments implicated are obviously unwilling to cooperate, the Committee may recommend, as an exceptional measure, that wider publicity be given to the allegations, to the recommendations of the Governing Body and to the negative attitude of the governments concerned.

63. The procedure for the examination of complaints of alleged infringements of the exercise of trade union rights provides for the examination of complaints presented against member States of the ILO. Evidently, it is possible for the consequences of events which gave rise to the presentation of the initial complaint to continue after the setting up of a new State which has become a Member of the ILO, but if such a case should arise, the complainants would be able to have recourse, in respect of the new State, to the procedure established for the examination of complaints relating to infringements of the exercise of trade union rights.

64. There exists a link of continuity between successive governments of the same State and, while a government cannot be held responsible for events which took place under a former government, it is clearly responsible for any continuing consequences which these events may have had since its accession to power.

65. Where a change of regime has taken place in a country, the new government should take all necessary steps to remedy any continuing effects which the events on which the complaint is based may have had since its accession to power, even though those events took place under its predecessor.

Requests for the postponement of the examination of cases

66. With regard to requests for the postponement of the examination of cases by the complainant organization or the government concerned, the practice followed by the Committee consists of deciding the question in full freedom when the reasons given for the request have been evaluated and taking into account the circumstances of the case.[11]

On-the-spot missions

67. At various stages in the procedure, an ILO representative may be sent to the country concerned, for example in the context of direct contacts, with a view to seeking a solution to the difficulties encountered, either during the examination of the case or at the stage of the action to be taken on the recommendations of the Governing Body. Such contacts, however, can only be established at the invitation of the governments concerned or at least with their consent. In addition, upon the receipt of a complaint containing allegations of a particularly serious nature, and after having received the prior approval of the chairman of the Committee, the Director-General may appoint a representative whose mandate would be to carry out preliminary contacts for the following purposes, viz: to transmit to the competent authorities in the country the concern to which the events described in the complaint have given rise; to explain to these authorities the principles of freedom of association involved; to obtain from the authorities their initial reaction, as well as any comments and information with regard to the matters raised in the complaint; to explain to the authorities the special procedure in cases of alleged infringements of trade union rights and, in particular, the direct contact method which may subsequently be requested by the government in order to facilitate a full appraisal of the situation

[11] See 274th Report, Cases Nos. 1455, 1456, 1696 and 1515, para. 10.

by the Committee and the Governing Body; to request and encourage the authorities to communicate as soon as possible a detailed reply containing the observations of the government on the complaint. The report of the representative of the Director-General is submitted to the Committee at its next meeting for consideration together with all the other information made available. The ILO representative can be an ILO official or an independent person appointed by the Director-General. It goes without saying, however, that the mission of the ILO representative is above all to ascertain the facts and to seek possible solutions on the spot. The Committee and the Governing Body remain fully competent to appraise the situation at the outcome of these direct contacts.

68. The representative of the Director-General charged with an on-the-spot mission will not be able to perform his task properly and therefore be fully and objectively informed on all aspects of the case if he is not able to meet freely with all the parties involved.[12]

Hearing of the parties

69. The Committee will decide, in the appropriate instances and taking into account all the circumstances of the case, whether it should hear the parties, or one of them, during its sessions so as to obtain more complete information on the matter. It may do this especially: (a) in appropriate cases where the complainants and the governments have submitted contradictory statements on the substance of the matters at issue, and where the Committee might consider it useful for the representatives of the parties to furnish orally more detailed information as requested by the Committee; (b) in cases in which the Committee might consider it useful to have an exchange of views with the governments in question, on the one hand, and with the complainants, on the other, on certain important matters in order to appreciate more fully the factual situation and the eventual developments in the situation which might lead to a solution of the problems involved, and to seek to conciliate on the basis of the principles of freedom of association; (c) in other cases where particular difficulties have arisen in the examination of the questions involved or in the implementation of its recommendations, and where the Committee might consider it appropriate to discuss the matters with the representative of the government concerned.

Effect given to the Committee's recommendations

70. In all cases where it suggests that the Governing Body should make recommendations to a government, the Committee adds to its conclusions on such cases a paragraph proposing that the government concerned be invited to state, after a reasonable period has elapsed and taking account of the circumstances of the case, what action it has been able to take on the recommendations made to it.

71. A distinction is made between countries which have ratified one or more Conventions on freedom of association and those which have not.

72. In the first case (ratified Conventions) examination of the action taken on the recommendations of the Governing Body is normally entrusted to the Committee

[12] See 229th Report, Case No. 1097, para. 51.

of Experts on the Application of Conventions and Recommendations, whose attention is specifically drawn in the concluding paragraph of the Committee's reports to discrepancies between national laws and practice and the terms of the Conventions, or to the incompatibility of a given situation with the provisions of these instruments. Clearly, this possibility is not such as to hinder the Committee from examining, through the procedure outlined below, the effect given to certain recommendations made by it; this can be of use taking into account the nature or urgency of certain questions.

73. In the second case (non-ratified Conventions), if there is no reply, or if the reply given is partly or entirely unsatisfactory, the matter may be followed up periodically, the Committee instructing the Director-General at suitable intervals, according to the nature of each case, to remind the government concerned of the matter and to request it to supply information as to the action taken on the recommendations approved by the Governing Body. The Committee itself, from time to time, reports on the situation.

74. The Committee may recommend the Governing Body to attempt to secure the consent of the government concerned to the reference of the case to the Fact-Finding and Conciliation Commission. The Committee submits to each session of the Governing Body a progress report on all cases which the Governing Body has determined warrant further examination. In every case in which the government against which the complaint is made has refused to consent to referral to the Fact-Finding and Conciliation Commission or has not within four months replied to a request for such consent, the Committee may include in its report to the Governing Body recommendations as to the "appropriate alternative action" which, in the opinion of the Committee, the Governing Body might take. In certain cases, the Governing Body itself has discussed the measures to be taken where a government has not consented to a referral to the Fact-Finding and Conciliation Commission.

Chronological index of cases

Annex II

No.	Country
1	Peru
2	Venezuela
3	Dominican Republic
4	Egypt
5	India
6	Iran
7	Italy
8	Israel
9	Netherlands
10	Chile
11	Brazil
12	Argentina
13	Bolivia
14	Czechoslovakia
15	France
16	France/Morocco
17	France/Tunisia
18	Greece
19	Hungary
20	Lebanon
21	New Zealand
22	Philippines
23	United Kingdom/ Anglo-Egyptian Sudan
24	United Kingdom/Cyprus
25	United Kingdom/Gold Coast
26	United Kingdom/Grenada
27	United Kingdom/Hong Kong
28	United Kingdom/Jamaica
29	United Kingdom/Kenya
30	United Kingdom/Malaysia
31	United Kingdom/Nigeria
32	United Kingdom/Uganda
33	United States
34	Ceylon
35	Hungary
36	Saudi Arabia
37	United Kingdom/British Honduras
38	United Kingdom/Cyprus
39	Bolivia and Peru
40	France/Tunisia
41	United Kingdom/British Guyana
42	United States/Panama Canal one
43	Chile
44	Colombia
45	United States and Greece
46	United States
47	India
48	Japan
49	Pakistan
50	Turkey
51	Saar
52	Trieste
53	Spain
54	Argentina
55	Greece
56	Uruguay

No.	Country
57	United Kingdom/British Guyana
58	Poland
59	United Kingdom/Cyprus
60	Japan
61	France/Tunisia
62	Netherlands
63	Union of South Africa
64	Italy
65	Cuba
66	Greece
67	Egypt
68	Colombia
69	France
70	United States and Greece
71	United States
72	Venezuela
73	United Kingdom/British Honduras
74	Burma
75	France/Madagascar
76	Costa Rica
77	France/various African territories
78	Switzerland
79	Belgium
80	Federal Republic of Germany
81	Chile
82	Lebanon
83	Brazil
84	Mexico
85	Austria
86	Italy
87	India
88	France/Sudan
89	United States
90	France
91	United Kingdom/British Guyana
92	Peru
93	Iran
94	Cuba
95	United States
96	United Kingdom
97	India

No.	Country
98	France/Tunisia
99	France
100	El Salvador
101	United Kingdom/British Guyana
102	Union of South Africa
103	United Kingdom/Southern Rhodesia
104	Iran
105	Greece
106	Argentina
107	Burma
108	Costa Rica
109	Guatemala
110	Pakistan
111	USSR
112	Greece
113	France/Morocco
114	United States
115	Greece
116	Iran
117	Argentina
118	France
119	Union of South Africa
120	France
121	Greece
122	Venezuela
123	German Democratic Republic
124	Colombia
125	Brazil
126	Costa Rica
127	Guatemala
128	Netherlands
129	Peru
130	Switzerland
131	Guatemala
132	Greece
133	Netherlands/Netherlands Antilles
134	Chile
135	Burma
136	United Kingdom/Cyprus
137	Brazil
138	United States and Greece

No.	Country
139	Austria
140	Argentina
141	Chile
142	Honduras
143	Spain
144	Guatemala
145	Union of South Africa
146	Colombia
147	Union of South Africa
148	Poland
149	India
150	United Kingdom/Jamaica
151	Dominican Republic
152	United Kingdom/Northern Rhodesia
153	Chile
154	Chile
155	USSR
156	France/Algeria
157	Greece
158	Hungary
159	Cuba
160	Hungary
161	France/Cameroon
162	United Kingdom
163	Burma
164	United States and Greece
165	Argentina
166	Greece
167	Jordan
168	Paraguay
169	Turkey
170	France/Madagascar
171	Canada
172	Argentina
173	United States and Greece
174	Greece
175	Yugoslavia
176	Greece
177	Honduras
178	United Kingdom/Aden
179	Japan

No.	Country
180	United Kingdom/Singapore
181	Ecuador
182	United Kingdom
183	Union of South Africa
184	Haiti
185	Greece
186	Bolivia
187	United Kingdom/Northern Rhodesia
188	Denmark
189	Honduras
190	Argentina
191	Sudan
192	Argentina
193	Burma
194	United Kingdom/Singapore
195	France
196	Greece
197	Pakistan
198	Greece
199	Argentina
200	Union of South Africa
201	Greece
202	Thailand
203	Hungary
204	India
205	Brazil
206	Uruguay
207	Greece
208	France/Ivory Coast
209	United Arab Republic
210	Haiti
211	Canada
212	United States
213	Federal Republic of Germany
214	Guinea
215	Greece
216	Argentina
217	Paraguay
218	France/Cameroon
219	Iran
220	Argentina

No.	Country
221	United Kingdom/Aden
222	Greece
223	Morocco
224	Greece
225	Mexico
226	Haiti, Nicaragua and Paraguay
227	Chile
228	Greece
229	Union of South Africa
230	Paraguay
231	Argentina
232	Morocco
233	France/Congo
234	Greece
235	Cameroon
236	Iran
237	Morocco
238	Greece
239	Costa Rica
240	Greece
241	France
242	Morocco
243	Burma
244	Belgium
245	Greece
246	Cuba
247	Greece
248	Senegal
249	Greece
250	Belgium
251	United Kingdom/Southern Rhodesia
252	United Kingdom/Gambia
253	Cuba
254	Congo (Leopoldville)
255	Morocco
256	Greece
257	France/French Somaliland
258	Argentina
259	Argentina
260	Iran
261	Union of South Africa

No.	Country
262	Cameroon
263	Greece
264	Uruguay
265	Iran
266	Portugal
267	Argentina
268	Argentina
269	Burma
270	Chile
271	Chile
272	Republic of South Africa
273	Argentina
274	Libya
275	United Kingdom/Aden
276	Jordan
277	Senegal
278	Republic of South Africa
279	United Kingdom
280	France
281	Belgium
282	Belgium/Burundi
283	Cuba
284	Republic of South Africa
285	Peru
286	Portugal
287	India
288	Republic of South Africa
289	Senegal
290	Congo (Leopoldville)
291	United Kingdom/Aden
292	United Kingdom
293	Federal Republic of Germany
294	Spain
295	Greece
296	Pakistan
297	USSR
298	United Kingdom/Southern Rhodesia
299	Greece
300	Republic of South Africa
301	Liberia
302	Morocco

No.	Country
303	Ghana
304	Spain, Portugal, Republic of South Africa, Iran and Greece
305	Chile
306	Syrian Arab Republic
307	Somalia
308	Argentina
309	Greece
310	Japan
311	Republic of South Africa
312	Dominican Republic
313	Dahomey
314	Republic of South Africa
315	United Kingdom/Aden
316	Ecuador
317	Norway
318	Morocco
319	El Salvador
320	Pakistan
321	Republic of South Africa
322	Sierra Leone
323	Peru
324	Italy
325	United Kingdom/Singapore
326	Upper Volta
327	Congo (Leopoldville)
328	Finland
329	Cuba
330	Iraq
331	Peru
332	Brazil
333	Greece
334	Argentina
335	Peru
336	Dahomey
337	France/French Somaliland
338	Cameroon
339	Morocco
340	Republic of South Africa
341	Greece
342	Iraq

No.	Country
343	Ceylon
344	Mali
345	United Kingdom/Swaziland
346	Argentina
347	Venezuela
348	Honduras
349	Panama
350	Dominican Republic
351	Spain
352	Guatemala
353	Greece
354	Chile
355	Jamaica
356	Spain
357	Congo (Leopoldville)
358	Mexico
359	Morocco
360	Dominican Republic
361	Morocco
362	Morocco
363	Colombia
364	Ecuador
365	Congo (Leopoldville)
366	United Kingdom/British Guyana
367	Congo (Leopoldville)
368	Austria
369	Argentina
370	Portugal
371	Federal Republic of Germany
372	Congo (Leopoldville)
373	Haiti
374	Costa Rica
375	Cyprus
376	Belgium
377	Congo (Leopoldville)
378	Honduras
379	Costa Rica
380	United Kingdom/Southern Rhodesia
381	Honduras
382	Greece
383	Spain

No.	Country
384	Ecuador
385	Brazil
386	India
387	Viet Nam
388	Costa Rica
389	Cameroon
390	Venezuela
391	Ecuador
392	Congo (Leopoldville)
393	Syrian Arab Republic
394	Mexico
395	Colombia
396	Guatemala
397	Spain
398	Japan
399	Argentina
400	Spain
401	Burundi
402	Congo (Leopoldville)
403	Upper Volta
404	Republic of South Africa
405	Peru
406	United Kingdom/British Guyana
407	Pakistan
408	Honduras
409	Bolivia
410	Paraguay
411	Dominican Republic
412	Netherlands/Netherlands Antilles
413	Greece
414	United Kingdom/Southern Rhodesia
415	United Kingdom/Saint Vincent
416	Pakistan
417	Viet Nam
418	Cameroon
419	Congo (Brazzaville)
420	India
421	United Kingdom/Aden
422	Ecuador
423	Honduras
424	India

No.	Country
425	Cuba
426	Greece
427	Congo (Leopoldville)
428	Dominican Republic
429	Spain
430	United States/Puerto Rico
431	Malta
432	Portugal
433	Ecuador
434	Colombia
435	Bahrain
436	India
437	Congo (Leopoldville)
438	Greece
439	Paraguay
440	United States/Panama Canal Zone
441	Paraguay
442	Guatemala
443	Bolivia
444	Costa Rica
445	Morocco
446	Panama
447	Dominican Republic
448	Uganda
449	United Kingdom/Saint Kitts
450	El Salvador
451	Bolivia
452	Colombia
453	Greece
454	Honduras
455	Ireland
456	Bolivia
457	Mexico
458	Cuba
459	Uruguay
460	Mexico
461	Spain
462	Venezuela
463	Congo (Leopoldville)
464	Greece
465	United Kingdom/Aden

No.	Country
466	Panama
467	Dominican Republic
468	Congo (Leopoldville)
469	Cuba
470	Greece
471	Italy
472	Republic of South Africa
473	Ecuador
474	Ecuador
475	Chile
476	Peru
477	Ecuador
478	United Kingdom/Aden
479	Nicaragua
480	Tunisia
481	Greece
482	Cyprus
483	Viet Nam
484	India
485	Venezuela
486	Morocco
487	Spain
488	Belgium
489	Greece
490	Colombia
491	Ceylon
492	Mexico
493	India
494	Sudan
495	France/New Caledonia
496	Honduras
497	Spain
498	Greece
499	France/French Somaliland
500	Congo (Kinshasa)
501	Indonesia
502	Jordan
503	Argentina
504	Spain
505	Morocco
506	Liberia

No.	Country
507	Spain
508	Greece
509	Spain
510	Paraguay
511	Nicaragua
512	Cyprus
513	Morocco
514	Colombia
515	France/French Somaliland
516	Peru
517	Greece
518	Colombia
519	Greece
520	Spain
521	United Kingdom/Saint Vincent
522	Dominican Republic
523	Canada
524	Morocco
525	United Kingdom/Bermuda
526	Bolivia
527	Colombia
528	Morocco
529	Peru
530	Uruguay
531	Panama
532	Peru
533	India
534	Colombia
535	Venezuela
536	Gabon
537	Indonesia
538	India
539	El Salvador
540	Spain
541	Argentina
542	Dahomey
543	Turkey
544	Dominican Republic
545	Viet Nam
546	Colombia
547	Peru

No.	Country
548	Haiti
549	Chile
550	Guatemala
551	Cuba
552	Argentina
553	Argentina
554	Brazil
555	Libya
556	Morocco
557	Dominican Republic
558	Brazil
559	Trinidad and Tobago
560	Morocco
561	Uruguay
562	Dominican Republic
563	Costa Rica
564	Nicaragua
565	France
566	Dominican Republic
567	Israel
568	Morocco
569	Chad
570	Nicaragua
571	Bolivia
572	Panama
573	Bolivia
574	Argentina
575	India
576	Argentina
577	Morocco
578	Ghana
579	Guatemala
580	United States
581	Panama
582	Brazil
583	Argentina
584	Nicaragua
585	Pakistan
586	Panama
587	Costa Rica
588	Argentina

No.	Country
589	India
590	Luxembourg
591	Senegal
592	Jamaica
593	Argentina
594	India
595	Brazil
596	Panama
597	Togo
598	Ecuador
599	Netherlands/Netherlands Antilles
600	Yemen
601	Colombia
602	Guyana
603	Mexico
604	Uruguay
605	Jamaica
606	Paraguay
607	Uruguay
608	India
609	Guatemala, Argentina and Uruguay
610	Panama
611	Costa Rica
612	Spain
613	Mauritius
614	Peru
615	Dominican Republic
616	Brazil
617	Venezuela
618	Malaysia
619	Honduras
620	Panama
621	Sweden
622	Spain
623	Brazil
624	United Kingdom/British Honduras
625	Venezuela
626	Guatemala
627	United States
628	Venezuela
629	Nicaragua

No.	Country
630	Spain
631	Turkey
632	Brazil
633	Argentina
634	Italy
635	Costa Rica
636	Argentina
637	Spain
638	Lesotho
639	United States
640	India
641	Colombia
642	United Kingdom/British Honduras
643	Colombia
644	Mali
645	Ecuador
646	Costa Rica
647	Portugal
648	United Kingdom/Saint Vincent
649	El Salvador
650	El Salvador
651	Argentina
652	Philippines
653	Argentina
654	Portugal
655	Belgium
656	Argentina
657	Spain
658	Spain
659	Guatemala
660	Mauritania
661	Spain
662	Nicaragua
663	Paraguay
664	Colombia
665	Costa Rica
666	Portugal
667	Spain
668	Jordan
669	Argentina
670	Cyprus

No.	Country
671	Bolivia
672	Dominican Republic
673	Madagascar
674	Indonesia
675	Colombia
676	Nicaragua
677	Sudan
678	Spain
679	Spain
680	United Kingdom
681	Central African Republic
682	Costa Rica
683	Ecuador
684	Spain
685	Bolivia
686	Japan
687	Colombia
688	Chile
689	Mauritius
690	United Kingdom/British Honduras
691	Argentina
692	Brazil
693	Uruguay
694	Honduras
695	India
696	Mexico
697	Spain
698	Senegal
699	Canada
700	Guyana
701	Colombia
702	Costa Rica
703	Chile
704	Spain
705	United States
706	Uruguay
707	Argentina
708	Bulgaria
709	Mauritius
710	Argentina
711	Morocco

No.	Country
712	Guatemala
713	Peru
714	Ecuador
715	Nicaragua
716	United Kingdom/Saint Vincent
717	Costa Rica
718	Dominican Republic
719	Colombia
720	India
721	India
722	Spain
723	Colombia
724	Philippines
725	Japan
726	Uruguay
727	Nigeria
728	Jamaica
729	Bangladesh
730	Jordan
731	Argentina
732	Togo
733	Guatemala
734	Colombia
735	Spain
736	Spain
737	Japan
738	Japan
739	Japan
740	Japan
741	Japan
742	Japan
743	Japan
744	Japan
745	Japan
746	Canada
747	Guatemala
748	Brazil
749	Senegal
750	Spain
751	Viet Nam
752	El Salvador

No.	Country
753	Japan
754	Jamaica
755	Japan
756	India
757	Australia
758	Costa Rica
759	United Kingdom/British Honduras
760	Spain
761	Mauritius
762	Peru
763	Uruguay
764	Colombia
765	Chile
766	Yemen
767	Republic of South Africa
768	Dominican Republic
769	Nicaragua
770	Greece
771	Uruguay
772	Israel
773	Mexico
774	Central African Republic
775	Uganda
776	Jamaica
777	India
778	France
779	Argentina
780	Spain
781	Bolivia
782	Liberia
783	Costa Rica
784	Greece
785	Colombia
786	Uruguay
787	Brazil
788	Peru
789	Guatemala
790	Jamaica
791	Israel
792	Japan
793	India

No.	Country
794	Greece
795	Liberia
796	Bahamas
797	Jordan
798	Cyprus
799	Turkey
800	Brazil
801	Uruguay
802	Dominican Republic
803	Spain
804	Pakistan
805	Malta
806	Bolivia
807	United States/Puerto Rico
808	Ivory Coast
809	Argentina
810	France/Guyana
811	Jordan
812	Spain
813	Colombia
814	Bolivia
815	Ethiopia
816	Bangladesh
817	France/Territory of the Afars and the Issas
818	Canada
819	Dominican Republic
820	Honduras
821	Costa Rica
822	Dominican Republic
823	Chile
824	Dahomey
825	Nicaragua
826	Costa Rica
827	Mexico
828	India
829	Italy
830	Brazil
831	Mexico
832	India
833	India
834	Greece
835	Spain
836	Argentina
837	India
838	Spain
839	Jordan
840	Sudan
841	Canada
842	Argentina
843	India
844	El Salvador
845	Canada
846	Australia
847	Dominican Republic
848	Spain
849	Nicaragua
850	Colombia
851	Greece
852	Republic of South Africa
853	Chad
854	Paraguay
855	Honduras
856	Guatemala
857	United Kingdom/Antigua
858	Ecuador
859	Costa Rica
860	United Kingdom/Saint Vincent
861	Bangladesh
862	India
863	Turkey
864	Spain
865	Ecuador
866	France
867	United Kingdom/Belize
868	Peru
869	India
870	Peru
871	Colombia
872	Greece
873	El Salvador
874	Spain

No.	Country
875	Costa Rica
876	Greece
877	Greece
878	Nigeria
879	Malaysia
880	Madagascar
881	India
882	United Kingdom/Saint Vincent
883	United Kingdom/Belize
884	Peru
885	Ecuador
886	Canada
887	Ethiopia
888	Ecuador
889	Colombia
890	Guyana
891	Guatemala
892	Fiji
893	Canada
894	Ecuador
895	Morocco
896	Honduras
897	Paraguay
898	United States/Puerto Rico
899	Tunisia
900	Spain
901	Nicaragua
902	Australia
903	Canada
904	El Salvador
905	USSR
906	Peru
907	Colombia
908	Morocco
909	Poland
910	Greece
911	Malaysia
912	Peru
913	Sri Lanka
914	Nicaragua
915	Spain

No.	Country
916	Peru
917	Costa Rica
918	Belgium
919	Colombia
920	United Kingdom/Antigua
921	Greece
922	India
923	Spain
924	Guatemala
925	Yemen
926	Italy
927	Brazil
928	Malaysia
929	Honduras
930	Turkey
931	Canada
932	Greece
933	Peru
934	Morocco
935	Greece
936	New Zealand
937	Spain
938	Honduras
939	Greece
940	Sudan
941	Guyana
942	India
943	Dominican Republic
944	Egypt
945	Argentina
946	Paraguay
947	Greece
948	Colombia
949	Malta
950	Dominican Republic
951	Peru
952	Spain
953	El Salvador
954	Guatemala
955	Bangladesh
956	New Zealand

No.	Country
957	Guatemala
958	Brazil
959	Honduras
960	Peru
961	Greece
962	Turkey
963	Grenada
964	Canada
965	Malaysia
966	Portugal
967	Peru
968	Greece
969	Peru
970	Greece
971	Dominican Republic
972	Peru
973	El Salvador
974	Peru
975	Guatemala
976	Greece
977	Colombia
978	Guatemala
979	Spain
980	Costa Rica
981	Belgium
982	Costa Rica
983	Bolivia
984	Kenya
985	Turkey
986	Dominican Republic
987	El Salvador
988	Sri Lanka
989	Greece
990	Sri Lanka
991	Costa Rica
992	Morocco
993	Morocco
994	Colombia
995	India
996	Greece
997	Turkey

No.	Country
998	Greece
999	Turkey
1000	El Salvador
1001	Spain
1002	Brazil
1003	Sri Lanka
1004	Haiti
1005	United Kingdom (Hong Kong)
1006	Greece
1007	Nicaragua
1008	Greece
1009	Colombia
1010	Spain
1011	Senegal
1012	Ecuador
1013	Upper Volta
1014	Dominican Republic
1015	Thailand
1016	El Salvador
1017	Morocco
1018	Morocco
1019	Greece
1020	Mali
1021	Greece
1022	Malaysia
1023	Colombia
1024	India
1025	Haiti
1026	Guatemala
1027	Paraguay
1028	Chile
1029	Turkey
1030	France/Guyana and Martinique
1031	Nicaragua
1032	Ecuador
1033	Jamaica
1034	Brazil
1035	India
1036	Colombia
1037	Sudan
1038	United Kingdom

No.	Country
1039	Spain
1040	Central African Republic
1041	Brazil
1042	Portugal
1043	Bahrain
1044	Dominican Republic
1045	Portugal
1046	Chile
1047	Nicaragua
1048	Pakistan
1049	Peru
1050	India
1051	Chile
1052	Panama
1053	Dominican Republic
1054	Morocco
1055	Canada
1056	Honduras
1057	Greece
1058	Greece
1059	Dominican Republic
1060	Argentina
1061	Spain
1062	Greece
1063	Costa Rica
1064	Uruguay
1065	Colombia
1066	Romania
1067	Argentina
1068	Greece
1069	India
1070	Canada (Nova Scotia)
1071	Canada (Ontario)
1072	Colombia
1073	Colombia
1074	United States
1075	Pakistan
1076	Bolivia
1077	Morocco
1078	Spain
1079	Colombia

No.	Country
1080	Zambia
1081	Peru
1082	Greece
1083	Colombia
1084	Nicaragua
1085	Colombia
1086	Greece
1087	Portugal
1088	Mauritania
1089	Upper Volta
1090	Spain
1091	India
1092	Uruguay
1093	Bolivia
1094	Chile
1095	Chile
1096	Chile
1097	Poland
1098	Uruguay
1099	Norway
1100	India
1101	Colombia
1102	Panama
1103	Nicaragua
1104	Bolivia
1105	Colombia
1106	Dominican Republic
1107	India
1108	Costa Rica
1109	Chile
1110	Thailand
1111	India
1112	Bolivia
1113	India
1114	Nicaragua
1115	Morocco
1116	Morocco
1117	Chile
1118	Dominican Republic
1119	Argentina
1120	Spain

No.	Country
1121	Sierra Leone
1122	Costa Rica
1123	Nicaragua
1124	Bolivia
1125	Argentina
1126	Chile
1127	Colombia
1128	Bolivia
1129	Nicaragua
1130	United States
1131	Upper Volta
1132	Uruguay
1133	Nicaragua
1134	Cyprus
1135	Ghana
1136	Chile
1137	Chile
1138	Peru
1139	Jordan
1140	Colombia
1141	Venezuela
1142	Thailand
1143	United States
1144	Chile
1145	Honduras
1146	Iraq
1147	Canada
1148	Nicaragua
1149	Honduras
1150	El Salvador
1151	Japan
1152	Chile
1153	Uruguay
1154	Cameroon
1155	Colombia
1156	Chile
1157	Philippines
1158	Jamaica
1159	Nicaragua
1160	Suriname
1161	Bolivia

No.	Country
1162	Chile
1163	Cyprus
1164	Malta
1165	Japan
1166	Honduras
1167	Greece
1168	El Salvador
1169	Nicaragua
1170	Chile
1171	Canada (Quebec)
1172	Canada (Ontario)
1173	Canada (British Columbia)
1174	Portugal
1175	Pakistan
1176	Guatemala
1177	Dominican Republic
1178	Israel
1179	Dominican Republic
1180	Australia
1181	Peru
1182	Belgium
1183	Chile
1184	Chile
1185	Nicaragua
1186	Chile
1187	Islamic Republic of Iran
1188	Dominican Republic
1189	Kenya
1190	Peru
1191	Chile
1192	Philippines
1193	Greece
1194	Chile
1195	Guatemala
1196	Morocco
1197	Jordan
1198	Cuba
1199	Peru
1200	Chile
1201	Morocco
1202	Greece

No.	Country
1203	Spain
1204	Paraguay
1205	Chile
1206	Peru
1207	Uruguay
1208	Nicaragua
1209	Uruguay
1210	Colombia
1211	Bahrain
1212	Chile
1213	Greece
1214	Bangladesh
1215	Guatemala
1216	Honduras
1217	Chile
1218	Costa Rica
1219	Liberia
1220	Argentina
1221	Dominican Republic
1222	Bahamas
1223	Djibouti
1224	Greece
1225	Brazil
1226	Canada
1227	India
1228	Peru
1229	Chile
1230	Ecuador
1231	Peru
1232	India
1233	El Salvador
1234	Canada
1235	Canada (British Columbia)
1236	Uruguay
1237	Brazil
1238	Greece
1239	Colombia
1240	Colombia
1241	Australia (Northern Territory)
1242	Costa Rica
1243	Grenada

No.	Country
1244	Spain
1245	Cyprus
1246	Bangladesh
1247	Canada (Alberta)
1248	Colombia
1249	Spain
1250	Belgium
1251	Portugal
1252	Colombia
1253	Morocco
1254	Uruguay
1255	Norway
1256	Portugal
1257	Uruguay
1258	El Salvador
1259	Bangladesh
1260	Canada (Newfoundland)
1261	United Kingdom
1262	Guatemala
1263	Japan
1264	Barbados
1265	United States
1266	Upper Volta
1267	Papua New Guinea
1268	Honduras
1269	El Salvador
1270	Brazil
1271	Honduras
1272	Chile
1273	El Salvador
1274	Uruguay
1275	Paraguay
1276	Chile
1277	Dominican Republic
1278	Chile
1279	Portugal
1280	Chile
1281	El Salvador
1282	Morocco
1283	Nicaragua
1284	Grenada

No.	Country
1285	Chile
1286	El Salvador
1287	Costa Rica
1288	Dominican Republic
1289	Peru
1290	Uruguay
1291	Colombia
1292	Spain
1293	Dominican Republic
1294	Brazil
1295	United Kingdom/Montserrat
1296	Antigua
1297	Chile
1298	Nicaragua
1299	Uruguay
1300	Costa Rica
1301	Paraguay
1302	Colombia
1303	Portugal
1304	Costa Rica
1305	Costa Rica
1306	Mauritania
1307	Honduras
1308	Grenada
1309	Chile
1310	Costa Rica
1311	Guatemala
1312	Greece
1313	Brazil
1314	Portugal
1315	Portugal
1316	Uruguay
1317	Nicaragua
1318	Federal Republic of Germany
1319	Ecuador
1320	Spain
1321	Peru
1322	Dominican Republic
1323	Philippines
1324	Australia
1325	Sudan

No.	Country
1326	Bangladesh
1327	Tunisia
1328	Paraguay
1329	Canada (British Columbia)
1330	Guyana
1331	Brazil
1332	Pakistan
1333	Jordan
1334	New Zealand
1335	Malta
1336	Mauritius
1337	Nepal
1338	Denmark
1339	Dominican Republic
1340	Morocco
1341	Paraguay
1342	Spain
1343	Colombia
1344	Nicaragua
1345	Australia
1346	India
1347	Bolivia
1348	Ecuador
1349	Malta
1350	Canada (British Columbia)
1351	Nicaragua
1352	Israel
1353	Philippines
1354	Greece
1355	Senegal
1356	Canada (Quebec)
1357	Greece
1358	Spain
1359	Pakistan
1360	Dominican Republic
1361	Nicaragua
1362	Spain
1363	Peru
1364	France
1365	Portugal
1366	Spain

No.	Country
1367	Peru
1368	Paraguay
1369	Honduras
1370	Portugal
1371	Australia
1372	Nicaragua
1373	Belgium
1374	Spain
1375	Spain
1376	Colombia
1377	Brazil
1378	Bolivia
1379	Fiji
1380	Malaysia
1381	Ecuador
1382	Portugal
1383	Pakistan
1384	Greece
1385	New Zealand
1386	Peru
1387	Ireland
1388	Morocco
1389	Norway
1390	Israel
1391	United Kingdom
1392	Venezuela
1393	Dominican Republic
1394	Canada
1395	Costa Rica
1396	Haiti
1397	Argentina
1398	Honduras
1399	Spain
1400	Ecuador
1401	United States
1402	Czechoslovakia
1403	Uruguay
1404	Uruguay
1405	Burkina Faso
1406	Zambia
1407	Mexico

No.	Country
1408	Venezuela
1409	Argentina
1410	Liberia
1411	Ecuador
1412	Venezuela
1413	Bahrain
1414	Israel
1415	Australia
1416	United States
1417	Brazil
1418	Denmark
1419	Panama
1420	United States (Puerto Rico)
1421	Denmark
1422	Colombia
1423	Côte d'Ivoire
1424	Portugal
1425	Fiji
1426	Philippines
1427	Brazil
1428	India
1429	Colombia
1430	Canada
1431	Indonesia
1432	Peru
1433	Spain
1434	Colombia
1435	Paraguay
1436	Colombia
1437	United States
1438	Canada
1439	United Kingdom
1440	Paraguay
1441	El Salvador
1442	Nicaragua
1443	Denmark
1444	Philippines
1445	Peru
1446	Paraguay
1447	Saint Lucia
1448	Norway

No.	Country
1449	Mali
1450	Peru
1451	Canada
1452	Ecuador
1453	Venezuela
1454	Nicaragua
1455	Argentina
1456	Argentina
1457	Colombia
1458	Iceland
1459	Guatemala
1460	Uruguay
1461	Brazil
1462	Burkina Faso
1463	Liberia
1464	Honduras
1465	Colombia
1466	Spain
1467	United States
1468	India
1469	Netherlands
1470	Denmark
1471	India
1472	Spain
1473	Morocco
1474	Spain
1475	Panama
1476	Panama
1477	Colombia
1478	Peru
1479	India
1480	Malaysia
1481	Brazil
1482	Paraguay
1483	Costa Rica
1484	Peru
1485	Venezuela
1486	Portugal
1487	Brazil
1488	Guatemala
1489	Cyprus

No.	Country
1490	Morocco
1491	Trinidad and Tobago
1492	Romania
1493	Cyprus
1494	El Salvador
1495	Philippines
1496	Argentina
1497	Portugal
1498	Ecuador
1499	Morocco
1500	China
1501	Venezuela
1502	Peru
1503	Peru
1504	Dominican Republic
1505	Barbados
1506	El Salvador
1507	Turkey
1508	Sudan
1509	Brazil
1510	Paraguay
1511	Australia
1512	Guatemala
1513	Malta
1514	India
1515	Argentina
1516	Bolivia
1517	India
1518	United Kingdom
1519	Paraguay
1520	Haiti
1521	Turkey
1522	Colombia
1523	United States
1524	El Salvador
1525	Pakistan
1526	Canada
1527	Peru
1528	Federal Republic of Germany
1529	Philippines
1530	Nigeria

No.	Country
1531	Panama
1532	Argentina
1533	Venezuela
1534	Pakistan
1535	Venezuela
1536	Spain
1537	Niger
1538	Honduras
1539	Guatemala
1540	United Kingdom
1541	Peru
1542	Malaysia
1543	United States
1544	Ecuador
1545	Poland
1546	Paraguay
1547	Canada
1548	Peru
1549	Dominican Republic
1550	India
1551	Argentina
1552	Malaysia
1553	United Kingdom (Hong Kong)
1554	Honduras
1555	Colombia
1556	Iraq
1557	United States
1558	Ecuador
1559	Australia
1560	Argentina
1561	Spain
1562	Colombia
1563	Iceland
1564	Sierra Leone
1565	Greece
1566	Peru
1567	Argentina
1568	Honduras
1569	Panama
1570	Philippines
1571	Romania

No.	Country
1572	Philippines
1573	Paraguay
1574	Morocco
1575	Zambia
1576	Norway
1577	Turkey
1578	Venezuela
1579	Peru
1580	Panama
1581	Thailand
1582	Turkey
1583	Turkey
1584	Greece
1585	Philippines
1586	Nicaragua
1587	Canada (British Columbia)
1588	Guatemala
1589	Morocco
1590	Lesotho
1591	India
1592	Chad
1593	Central African Republic
1594	Côte d'Ivoire
1595	Guatemala
1596	Uruguay
1597	Mauritania
1598	Peru
1599	Gabon
1600	Czechoslovakia
1601	Canada (Quebec)
1602	Spain
1603	Canada (British Columbia)
1604	Canada (Manitoba)
1605	Canada (New Brunswick)
1606	Canada (Nova Scotia)
1607	Canada (Newfoundland)
1608	Lebanon
1609	Peru
1610	Philippines
1611	Venezuela
1612	Venezuela

No.	Country
1613	Spain
1614	Peru
1615	Philippines
1616	Canada
1617	Ecuador
1618	United Kingdom
1619	United Kingdom
1620	Colombia
1621	Sri Lanka
1622	Fiji
1623	Bulgaria
1624	Canada (Nova Scotia)
1625	Colombia
1626	Venezuela
1627	Uruguay
1628	Cuba
1629	Korea
1630	Malta
1631	Colombia
1632	Greece
1633	United Kingdom (Isle of Man)
1634	Russian Federation
1635	Portugal
1636	Venezuela
1637	Togo
1638	Malawi
1639	Argentina
1640	Morocco
1641	Denmark
1642	Peru
1643	Morocco
1644	Poland
1645	Central African Republic
1646	Morocco
1647	Côte d'Ivoire
1648	Peru
1649	Nicaragua
1650	Peru
1651	India
1652	China
1653	Argentina

No.	Country
1654	Paraguay
1655	Nicaragua
1656	Paraguay
1657	Portugal
1658	Dominican Republic
1659	El Salvador
1660	Argentina
1661	Peru
1662	Argentina
1663	Peru
1664	Ecuador
1665	Ecuador
1666	Guatemala
1667	Ecuador
1668	Cyprus
1669	Chad
1670	Canada
1671	Morocco
1672	Venezuela
1673	Nicaragua
1674	Denmark
1675	Senegal
1676	Venezuela
1677	Poland
1678	Costa Rica
1679	Argentina
1680	Norway
1681	Canada
1682	Haiti
1683	Russian Federation
1684	Argentina
1685	Venezuela
1686	Colombia
1687	Morocco
1688	Sudan
1689	Côte d'Ivoire
1690	Peru
1691	Morocco
1692	Germany
1693	El Salvador
1694	Portugal

No.	Country
1695	Costa Rica
1696	Pakistan
1697	Turkey
1698	New Zealand
1699	Cameroon
1700	Nicaragua
1701	Egypt
1702	Colombia
1703	Guinea
1704	Lebanon
1705	Paraguay
1706	Peru
1707	Malta
1708	Peru
1709	Morocco
1710	Chile
1711	Haiti
1712	Morocco
1713	Kenya
1714	Morocco
1715	Canada
1716	Haiti
1717	Cape Verde
1718	Philippines
1719	Nicaragua
1720	Brazil
1721	Colombia
1722	Canada (Ontario)
1723	Argentina
1724	Morocco
1725	Denmark
1726	Pakistan
1727	Turkey
1728	Argentina
1729	Ecuador
1730	United Kingdom
1731	Peru
1732	Dominican Republic
1733	Canada (Quebec)
1734	Guatemala
1735	Canada (Ontario)

No.	Country
1736	Argentina
1737	Canada
1738	Canada (Newfoundland)
1739	Venezuela
1740	Guatemala
1741	Argentina
1742	Hungary
1743	Canada (Quebec)
1744	Argentina
1745	Argentina
1746	Ecuador
1747	Canada
1748	Canada (Quebec)
1749	Canada (Quebec)
1750	Canada (Quebec)
1751	Dominican Republic
1752	Myanmar
1753	Burundi
1754	El Salvador
1755	Turkey
1756	Indonesia
1757	El Salvador
1758	Canada
1759	Peru
1760	Sweden
1761	Colombia
1762	Czech Republic
1763	Norway
1764	Nicaragua
1765	Bulgaria
1766	Portugal
1767	Ecuador
1768	Iceland
1769	Russian Federation
1770	Costa Rica
1771	Pakistan
1772	Cameroon
1773	Indonesia
1774	Australia
1775	Belize
1776	Nicaragua

No.	Country
1777	Argentina
1778	Guatemala
1779	Canada (Prince Edward Island)
1780	Costa Rica
1781	Costa Rica
1782	Portugal
1783	Paraguay
1784	Peru
1785	Poland
1786	Guatemala
1787	Colombia
1788	Romania
1789	Republic of Korea
1790	Paraguay
1791	Chad
1792	Kenya
1793	Nigeria
1794	Peru
1795	Honduras
1796	Peru
1797	Venezuela
1798	Spain
1799	Kazakhstan
1800	Canada (Federal)
1801	Canada (Prince Edward Island)
1802	Canada (Nova Scotia)
1803	Djibouti
1804	Peru
1805	Cuba
1806	Canada (Yukon)
1807	Ukraine
1808	Costa Rica
1809	Kenya
1810	Turkey
1811	Paraguay
1812	Venezuela
1813	Peru
1814	Ecuador
1815	Spain
1816	Paraguay
1817	India

No.	Country
1818	Zaire
1819	China
1820	Germany
1821	Ethiopia
1822	Venezuela
1823	Guatemala
1824	El Salvador
1825	Morocco
1826	Philippines
1827	Venezuela
1828	Venezuela
1829	Chile
1830	Turkey
1831	Bolivia
1832	Argentina
1833	Democratic Republic of the Congo
1834	Kazakhstan
1835	Czech Republic
1836	Colombia
1837	Argentina
1838	Burkina Faso
1839	Brazil
1840	India
1841	Burundi
1842	El Salvador
1843	Sudan
1844	Mexico
1845	Peru
1846	Côte d'Ivoire
1847	Guatemala
1848	Ecuador
1849	Belarus
1850	Congo
1851	Djibouti
1852	United Kingdom
1853	El Salvador
1854	India
1855	Peru
1856	Uruguay
1857	Chad
1858	France (French Polynesia)

No.	Country
1859	Canada
1860	Dominican Republic
1861	Denmark
1862	Bangladesh
1863	Guinea
1864	Paraguay
1865	Korea, Republic of
1866	Brazil
1867	Argentina
1868	Costa Rica
1869	Latvia
1870	Congo
1871	Brazil
1872	Argentina
1873	Barbados
1874	El Salvador
1875	Costa Rica
1876	Guatemala
1877	Morocco
1878	Peru
1879	Costa Rica
1880	Peru
1881	Argentina
1882	Denmark
1883	Kenya
1884	Swaziland
1885	Belarus
1886	Uruguay
1887	Argentina
1888	Ethiopia
1889	Brazil
1890	India
1891	Romania
1892	Guatemala
1893	Chad
1894	Mauritania
1895	Venezuela
1896	Colombia
1897	Japan
1898	Guatemala
1899	Argentina

No.	Country
1900	Canada (Ontario)
1901	Costa Rica
1902	Venezuela
1903	Pakistan
1904	Romania
1905	Democratic Republic of the Congo
1906	Peru
1907	Mexico
1908	Ethiopia
1909	Zimbabwe
1910	Democratic Republic of the Congo
1911	Ecuador
1912	United Kingdom (Isle of Man)
1913	Panama
1914	Philippines
1915	Ecuador
1916	Colombia
1917	Comoros
1918	Croatia
1919	Spain
1920	Lebanon
1921	Niger
1922	Djibouti
1923	Croatia
1924	Argentina
1925	Colombia
1926	Peru
1927	Mexico
1928	Canada (Manitoba)
1929	France (French Guiana)
1930	China
1931	Panama
1932	Panama
1933	Denmark
1934	Cambodia
1935	Nigeria
1936	Guatemala
1937	Zimbabwe
1938	Croatia
1939	Argentina
1940	Mauritius

No.	Country
1941	Chile
1942	China – Hong Kong Special Administrative Region
1943	Canada (Ontario)
1944	Peru
1945	Chile
1946	Chile
1947	Argentina
1948	Colombia
1949	Bahrain
1950	Denmark
1951	Canada (Ontario)
1952	Venezuela
1953	Argentina
1954	Côte d'Ivoire
1955	Colombia
1956	Guinea-Bissau
1957	Bulgaria
1958	Denmark
1959	United Kingdom (Bermuda)
1960	Guatemala
1961	Cuba
1962	Colombia
1963	Australia
1964	Colombia
1965	Panama
1966	Costa Rica
1967	Panama
1968	Spain
1969	Cameroon
1970	Guatemala
1971	Denmark
1972	Poland
1973	Colombia
1974	Mexico
1975	Canada (Ontario)
1976	Zambia
1977	Togo
1978	Gabon
1979	Peru
1980	Luxembourg

No.	Country
1981	Turkey
1982	Brazil
1983	Portugal
1984	Costa Rica
1985	Canada
1986	Venezuela
1987	El Salvador
1988	Comoros
1989	Bulgaria
1990	Mexico
1991	Japan
1992	Brazil
1993	Venezuela
1994	Senegal
1995	Cameroon
1996	Uganda
1997	Brazil
1998	Bangladesh
1999	Canada (Saskatchewan)
2000	Morocco
2001	Ukraine
2002	Chile
2003	Peru
2004	Peru
2005	Central African Republic
2006	Pakistan
2007	Bolivia
2008	Guatemala
2009	Mauritius
2010	Ecuador
2011	Estonia
2012	Russian Federation
2013	Mexico
2014	Uruguay
2015	Colombia
2016	Brazil
2017	Guatemala
2018	Ukraine
2019	Swaziland
2020	Nicaragua
2021	Guatemala

No.	Country
2022	New Zealand
2023	Cape Verde
2024	Costa Rica
2025	Canada (Ontario)
2026	United States
2027	Zimbabwe
2028	Gabon
2029	Argentina
2030	Costa Rica
2031	China
2032	Guatemala
2033	Uruguay
2034	Nicaragua
2035	Haiti
2036	Paraguay
2037	Argentina
2038	Ukraine
2039	Mexico
2040	Spain
2041	Argentina
2042	Djibouti
2043	Russian Federation
2044	Cape Verde
2045	Argentina
2046	Colombia
2047	Bulgaria
2048	Morocco
2049	Peru
2050	Guatemala
2051	Colombia
2052	Haiti
2053	Bosnia and Herzegovina
2054	Argentina
2055	Morocco
2056	Central African Republic
2057	Romania
2058	Venezuela
2059	Peru
2060	Denmark
2061	New Zealand
2062	Argentina

No.	Country
2063	Paraguay
2064	Spain
2065	Argentina
2066	Malta
2067	Venezuela
2068	Colombia
2069	Costa Rica
2070	Mexico
2071	Togo
2072	Haiti
2073	Chile
2074	Cameroon
2075	Ukraine
2076	Peru
2077	El Salvador
2078	Lithuania
2079	Ukraine
2080	Venezuela
2081	Zimbabwe
2082	Morocco
2083	Canada (New Brunswick)
2084	Costa Rica
2085	El Salvador
2086	Paraguay
2087	Uruguay
2088	Venezuela
2089	Romania
2090	Belarus
2091	Romania
2092	Nicaragua
2093	Korea, Republic of
2094	Slovakia
2095	Argentina
2096	Pakistan
2097	Colombia
2098	Peru
2099	Brazil
2100	Honduras
2101	Nicaragua
2102	Bahamas
2103	Guatemala

No.	Country
2104	Costa Rica
2105	Paraguay
2106	Mauritius
2107	Chile
2108	Ecuador
2109	Morocco
2110	Cyprus
2111	Peru
2112	Nicaragua
2113	Mauritania
2114	Japan
2115	Mexico
2116	Indonesia
2117	Argentina
2118	Hungary
2119	Canada (Ontario)
2120	Nepal
2121	Spain
2122	Guatemala
2123	Spain
2124	Lebanon
2125	Thailand
2126	Turkey
2127	Bahamas
2128	Gabon
2129	Chad
2130	Argentina
2131	Argentina
2132	Madagascar
2133	The former Yugoslav Republic of
2134	Panama
2135	Chile
2136	Mexico
2137	Uruguay
2138	Ecuador
2139	Japan
2140	Bosnia and Herzegovina
2141	Chile
2142	Colombia
2143	Swaziland
2144	Georgia

No.	Country
2145	Canada (Ontario)
2146	Serbia and Montenegro
2147	Turkey
2148	Togo
2149	Romania
2150	Chile
2151	Colombia
2152	Mexico
2153	Algeria
2154	Venezuela
2155	Mexico
2156	Brazil
2157	Argentina
2158	India
2159	Colombia
2160	Venezuela
2161	Venezuela
2162	Peru
2163	Nicaragua
2164	Morocco
2165	El Salvador
2166	Canada (British Columbia)
2167	Guatemala
2168	Argentina
2169	Pakistan
2170	Iceland
2171	Sweden
2172	Chile
2173	Canada (British Columbia)
2174	Uruguay
2175	Morocco
2176	Japan
2177	Japan
2178	Denmark
2179	Guatemala
2180	Canada (British Columbia)
2181	Thailand
2182	Canada (Ontario)
2183	Japan
2184	Zimbabwe
2185	Russian Federation

No.	Country
2186	China - Hong Kong Special Administrative Region
2187	Guyana
2188	Bangladesh
2189	China
2190	El Salvador
2191	Venezuela
2192	Togo
2193	France
2194	Guatemala
2195	Philippines
2196	Canada (British Columbia)
2197	South Africa
2198	Kazakhstan
2199	Russian Federation
2200	Turkey
2201	Ecuador
2202	Venezuela
2203	Guatemala
2204	Argentina
2205	Nicaragua
2206	Nicaragua
2207	Mexico
2208	El Salvador
2209	Uruguay
2210	Spain
2211	Peru
2212	Greece
2213	Colombia
2214	El Salvador
2215	Chile
2216	Russian Federation
2217	Chile
2218	Chile
2219	Argentina
2220	Kenya
2221	Argentina
2222	Cambodia
2223	Argentina
2224	Argentina
2225	Bosnia and Herzegovina

No.	Country
2226	Colombia
2227	United States
2228	India
2229	Pakistan
2230	Guatemala
2231	Costa Rica
2232	Chile
2233	France
2234	Mexico
2235	Peru
2236	Indonesia
2237	Colombia
2238	Zimbabwe
2239	Colombia
2240	Argentina
2241	Guatemala
2242	Pakistan
2243	Morocco
2244	Russian Federation
2245	Chile
2246	Russian Federation
2247	Mexico
2248	Peru
2249	Venezuela
2250	Argentina
2251	Russian Federation
2252	Philippines
2253	China – Hong Kong Special Administrative Region
2254	Venezuela
2255	Sri Lanka
2256	Argentina
2257	Canada (Quebec)
2258	Cuba
2259	Guatemala
2260	Brazil
2261	Greece
2262	Cambodia
2263	Argentina
2264	Nicaragua
2265	Switzerland

No.	Country
2266	Lithuania
2267	Nigeria
2268	Myanmar
2269	Uruguay
2270	Uruguay
2271	Uruguay
2272	Costa Rica
2273	Pakistan
2274	Nicaragua
2275	Nicaragua
2276	Burundi
2277	Canada (Alberta)
2278	Canada (Quebec)
2279	Peru
2280	Uruguay
2281	Mauritius
2282	Mexico
2283	Argentina
2284	Peru
2285	Peru
2286	Peru
2287	Sri Lanka
2288	Niger
2289	Peru
2290	Chile
2291	Poland
2292	United States
2293	Peru
2294	Brazil
2295	Guatemala
2296	Chile
2297	Colombia
2298	Guatemala
2299	El Salvador
2300	Costa Rica
2301	Malaysia
2302	Argentina
2303	Turkey
2304	Japan
2305	Canada (Ontario)
2306	Belgium

No.	Country
2307	Chile
2308	Mexico
2309	United States
2310	Poland
2311	Nicaragua
2312	Argentina
2313	Zimbabwe
2314	Canada (Quebec)
2315	Japan
2316	Fiji
2317	Moldova, Republic of
2318	Cambodia
2319	Japan
2320	Chile
2321	Haiti
2322	Venezuela
2323	Iran, Islamic Republic of
2324	Canada (British Columbia)
2325	Portugal
2326	Australia
2327	Bangladesh
2328	Zimbabwe
2329	Turkey
2330	Honduras
2331	Colombia
2332	Poland
2333	Canada (Quebec)
2334	Portugal
2335	Chile
2336	Indonesia
2337	Chile
2338	Mexico
2339	Guatemala
2340	Nepal
2341	Guatemala
2342	Panama
2343	Canada (Quebec)
2344	Argentina
2345	Albania
2346	Mexico
2347	Mexico

No.	Country
2348	Iraq
2349	Canada (Newfoundland and Labrador)
2350	Moldova, Republic of
2351	Turkey
2352	Chile
2353	Venezuela
2354	Nicaragua
2355	Colombia
2356	Colombia
2357	Venezuela
2358	Romania
2359	Uruguay
2360	El Salvador
2361	Guatemala
2362	Colombia
2363	Colombia
2364	India
2365	Zimbabwe
2366	Turkey
2367	Costa Rica
2368	El Salvador
2369	Argentina
2370	Argentina
2371	Bangladesh
2372	Panama
2373	Argentina
2374	Cambodia
2375	Peru
2376	Côte d'Ivoire
2377	Argentina
2378	Uganda
2379	Netherlands
2380	Sri Lanka
2381	Lithuania
2382	Cameroon
2383	United Kingdom
2384	Colombia
2385	Costa Rica
2386	Peru
2387	Georgia

No.	Country
2388	Ukraine
2389	Peru
2390	Guatemala
2391	Madagascar
2392	Chile
2393	Mexico
2394	Nicaragua
2395	Poland
2396	El Salvador
2397	Guatemala
2398	Mauritius
2399	Pakistan
2400	Peru
2401	Canada (Quebec)
2402	Bangladesh
2403	Canada (Quebec)
2404	Morocco
2405	Canada (British Columbia)
2406	South Africa
2407	Benin
2408	Cape Verde
2409	Costa Rica
2410	Mexico
2411	Venezuela
2412	Nepal
2413	Guatemala
2414	Argentina
2415	Serbia and Montenegro
2416	Morocco
2417	Argentina
2418	El Salvador
2419	Sri Lanka
2420	Argentina
2421	Guatemala
2422	Venezuela
2423	El Salvador
2424	Colombia
2425	Burundi
2426	Burundi
2427	Brazil
2428	Venezuela

No.	Country
2429	Niger
2430	Canada (Ontario)
2431	Equatorial Guinea
2432	Nigeria
2433	Bahrain
2434	Colombia
2435	El Salvador
2436	Denmark
2437	United Kingdom
2438	Argentina
2439	Cameroon
2440	Argentina
2441	Indonesia
2442	Mexico
2443	Cambodia
2444	Mexico
2445	Guatemala
2446	Mexico
2447	Malta
2448	Colombia
2449	Eritrea
2450	Djibouti
2451	Indonesia
2452	Peru

No.	Country
2453	Iraq
2454	Serbia and Montenegro
2455	Morocco
2456	Argentina
2457	France
2458	Argentina
2459	Argentina
2460	United States
2461	Argentina
2462	Chile
2463	Argentina
2464	Barbados
2465	Chile
2466	Thailand
2467	Canada (Quebec)
2468	Cambodia
2469	Colombia
2470	Brazil
2471	Djibouti
2472	Indonesia
2473	United Kingdom (Jersey)
2474	Poland
2475	France